THE MINIMUM SECURITY CHRONICLES

RESISTANCE TO ECOCIDE

Stephanie McMillan

Seven Stories Press

NEW YORK

A Seven Stories Press First Edition

Seven Stories Press
140 Watts Street
New York, NY 10013
www.sevenstories.com

College professors may order examination copies of Seven Stories Press titles for a free. To order, visit http://www.sevenstories.com/textbook or send a fax on school letterhead to (212) 226-1411.

Library of Congress Cataloging-in-Publication Data
McMillan, Stephanie.
   The minimum security chronicles : resistance to ecocide / Stephanie McMillan. -- A Seven Stories Press First Edition.
      pages cm
   ISBN 978-1-60980-511-1 (pbk.)
   1. Protest movements--Comic books, strips, etc. 2. Nature conservation--Comic books, strips, etc. 3. Ecoterrorism--Comic books, strips, etc. 4. Graphic novels. I. Title.
   PN6727.M396M56 2013
   741.5'973--dc23
                       2013012768

Printed in China

9 8 7 6 5 4 3 2 1

FOREWORD

WHEN I BECAME EDITOR OF ACQUISITIONS AND Development for United Media, one of the top five newspaper syndicates in the United States, I had an agenda. There were several cartoonists whom I had long believed to be doing some of the best work in the United States, and I was determined to sign up their comics for national syndication. Stephanie McMillan's "Minimum Security" was one of them.

At the time, it wasn't a strip. It was a single panel gag cartoon—wickedly uncompromising and hilariously subversive—about the evils of capitalism and ecocide. There was nothing else like it.

Back then, though it was notoriously difficult to break into daily comics, it could provide a steady source of income for the one or two that each syndicate accepted each year (from thousands of submissions). I asked Stephanie if she was willing to develop a daily strip with recurring characters. "Would they expect me to compromise my politics?" she wanted to know. I assured her (and meant it) that no, she could—and should—be herself. And so Bunnista was born, along with Kranti, Bananabelle, and all their friends.

After a lengthy period of preparation and online distribution at United Media, "Minimum Security" was finally scheduled to be launched into formal print syndication. I made the happy phone call to let Stephanie know that it was next in line, and it would now be a mere matter of weeks until glossy sales kits were in the hands of newspaper editors all over the country.

And then came the Great Newspaper (and General US) Economic Collapse of 2008. The launch was postponed "until the situation improved." Which never happened.

Sorry, Stephanie. It's not my fault the housing bubble burst right then.

To Stephanie's credit, she didn't give up. Instead, she branched out into various related art forms, in print and online, including freelance illustrations, self-syndicated editorial cartoons, a graphic novel, and comics journalism. She decided to use "Minimum Security," which has a substantial audience on Universal Uclick's website gocomics.com (UU took over comics distribution from United Media in 2011), to try something new and unique: to serialize and game out how a group of environmentalists could save the earth from rapacious capitalists. It was a radical experiment both politically and artistically. It turned out to be awesome.

And here it is, all wrapped up, in your hands. As is your (our) future.

—Ted Rall

INTRODUCTION

HOW DO WE STOP OUR PLANET FROM BEING destroyed? In a state of acute agony over that question, I planned this story in early 2010, and on Earth Day began issuing the daily comic strips that would comprise a graphic novel two years later.

This would be a different story if I began writing it today. In 2010 the population was being primed, in subtle ways (if we can call major *New York Times* editorials subtle), to accept geo-engineering. I wanted to sound an alarm. Since then, that process is much further along, one more horrific aspect of ecocide that we now have to deal with alongside oil spills, radioactive fish, flammable tap water, and a rapidly heating planet. It has become so much worse, faster than even I (with my hyped-up tendency for catastrophic thinking) could have imagined.

What's more, in early 2010 the possibility of social change seemed remote. As the contradictions of global capitalism tightened, discontent simmered but remained confined beneath the surface. Today it's difficult to fully recall how subdued the mood was just that short time ago. Since then, there have been some significant changes in the world, starting with the boiling over of mass rebellion during the Arab Spring, which spread to Europe and elsewhere, and sparked the Occupy protests in the United States.

This story is a thought experiment about resistance, and about what it might take to transform society. Born in a time of mass passivity, out of frustration with a limited range of motion bounded by various ineffective forms of protest (pragmatism and activism (activity for its own sake) being the dominant forms of political practice), it examines the effects of political choices on personal relationships, the conflicting pressures toward loyalty and betrayal, complicity and rebellion, impulsiveness and prudence. It's about making mistakes and learning lessons, some of them painful.

I wrote it, also, to explore many of the common opinions, claims and disputes that characterized "the opposition" in that particular historical moment. It was intended to serve as a polemic against lifestyle activism and reformism (even of the "radical" type). It's an assertion that if we are to save the planet from certain destruction, we need to emancipate ourselves from the system of global capitalism.

How to destroy capitalism? I've wrestled with that question throughout my life. More than a critique of what doesn't work (though it is that), writing this book was my way of investigating various paths forward, even while I was aware of being mired in a period of general theoretical stagnation. It seemed that no one was able to fully grasp our situation and define viable strategies and tactics necessary for a successful movement to develop.

This was certainly true of myself as well. Rupturing with the limited ideology of a petit bourgeois radical is hard, and my own struggle with that is mirrored here in these pages. Over the course of the relatively short time that I worked on the story, my conclusions shifted several times, which twice resulted in discarding endings I had already written. I realize now, looking back, that my frustrations with the low level of political activity (in real life) at the start of the story drove me to set up a narrative logic chain promoting voluntarism: the (false) hope that with enough fortitude and willpower, a small group of dedicated individuals can take on the global system, and win. It is the dominant narrative structure: hero overcomes obstacle, in three acts.

The characters test out various strategies and tactics, from protesting to pacifism, sabotage to community gardening, political organizing to murder. Through their experiences, they learn that passion and drive cannot substitute for constructing an actual revolutionary movement. They are left with the task of constructing a theory to define what that is. Not exactly the happy ending that I had planned.

Though this conclusion left the ending unresolved (some might say: ruined it), I couldn't let them have the tidy victory I no longer believe is possible. (Victory is possible; but won't be simple, quick, or easy.) So while it may be a let-down that the big problems aren't solved for Bunnista and his friends, and that a long hard road lies ahead of them (and us), at least the reader can be confident that I'm not pushing illusions, not lying to you about what we need to do.

Since I began this story, I've developed along with the characters. Starting later the same year, I began working with others to build an anti-capitalist/anti-imperialist group called One Struggle, which as of this writing has three chapters. I'm also involved in other collective projects, like constructing and popularizing proletarian theory (to serve revolutionary practice). The experiences, people, and organizations connected to this work have influenced me profoundly.

Though our thinking changes and develops (along with reality itself), this doesn't mean we're chasing rainbows. If we remain focused on the goal of effectively impacting the fundamental social contradiction in which we're tangled, perhaps (and the future hinges on this fragile "perhaps") we can push it in our favor. Like the characters, I've come to appreciate the fact that the masses make history, and that there are no shortcuts. What they will find, through constructing their own theory (the topic for another book), is that the only class capable of leading society to a new stage is the international proletariat, and that anyone seriously interested in revolution must focus on the fundamental conflict between capital and labor.

This central contradiction of global capitalism is pushing us full speed into ecocide (omnicide, in fact), and we are not yet strong enough to stop this process. It appears we're in an impossible bind, and finding our way out is unlikely. But the only way to generate positive new possibilities is to take action, strategically and intelligently, while constructing theories capable of guiding us along the correct path. We will map the road as we walk it.

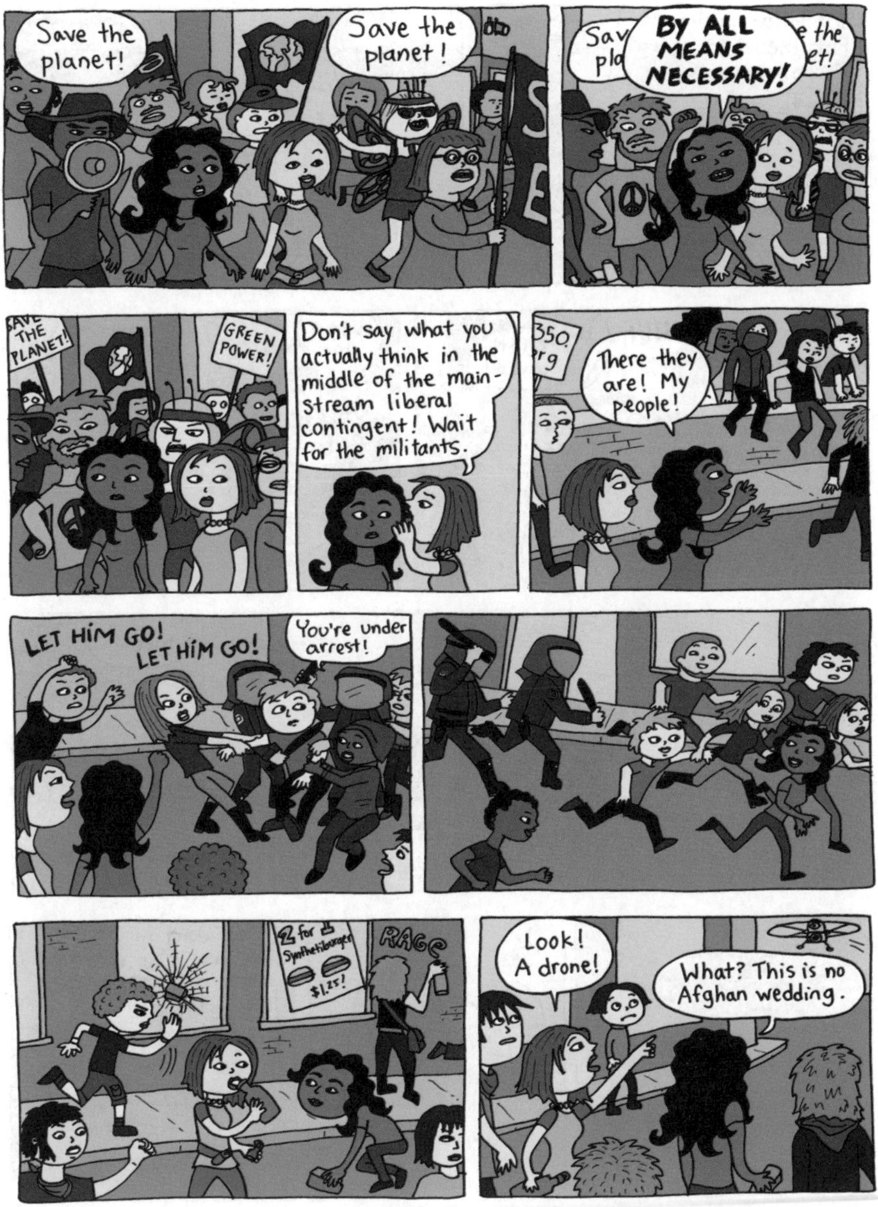
Save the planet!
Save the planet!
By ALL MEANS NECESSARY!
SAVE THE PLANET!
GREEN POWER!
Don't say what you actually think in the middle of the main-stream liberal contingent! Wait for the militants.
There they are! My people!
LET HIM GO!
LET HIM GO!
You're under arrest!
2 for Synthetiburger $1.25!
RAGE
Look! A drone!
What? This is no Afghan wedding.

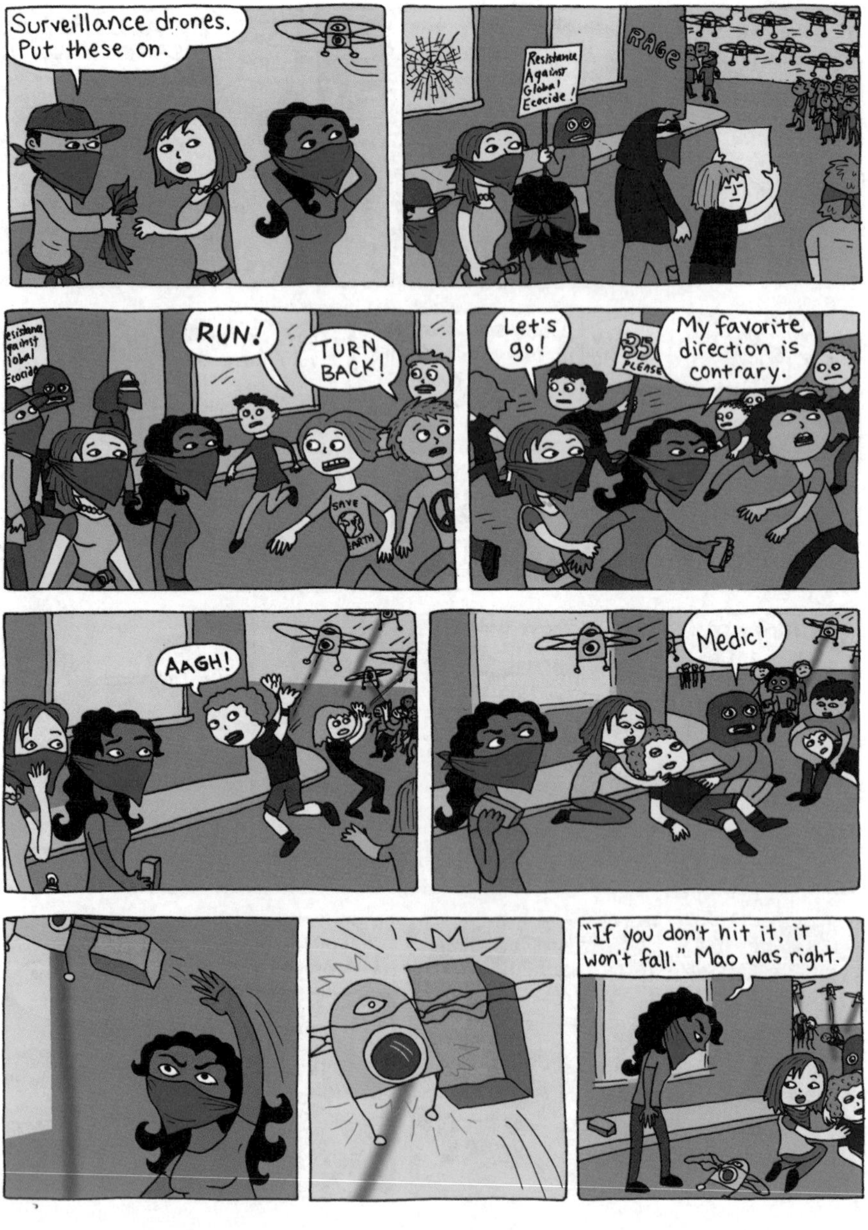
Surveillance drones. Put these on.
RAGE
Resistance Against Global Ecocide!
RUN!
TURN BACK!
SAVE EARTH
Let's go!
My favorite direction is contrary.
350 PLEASE
AAGH!
Medic!
"If you don't hit it, it won't fall." Mao was right.

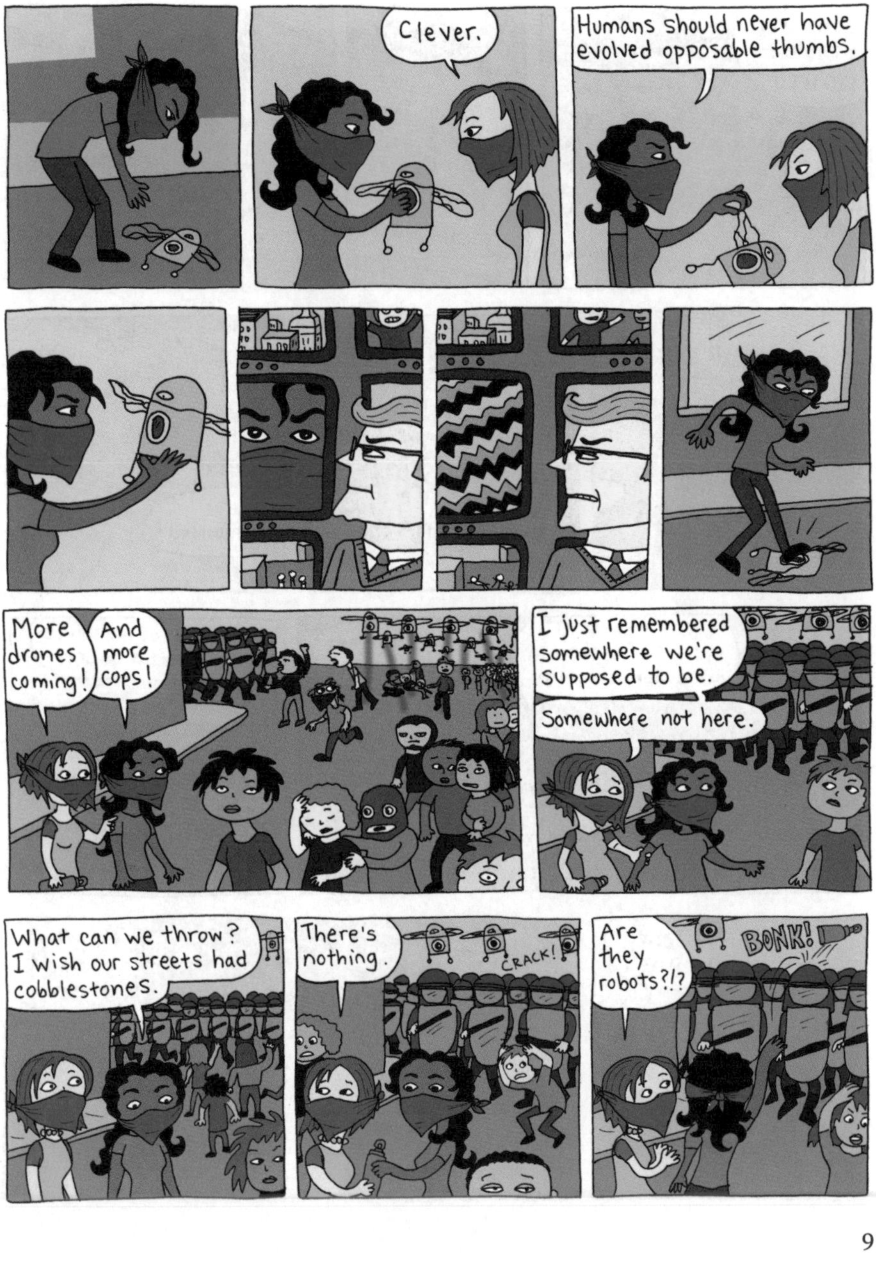
Clever.
Humans should never have evolved opposable thumbs.
More drones coming!
And more cops!
I just remembered somewhere we're supposed to be.
Somewhere not here.
What can we throw? I wish our streets had cobblestones.
There's nothing.
CRACK!
Are they robots?!?
BONK!

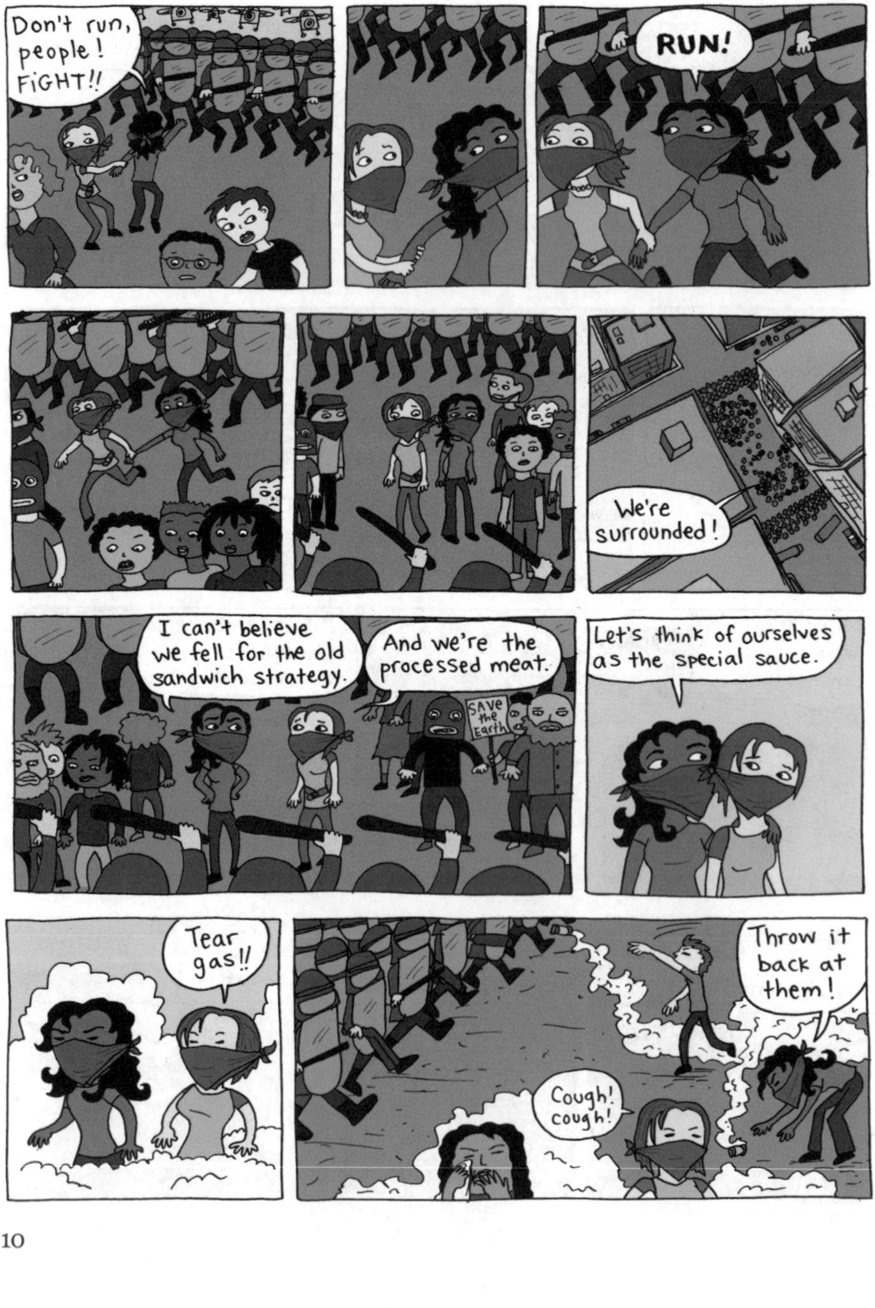
Don't run, people! FIGHT!!
RUN!
We're surrounded!
I can't believe we fell for the old sandwich strategy.
And we're the processed meat.
SAVE the Earth
Let's think of ourselves as the special sauce.
Tear gas!!
Throw it back at them!
Cough! cough!

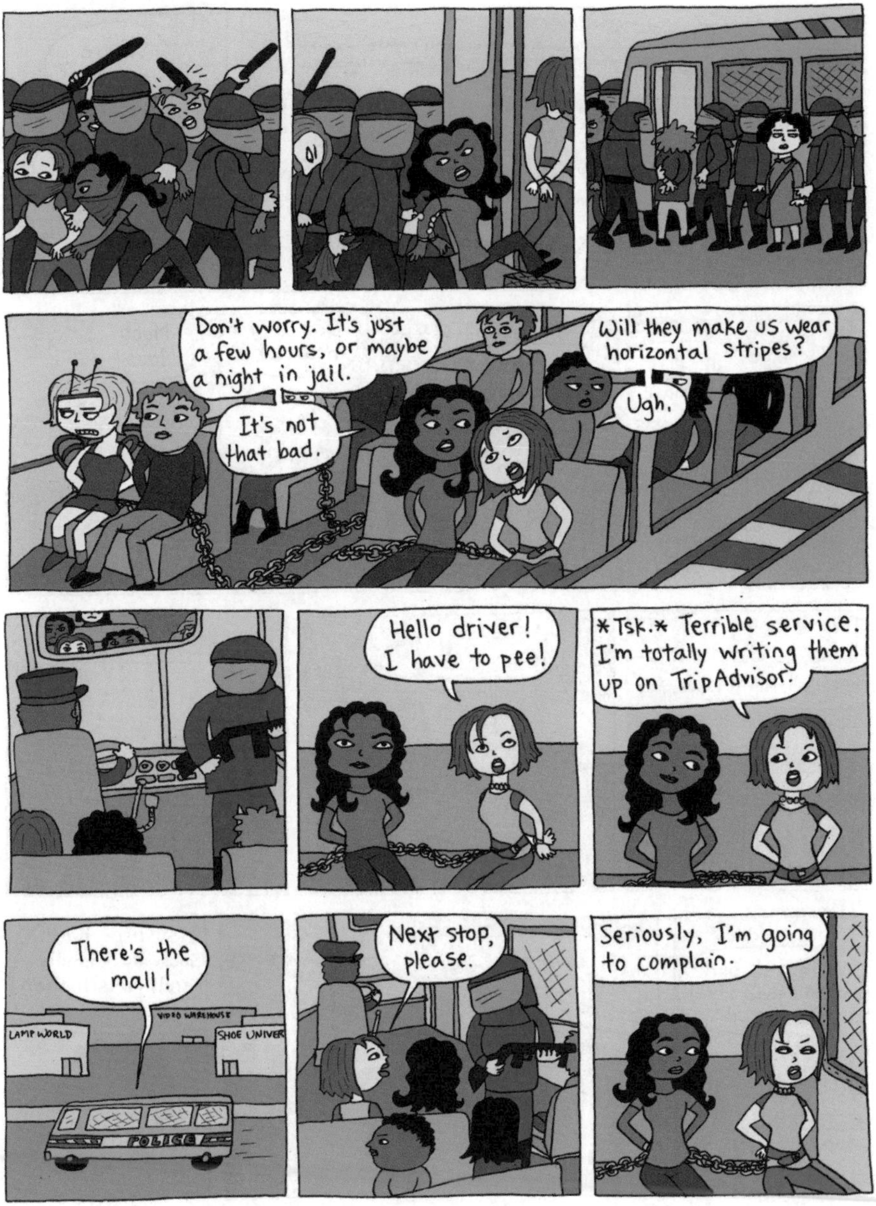
Don't worry. It's just a few hours, or maybe a night in jail.
It's not that bad.
Will they make us wear horizontal stripes?
Ugh.
Hello driver! I have to pee!
Tsk. Terrible service. I'm totally writing them up on TripAdvisor.
There's the mall!
LAMP WORLD
VIDEO WAREHOUSE
SHOE UNIVER
POLICE
Next stop, please.
Seriously, I'm going to complain.

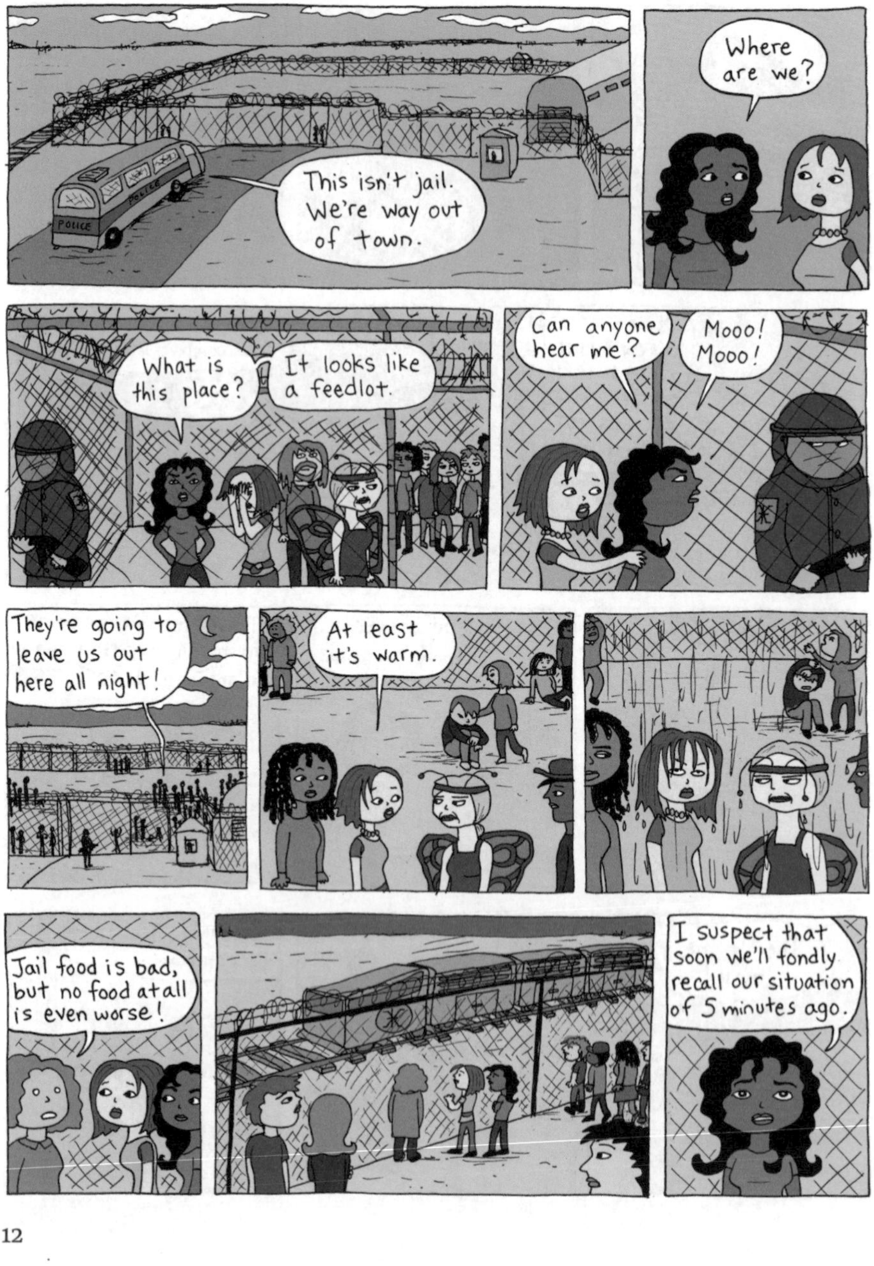
This isn't jail. We're way out of town.
Where are we?
What is this place?
It looks like a feedlot.
Can anyone hear me?
Mooo! Mooo!
They're going to leave us out here all night!
At least it's warm.
Jail food is bad, but no food at all is even worse!
I suspect that soon we'll fondly recall our situation of 5 minutes ago.

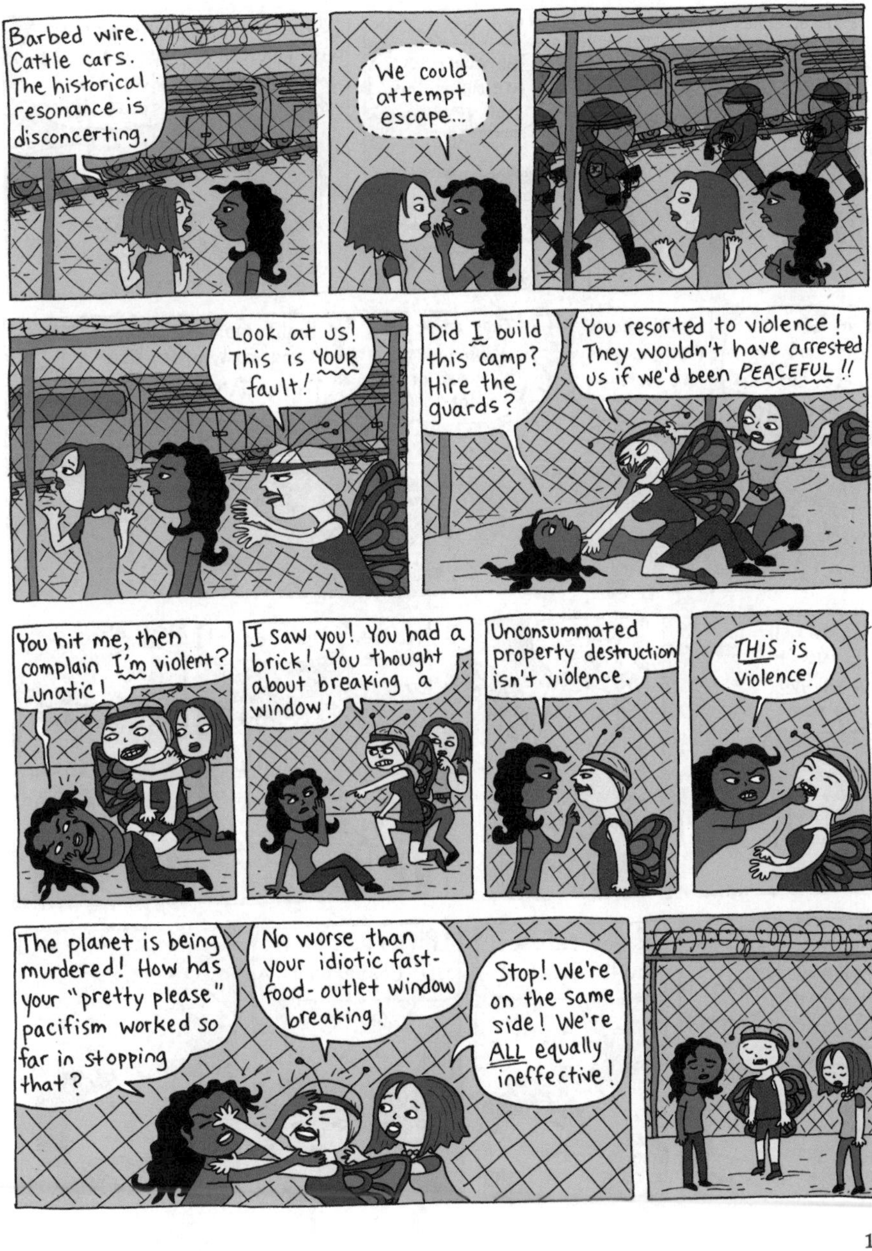
Barbed wire. Cattle cars. The historical resonance is disconcerting.
We could attempt escape...
Look at us! This is YOUR fault!
Did I build this camp? Hire the guards?
You resorted to violence! They wouldn't have arrested us if we'd been PEACEFUL!!
You hit me, then complain I'm violent? Lunatic!
I saw you! You had a brick! You thought about breaking a window!
Unconsummated property destruction isn't violence.
THIS is violence!
The planet is being murdered! How has your "pretty please" pacifism worked so far in stopping that?
No worse than your idiotic fast-food-outlet window breaking!
Stop! We're on the same side! We're ALL equally ineffective!

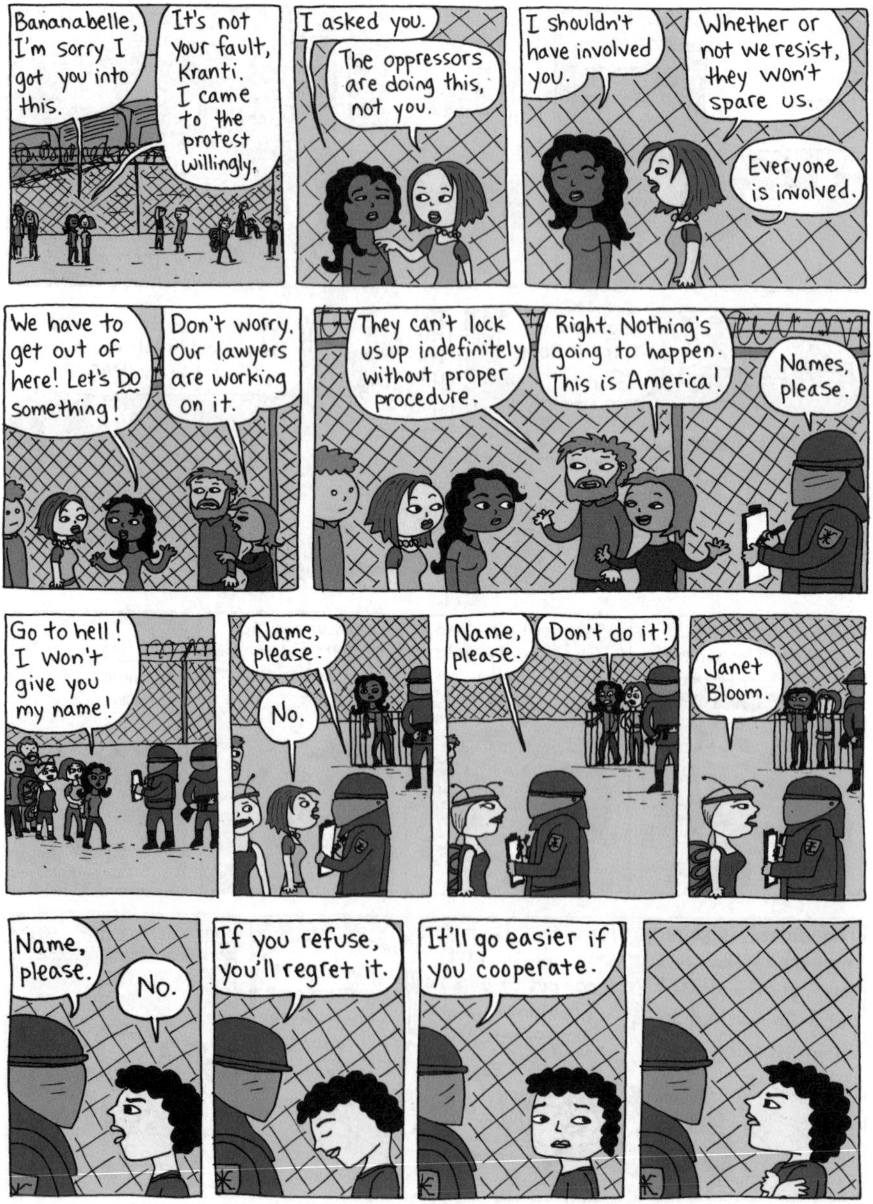

Bananabelle, I'm sorry I got you into this.
It's not your fault, Kranti. I came to the protest willingly,
I asked you.
The oppressors are doing this, not you.
I shouldn't have involved you.
Whether or not we resist, they won't spare us.
Everyone is involved.
We have to get out of here! Let's DO something!
Don't worry. Our lawyers are working on it.
They can't lock us up indefinitely without proper procedure.
Right. Nothing's going to happen. This is America!
Names, please.
Go to hell! I won't give you my name!
Name, please.
No.
Name, please.
Don't do it!
Janet Bloom.
Name, please.
No.
If you refuse, you'll regret it.
It'll go easier if you cooperate.

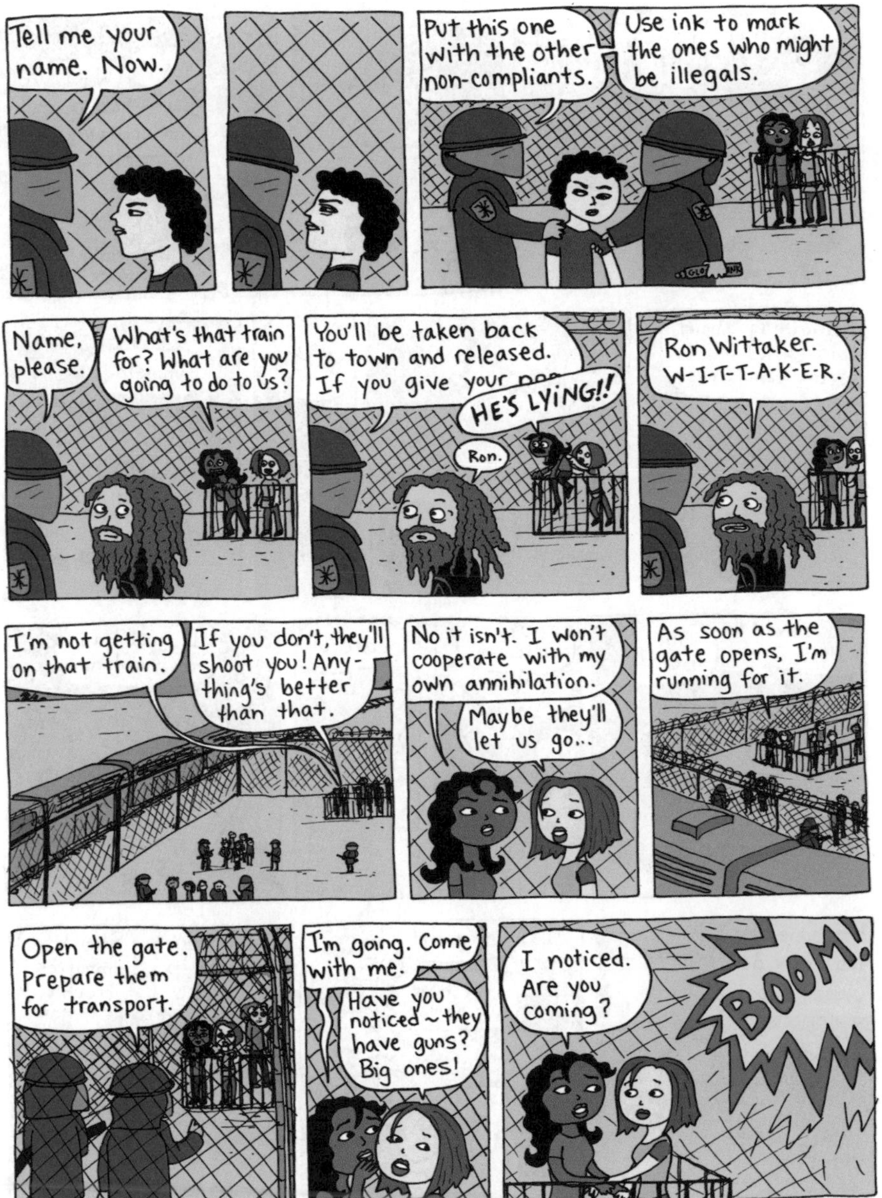
Tell me your name. Now.
Put this one with the other non-compliants.
Use ink to mark the ones who might be illegals.
Name, please.
What's that train for? What are you going to do to us?
You'll be taken back to town and released. If you give your nam
HE'S LYING!!
Ron.
Ron Wittaker. W-I-T-T-A-K-E-R.
I'm not getting on that train.
If you don't, they'll shoot you! Anything's better than that.
No it isn't. I won't cooperate with my own annihilation.
Maybe they'll let us go...
As soon as the gate opens, I'm running for it.
Open the gate. Prepare them for transport.
I'm going. Come with me.
Have you noticed ~ they have guns? Big ones!
I noticed. Are you coming?
BOOM!

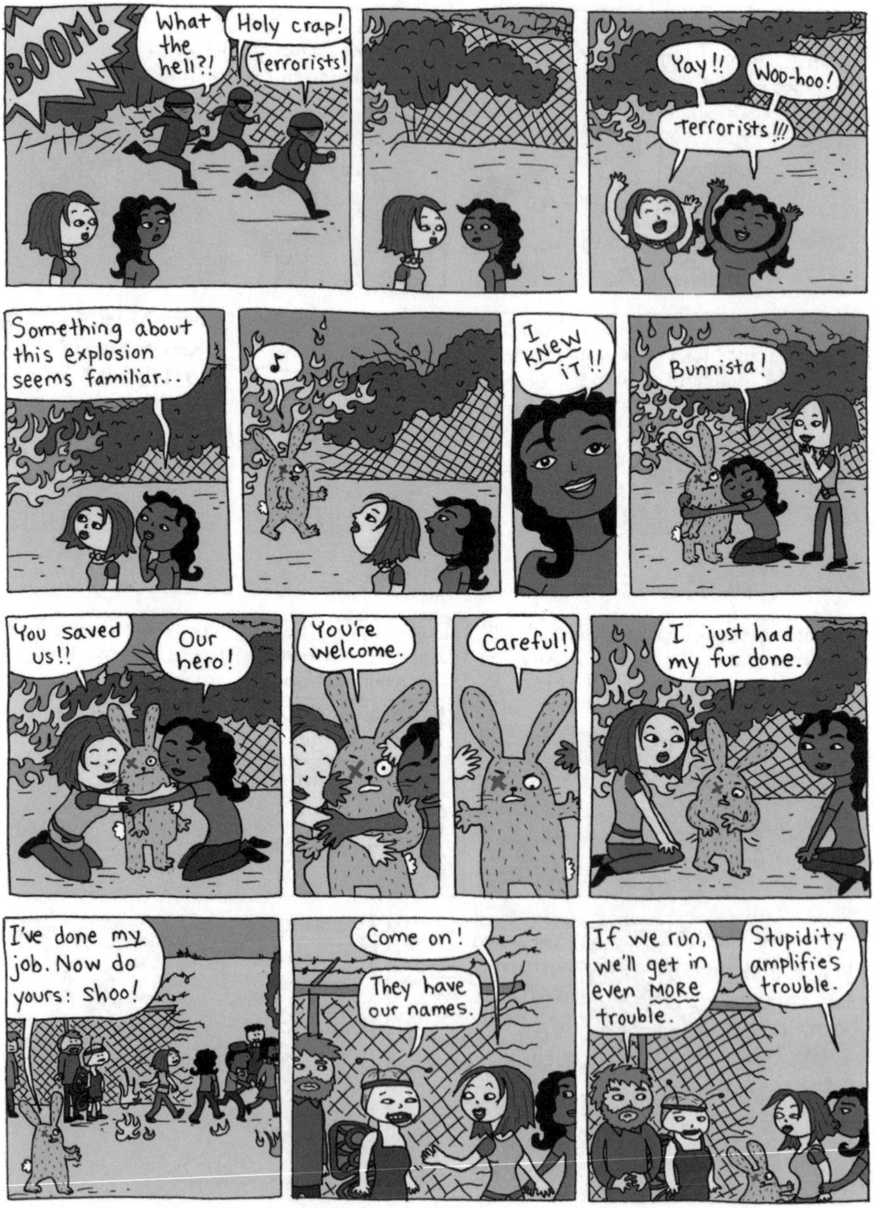
BOOM!
What the hell?!
Holy crap!
Terrorists!
Yay!!
Woo-hoo!
Terrorists!!!
Something about this explosion seems familiar...
♪
I KNEW IT!!
Bunnista!
You saved us!!
Our hero!
You're welcome.
Careful!
I just had my fur done.
I've done my job. Now do yours: Shoo!
Come on!
They have our names.
If we run, we'll get in even MORE trouble.
Stupidity amplifies trouble.

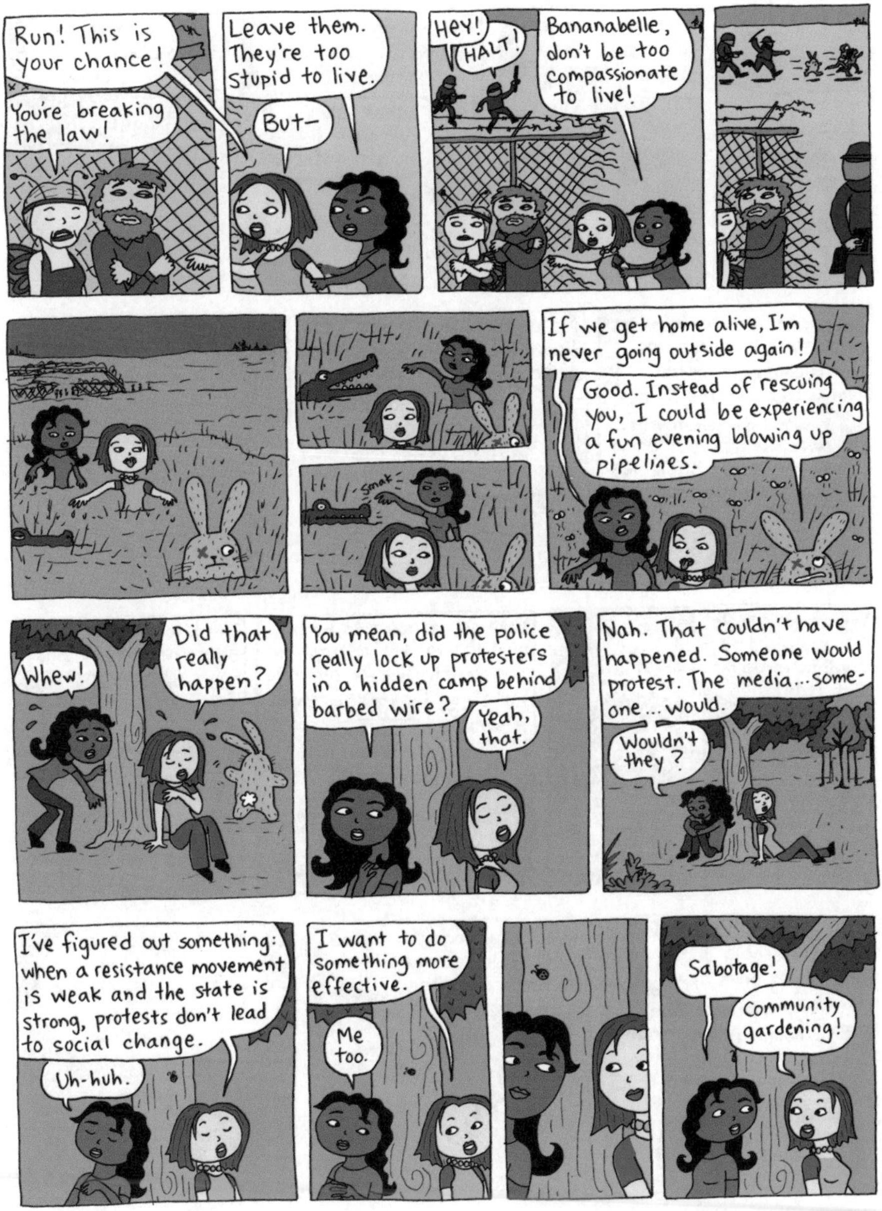
Run! This is your chance!
You're breaking the law!
Leave them. They're too stupid to live.
But–
HEY!
HALT!
Bananabelle, don't be too compassionate to live!
If we get home alive, I'm never going outside again!
Good. Instead of rescuing you, I could be experiencing a fun evening blowing up pipelines.
Whew!
Did that really happen?
You mean, did the police really lock up protesters in a hidden camp behind barbed wire?
Yeah, that.
Nah. That couldn't have happened. Someone would protest. The media... some-one... would.
Wouldn't they?
I've figured out something: when a resistance movement is weak and the state is strong, protests don't lead to social change.
Uh-huh.
I want to do something more effective.
Me too.
Sabotage!
Community gardening!

Community gardening?!

Lifestyle changes can't save the planet.

What can?

The problem is huge: industrial capitalism. Civilization itself!

What should we do ~ live as hunter-gatherers?

...Isn't that just the mother of all lifestyle changes?

The biggest.

You want to turn from protesting to gardening. Not because it would work. Because it's safe.

I won't throw my life away if it isn't going to make any difference.

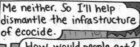

Me neither. So I'll help dismantle the infrastructure of ecocide.

How would people eat? Before they destroy the system, people must be able to survive without it.

Get real.

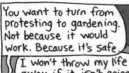

You expect people to renounce civilization and eat leaves?

Chomp Chomp

They aren't going to hate civilization for destroying the planet. They're going to hate you for making them miserable.

But that's irrational.

Chew chew

They won't smash the system ~ they'll smash you.

Mmm.

What could make people more miserable than languishing on a dead planet?

Someone telling them that everything they believe is wrong.

It's not enough to say we need to live sustainably. No one knows how.

You expect people to identify wild edible plants? Kids don't even know what common vegetables look like!

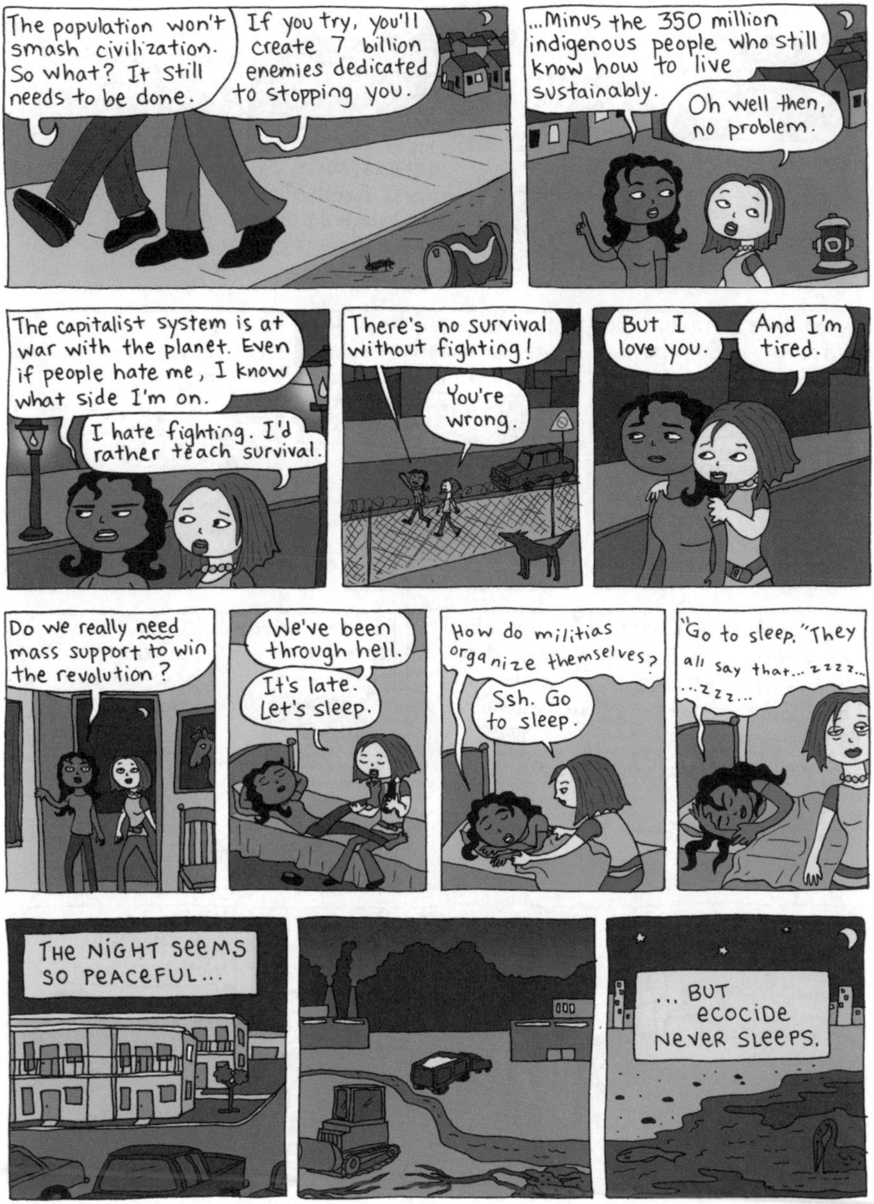

The population won't smash civilization. So what? It still needs to be done.
If you try, you'll create 7 billion enemies dedicated to stopping you.
...Minus the 350 million indigenous people who still know how to live sustainably.
Oh well then, no problem.
The capitalist system is at war with the planet. Even if people hate me, I know what side I'm on.
I hate fighting. I'd rather teach survival.
There's no survival without fighting!
You're wrong.
But I love you.
And I'm tired.
Do we really need mass support to win the revolution?
We've been through hell.
It's late. Let's sleep.
How do militias organize themselves?
Ssh. Go to sleep.
"Go to sleep," They all say that... zzzz... ...zzz...
THE NIGHT SEEMS SO PEACEFUL...
... BUT ECOCIDE NEVER SLEEPS.

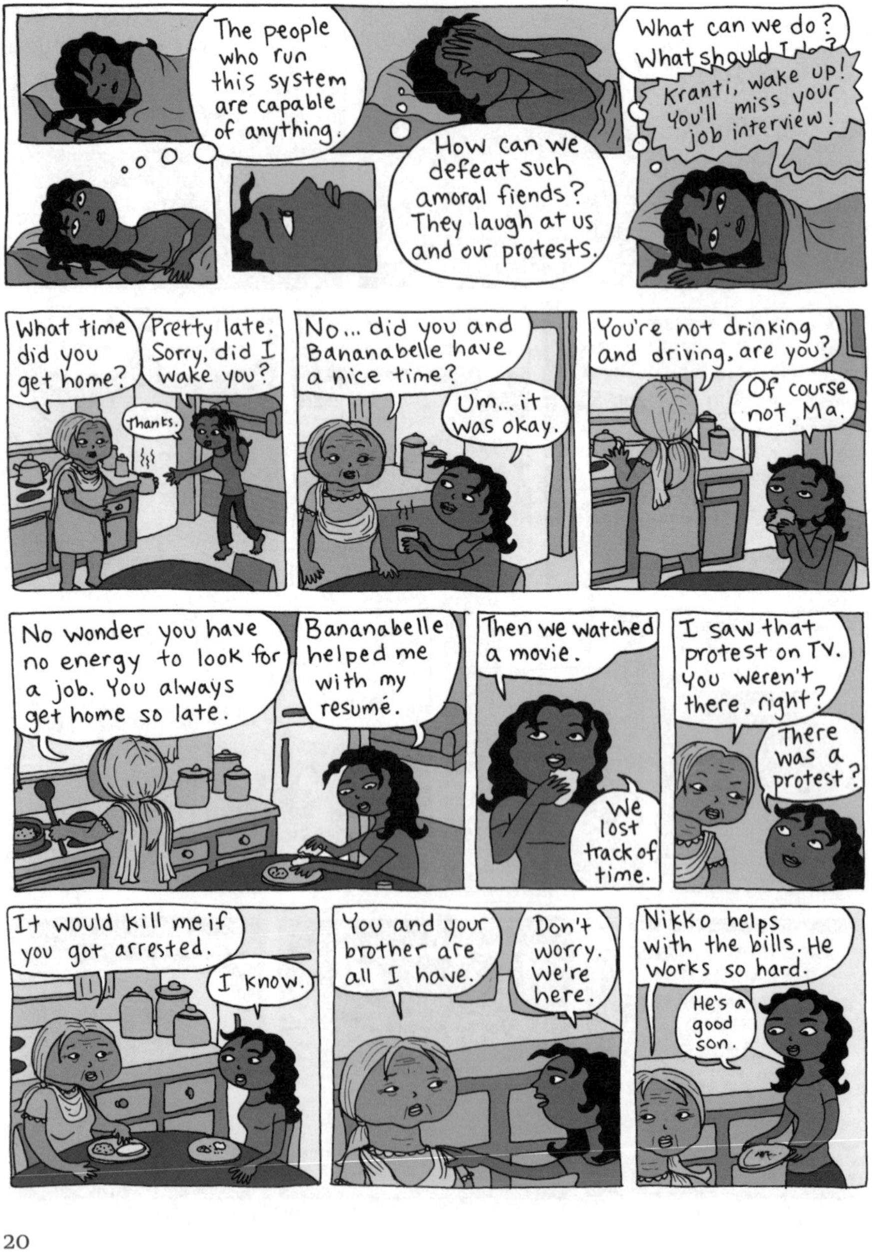

The people who run this system are capable of anything.
How can we defeat such amoral fiends? They laugh at us and our protests.
What can we do? What should I do?
Kranti, wake up! You'll miss your job interview!
What time did you get home?
Pretty late. Sorry, did I wake you?
Thanks.
No... did you and Bananabelle have a nice time?
Um... it was okay.
You're not drinking and driving, are you?
Of course not, Ma.
No wonder you have no energy to look for a job. You always get home so late.
Bananabelle helped me with my resumé.
Then we watched a movie.
We lost track of time.
I saw that protest on TV. You weren't there, right?
There was a protest?
It would kill me if you got arrested.
I know.
You and your brother are all I have.
Don't worry. We're here.
Nikko helps with the bills. He works so hard.
He's a good son.

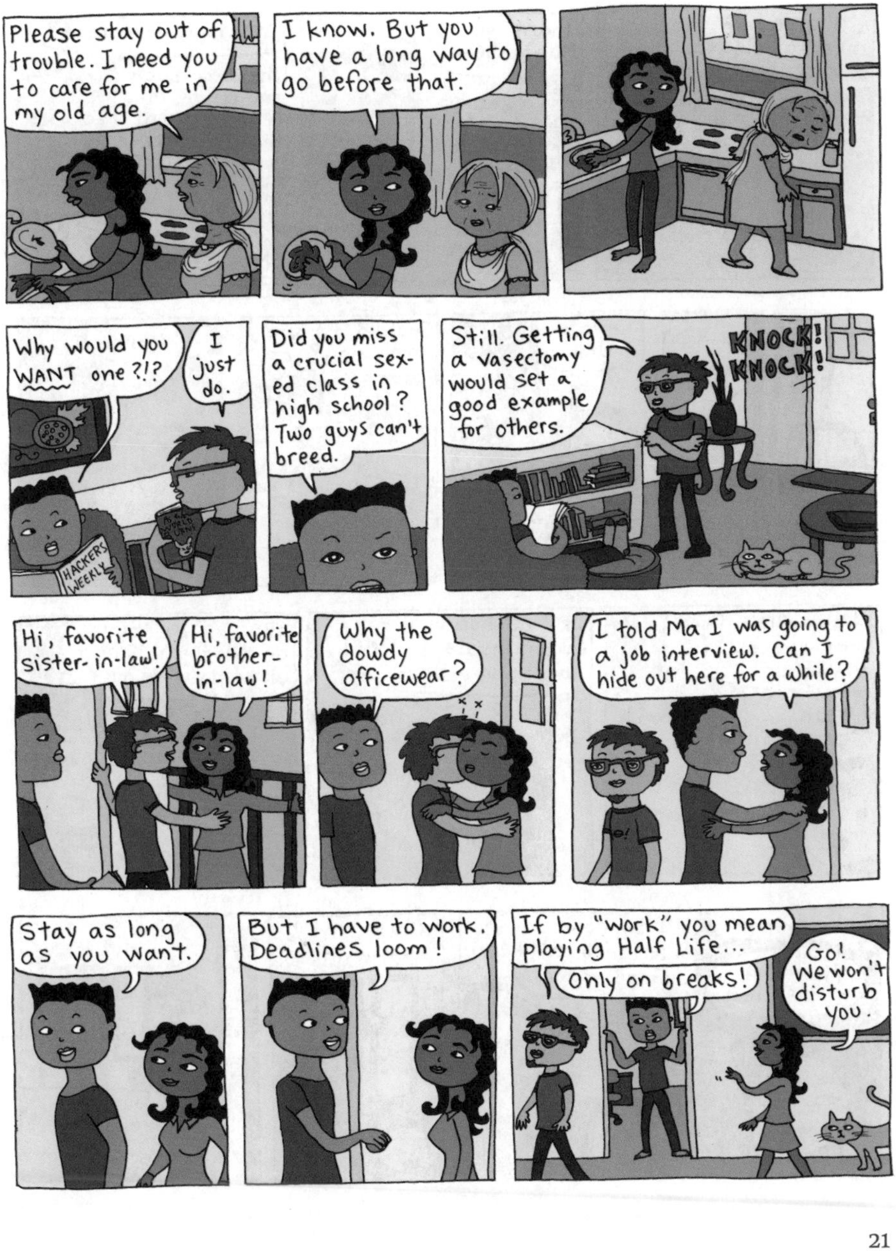
Please stay out of trouble. I need you to care for me in my old age.
I know. But you have a long way to go before that.
Why would you WANT one ?!?
I just do.
HACKERS WEEKLY
Did you miss a crucial sex-ed class in high school? Two guys can't breed.
Still. Getting a vasectomy would set a good example for others.
KNOCK! KNOCK!
Hi, favorite sister-in-law!
Hi, favorite brother-in-law!
Why the dowdy officewear?
I told Ma I was going to a job interview. Can I hide out here for a while?
Stay as long as you want.
But I have to work. Deadlines loom!
If by "work" you mean playing Half Life...
Only on breaks!
Go! We won't disturb you.

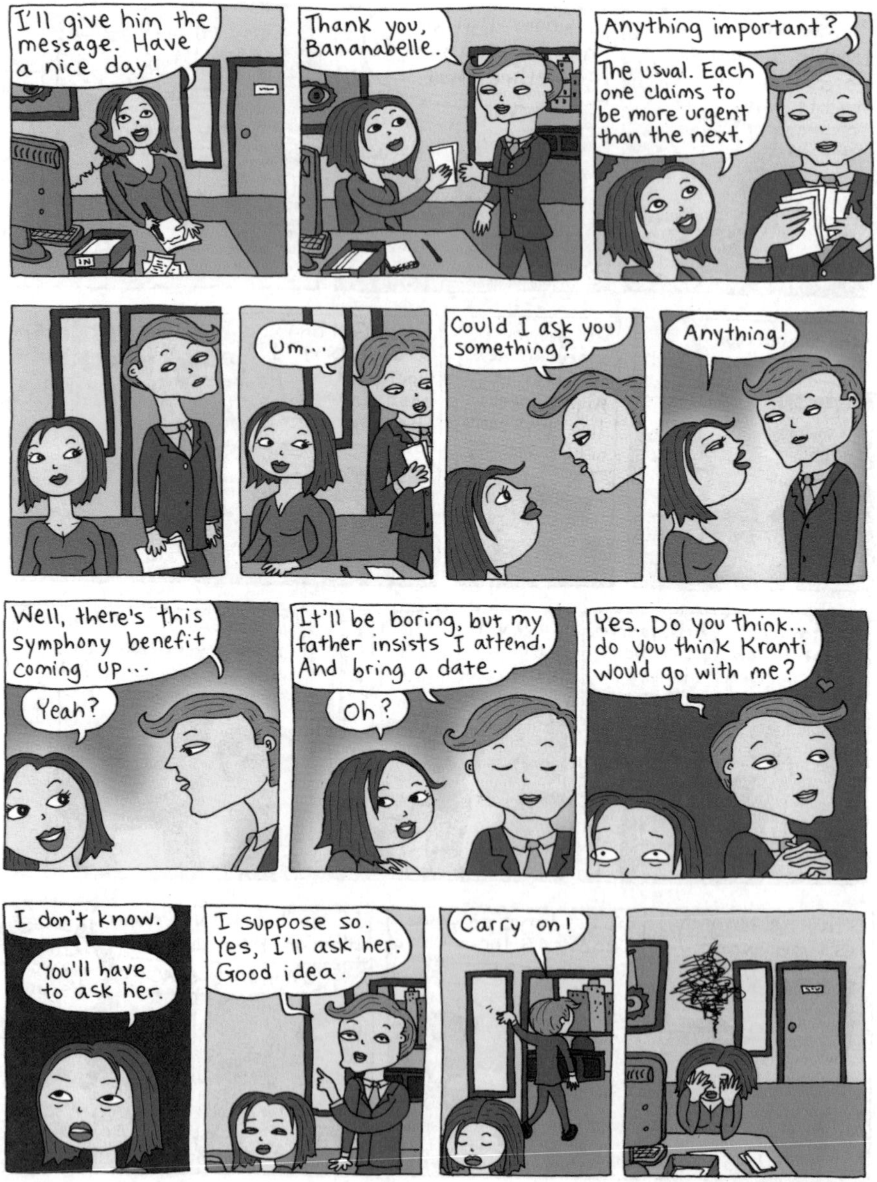
I'll give him the message. Have a nice day!
Thank you, Bananabelle.
Anything important?
The usual. Each one claims to be more urgent than the next.
Um...
Could I ask you something?
Anything!
Well, there's this symphony benefit coming up...
Yeah?
It'll be boring, but my father insists I attend. And bring a date.
Oh?
Yes. Do you think... do you think Kranti would go with me?
I don't know.
You'll have to ask her.
I suppose so. Yes, I'll ask her. Good idea.
Carry on!

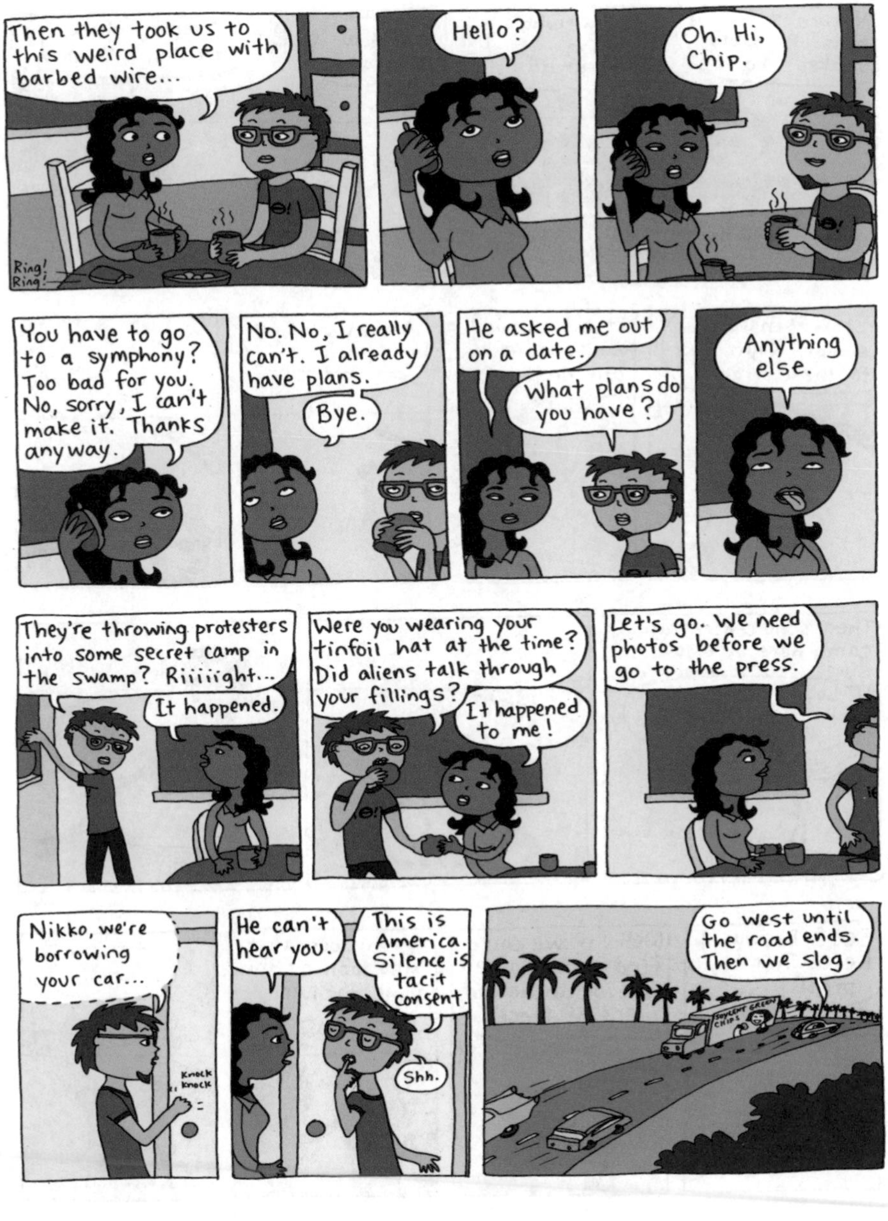
Then they took us to this weird place with barbed wire...
Ring! Ring!
Hello?
Oh. Hi, Chip.
You have to go to a symphony? Too bad for you. No, sorry, I can't make it. Thanks anyway.
No. No, I really can't. I already have plans.
Bye.
He asked me out on a date.
What plans do you have?
Anything else.
They're throwing protesters into some secret camp in the swamp? Riiiiight...
It happened.
Were you wearing your tinfoil hat at the time? Did aliens talk through your fillings?
It happened to me!
Let's go. We need photos before we go to the press.
Nikko, we're borrowing your car...
Knock knock
He can't hear you.
This is America. Silence is tacit consent.
Shh.
Go west until the road ends. Then we slog.

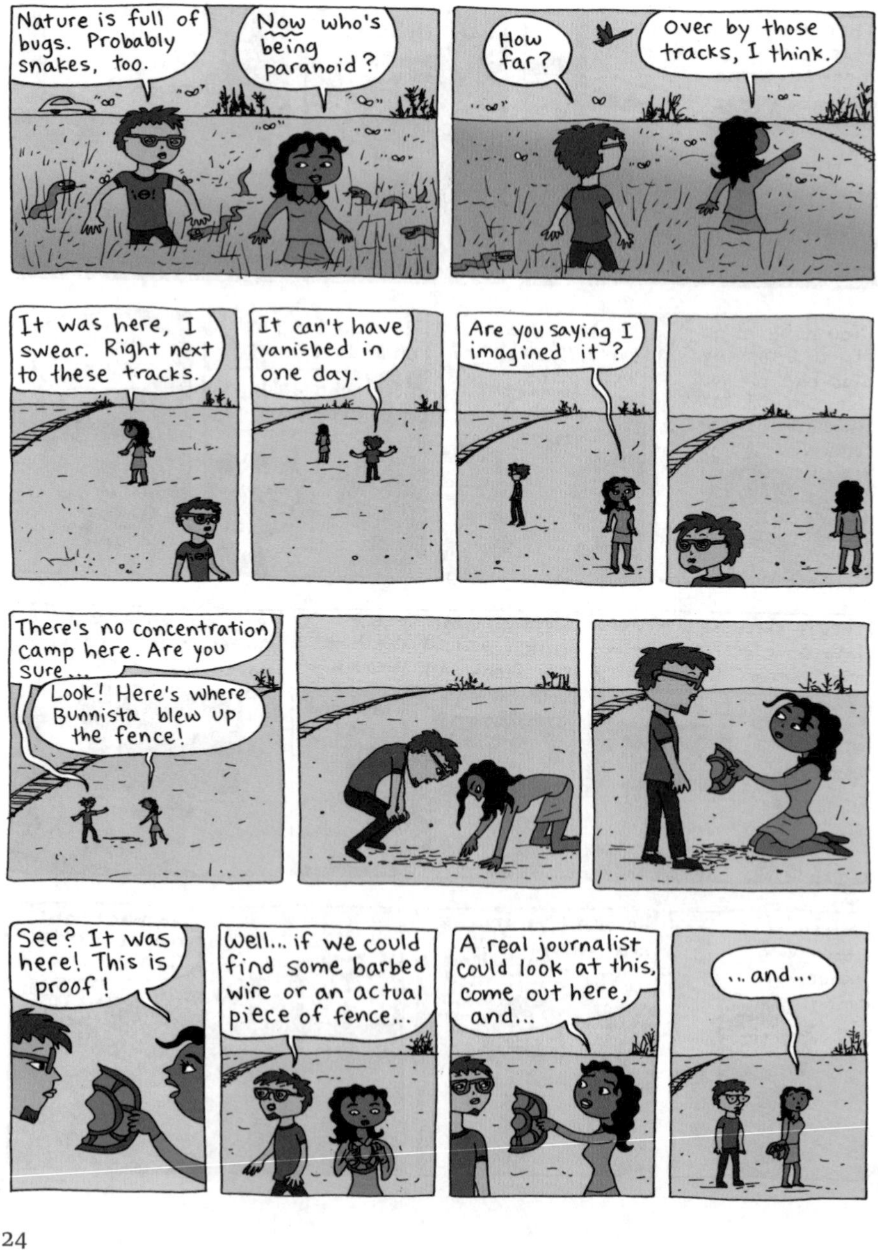
Nature is full of bugs. Probably snakes, too.
Now who's being paranoid?
How far?
Over by those tracks, I think.
It was here, I swear. Right next to these tracks.
It can't have vanished in one day.
Are you saying I imagined it?
There's no concentration camp here. Are you sure...
Look! Here's where Bunnista blew up the fence!
See? It was here! This is proof!
Well... if we could find some barbed wire or an actual piece of fence...
A real journalist could look at this, come out here, and...
...and...

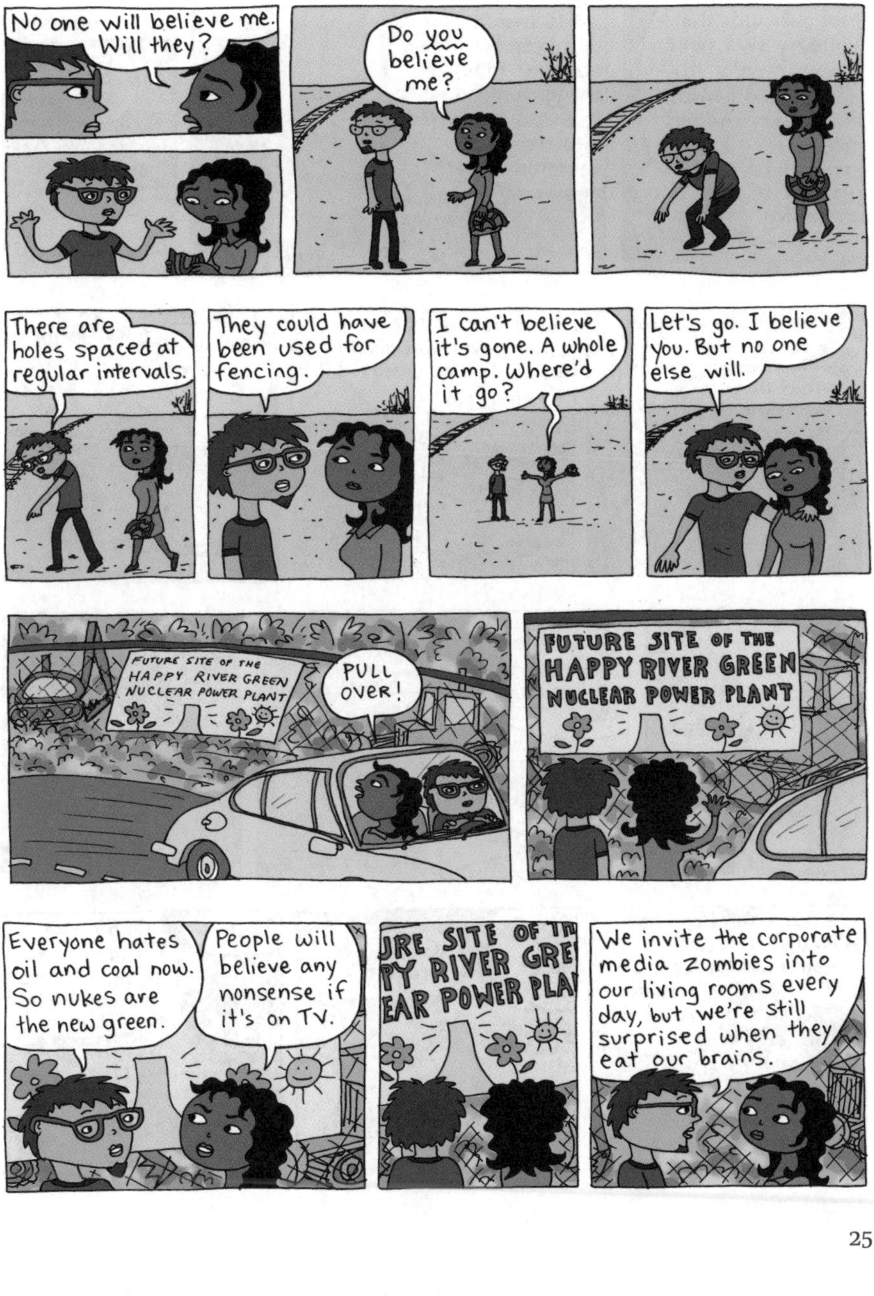

No one will believe me. Will they?
Do you believe me?
There are holes spaced at regular intervals.
They could have been used for fencing.
I can't believe it's gone. A whole camp. Where'd it go?
Let's go. I believe you. But no one else will.
FUTURE SITE OF THE HAPPY RIVER GREEN NUCLEAR POWER PLANT
PULL OVER!
FUTURE SITE OF THE HAPPY RIVER GREEN NUCLEAR POWER PLANT
Everyone hates oil and coal now. So nukes are the new green.
People will believe any nonsense if it's on TV.
URE SITE OF TH
PY RIVER GRE
EAR POWER PLA
We invite the corporate media zombies into our living rooms every day, but we're still surprised when they eat our brains.

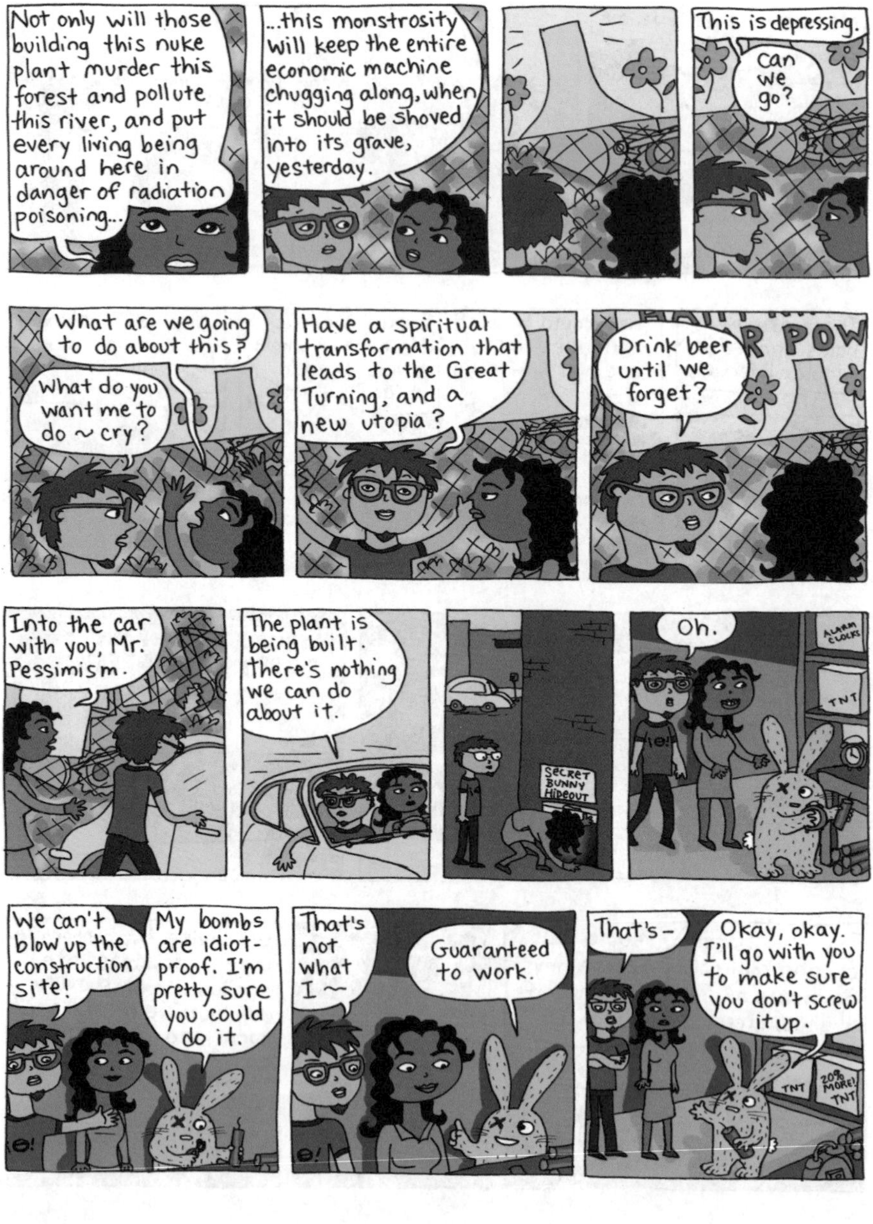
Not only will those building this nuke plant murder this forest and pollute this river, and put every living being around here in danger of radiation poisoning...
...this monstrosity will keep the entire economic machine chugging along, when it should be shoved into its grave, yesterday.
This is depressing.
Can we go?
What are we going to do about this?
What do you want me to do ~ cry?
Have a spiritual transformation that leads to the Great Turning, and a new utopia?
R POW
Drink beer until we forget?
Into the car with you, Mr. Pessimism.
The plant is being built. There's nothing we can do about it.
SECRET BUNNY HIDEOUT
Oh.
ALARM CLOCKS
TNT
We can't blow up the construction site!
My bombs are idiot-proof. I'm pretty sure you could do it.
That's not what I ~
Guaranteed to work.
That's -
Okay, okay. I'll go with you to make sure you don't screw it up.
TNT
20% MORE! TNT

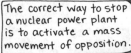 The correct way to stop a nuclear power plant is to activate a mass movement of opposition.

 To do what?

They will use civil disobedience to block the bulldozers.

Cool. Tell them to be out there by 8 am tomorrow.

 First, we start with public education and outreach. Then—

You're really testing me.

 Blowing up bulldozers is a bad strategy. You can't win with only willpower and passion. What happens when you get caught and you have no support network? POOF! You disappear, your efforts wasted.

I know we need mass resistance. But where is it? The world is being killed TODAY. There's no time left!

We can't let the plant get built! It'll poison the whole area!

We can't wait for a future mass resistance movement. We must deal with it now, ourselves.

 You're acting desperately instead of rationally. Like the Weather Underground and Red Army Faction did.

They went down in flames!

 At least they went down fighting. At least they tried.

 I'm a busy bunny. Are we going to blow that sucker up or not?

 Kranti, I don't want to TRY. I want to WIN. Without a militant mass movement, followed by the seizure of power, we have nothing.

 We can't win as individuals committing reckless acts.

Right. We can't win the revolution.

But we CAN stop this nuclear power plant from being built right now.

We could win that.

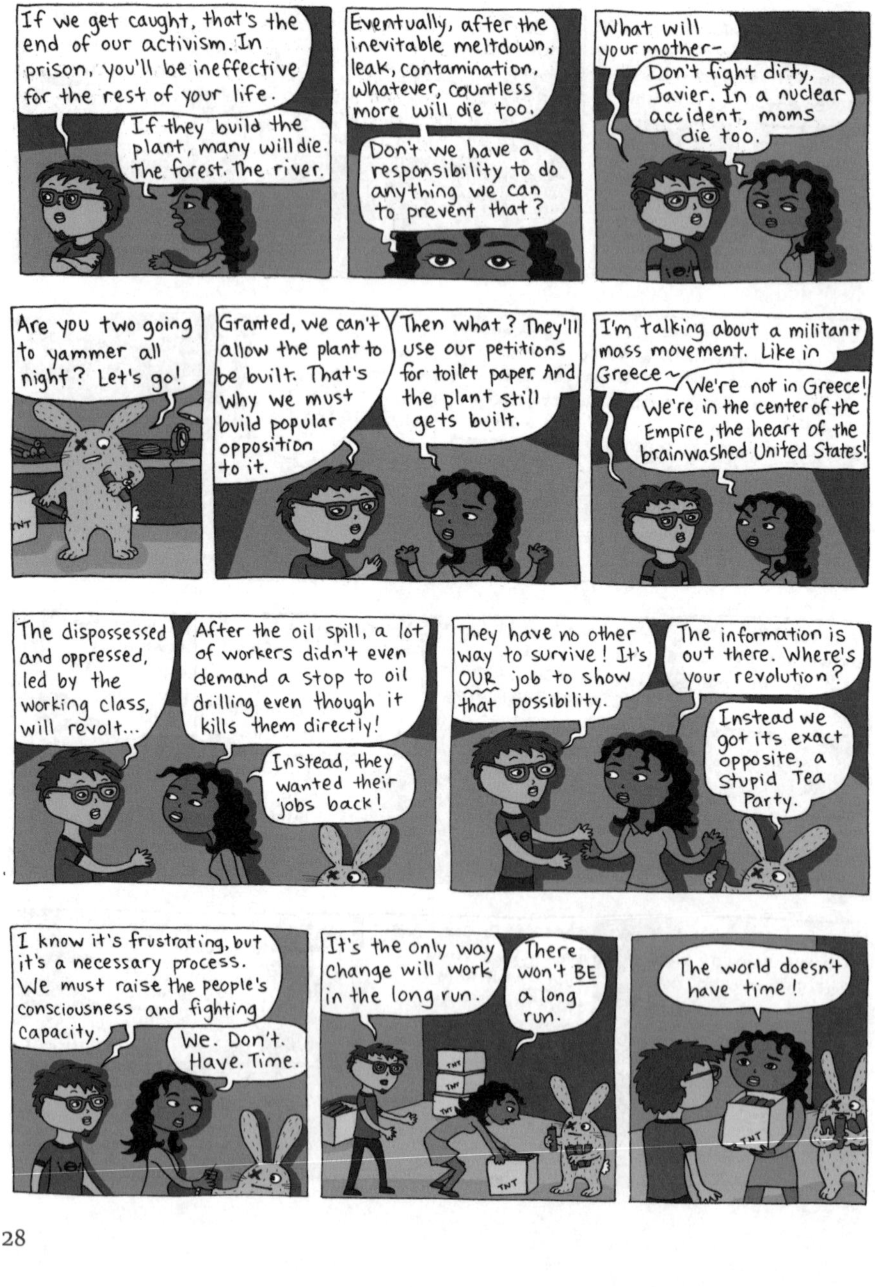
If we get caught, that's the end of our activism. In prison, you'll be ineffective for the rest of your life.
If they build the plant, many will die. The forest. The river.
Eventually, after the inevitable meltdown, leak, contamination, whatever, countless more will die too.
Don't we have a responsibility to do anything we can to prevent that?
What will your mother–
Don't fight dirty, Javier. In a nuclear accident, moms die too.
Are you two going to yammer all night? Let's go!
Granted, we can't allow the plant to be built. That's why we must build popular opposition to it.
Then what? They'll use our petitions for toilet paper. And the plant still gets built.
I'm talking about a militant mass movement. Like in Greece~
We're not in Greece! We're in the center of the Empire, the heart of the brainwashed United States!
The dispossessed and oppressed, led by the working class, will revolt...
After the oil spill, a lot of workers didn't even demand a stop to oil drilling even though it kills them directly!
Instead, they wanted their jobs back!
They have no other way to survive! It's OUR job to show that possibility.
The information is out there. Where's your revolution?
Instead we got its exact opposite, a stupid Tea Party.
I know it's frustrating, but it's a necessary process. We must raise the people's consciousness and fighting capacity.
We. Don't. Have. Time.
It's the only way change will work in the long run.
There won't BE a long run.
The world doesn't have time!

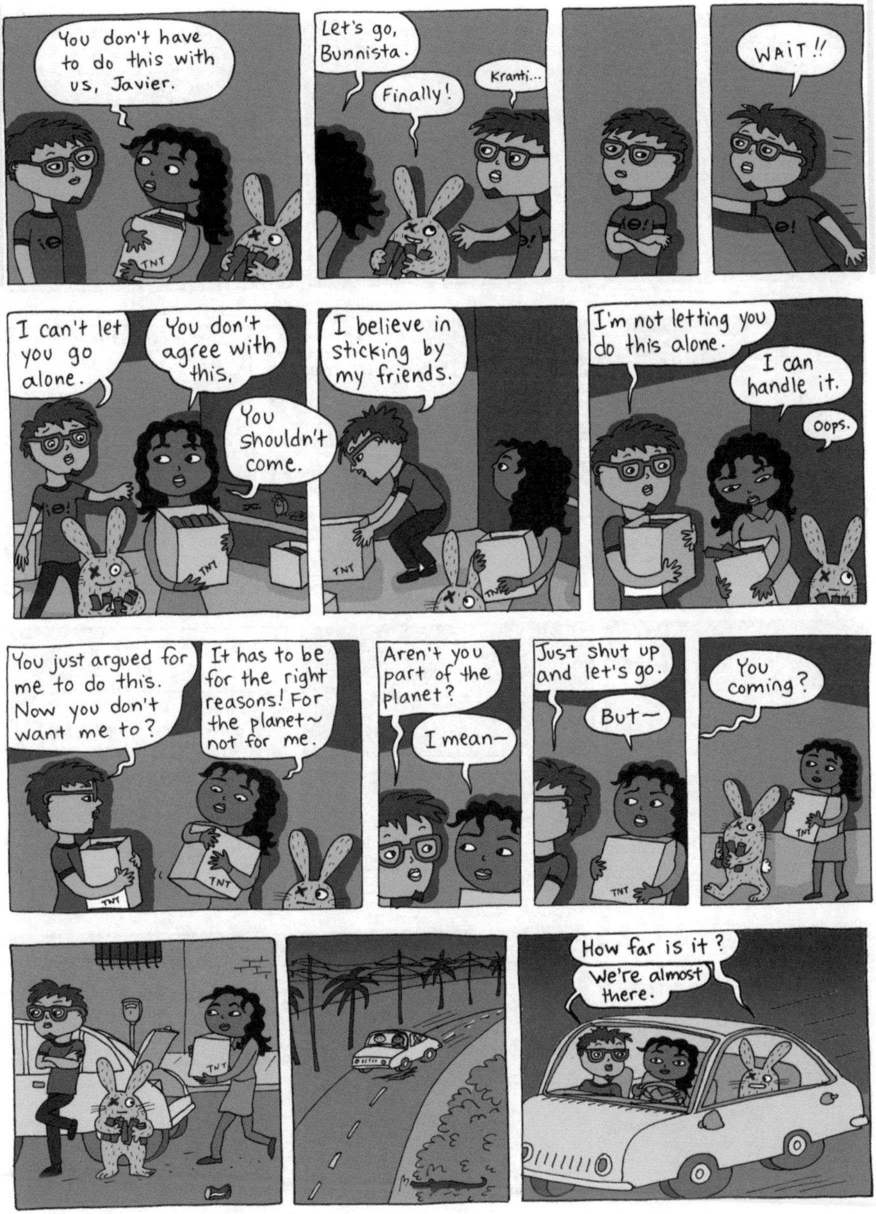
You don't have to do this with us, Javier.
Let's go, Bunnista.
Finally!
Kranti...
WAIT!!
I can't let you go alone.
You don't agree with this.
You shouldn't come.
I believe in sticking by my friends.
I'm not letting you do this alone.
I can handle it.
Oops.
You just argued for me to do this. Now you don't want me to?
It has to be for the right reasons! For the planet~ not for me.
Aren't you part of the planet?
I mean—
Just shut up and let's go.
But—
You coming?
How far is it?
We're almost there.

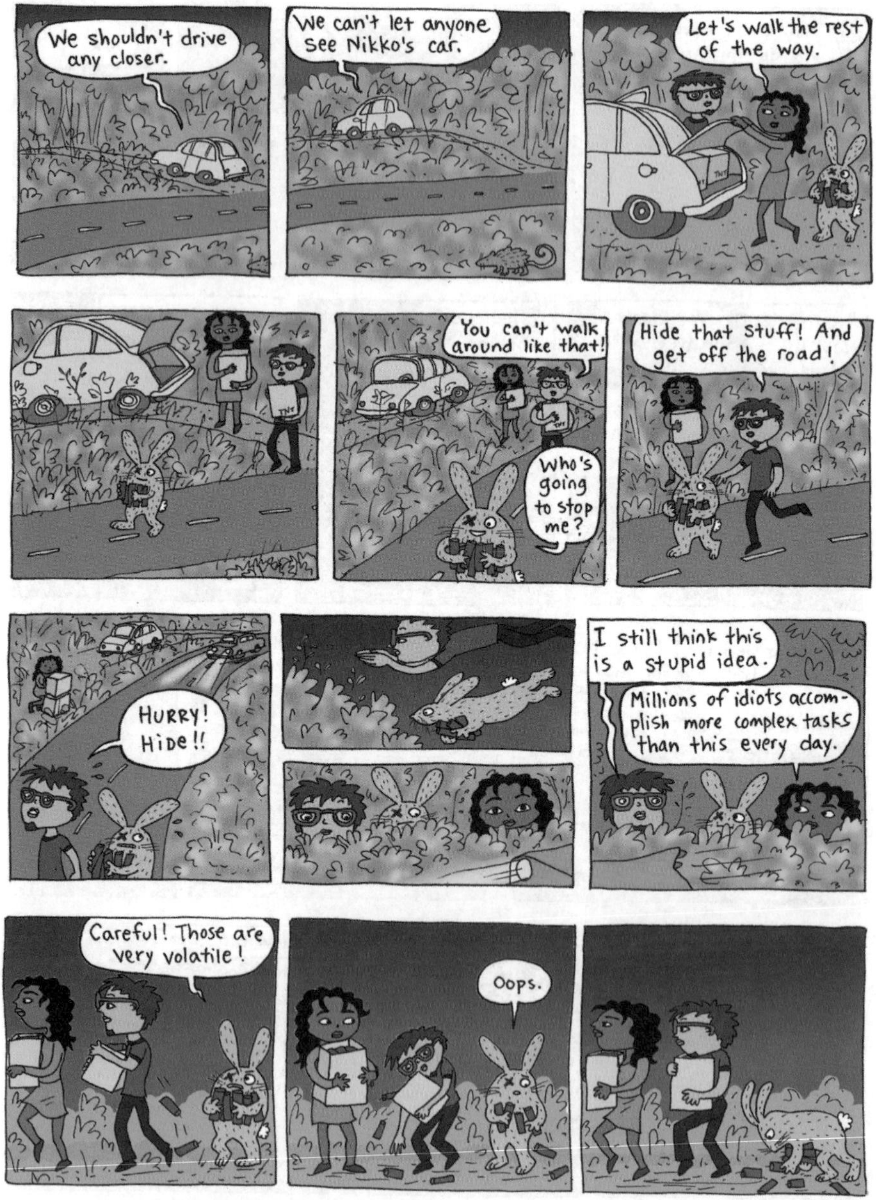
We shouldn't drive any closer.
We can't let anyone see Nikko's car.
Let's walk the rest of the way.
You can't walk around like that!
Who's going to stop me?
Hide that stuff! And get off the road!
HURRY! HIDE!!
I still think this is a stupid idea.
Millions of idiots accomplish more complex tasks than this every day.
Careful! Those are very volatile!
Oops.

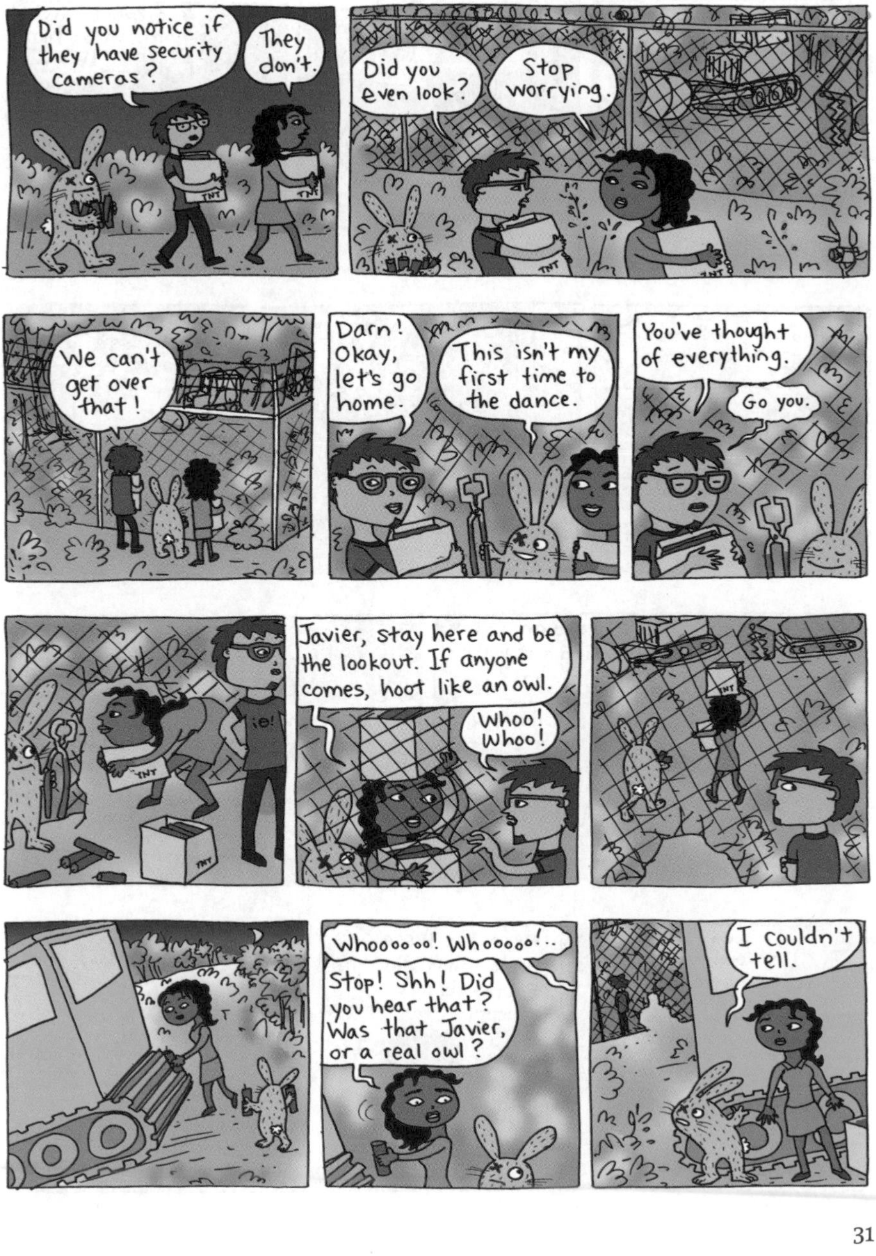

Did you notice if they have security cameras?
They don't.
TNT
TNT
Did you even look?
Stop worrying.
TNT
TNT
We can't get over that!
Darn! Okay, let's go home.
This isn't my first time to the dance.
You've thought of everything.
Go you.
TNT
TNT
Javier, stay here and be the lookout. If anyone comes, hoot like an owl.
Whoo! Whoo!
TNT
Whooooo! Whooooo!..
Stop! Shh! Did you hear that? Was that Javier, or a real owl?
I couldn't tell.

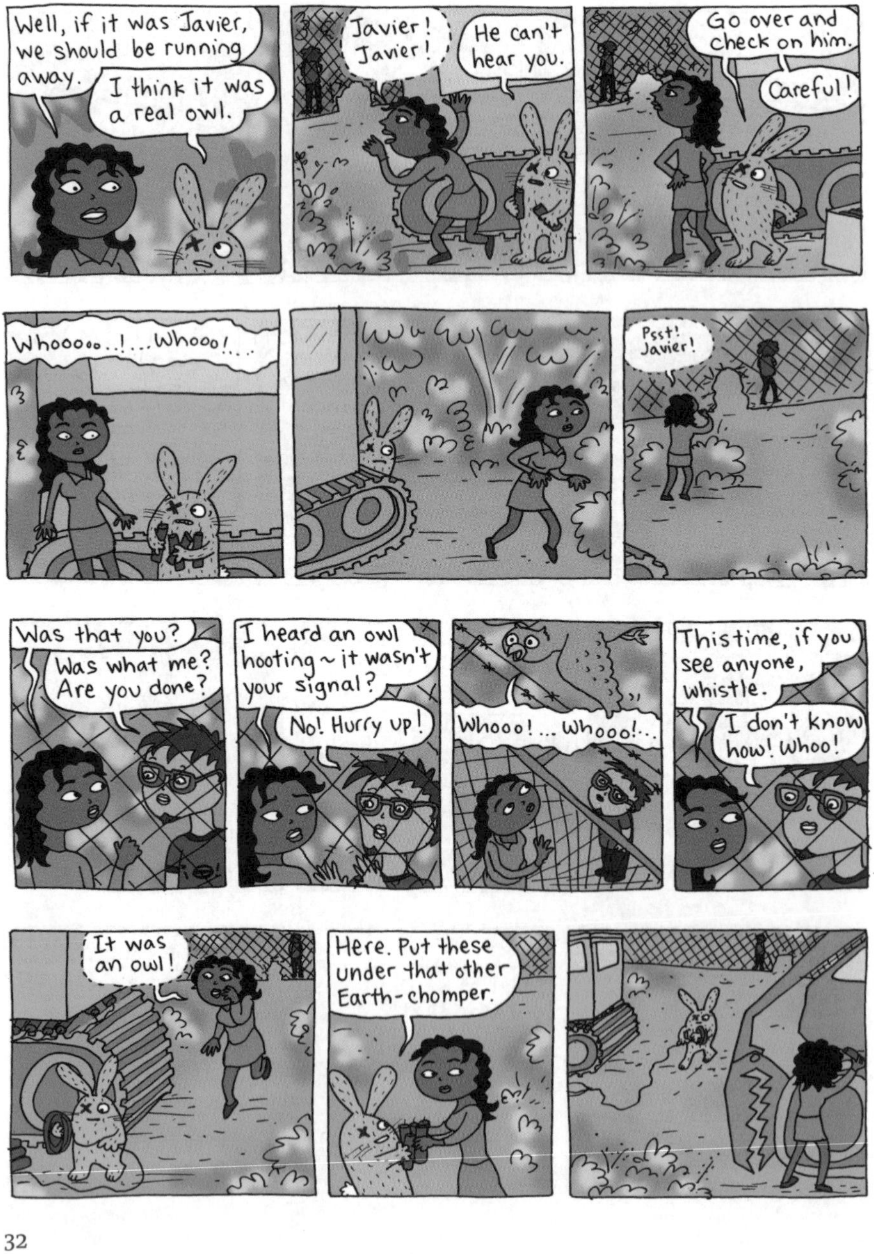

Well, if it was Javier, we should be running away.
I think it was a real owl.
Javier! Javier!
He can't hear you.
Go over and check on him.
Careful!
Whoooo..!...Whooo!...
Psst! Javier!
Was that you?
Was what me? Are you done?
I heard an owl hooting ~ it wasn't your signal?
No! Hurry up!
Whooo!...Whooo!...
This time, if you see anyone, whistle.
I don't know how! Whoo!
It was an owl!
Here. Put these under that other Earth-chomper.

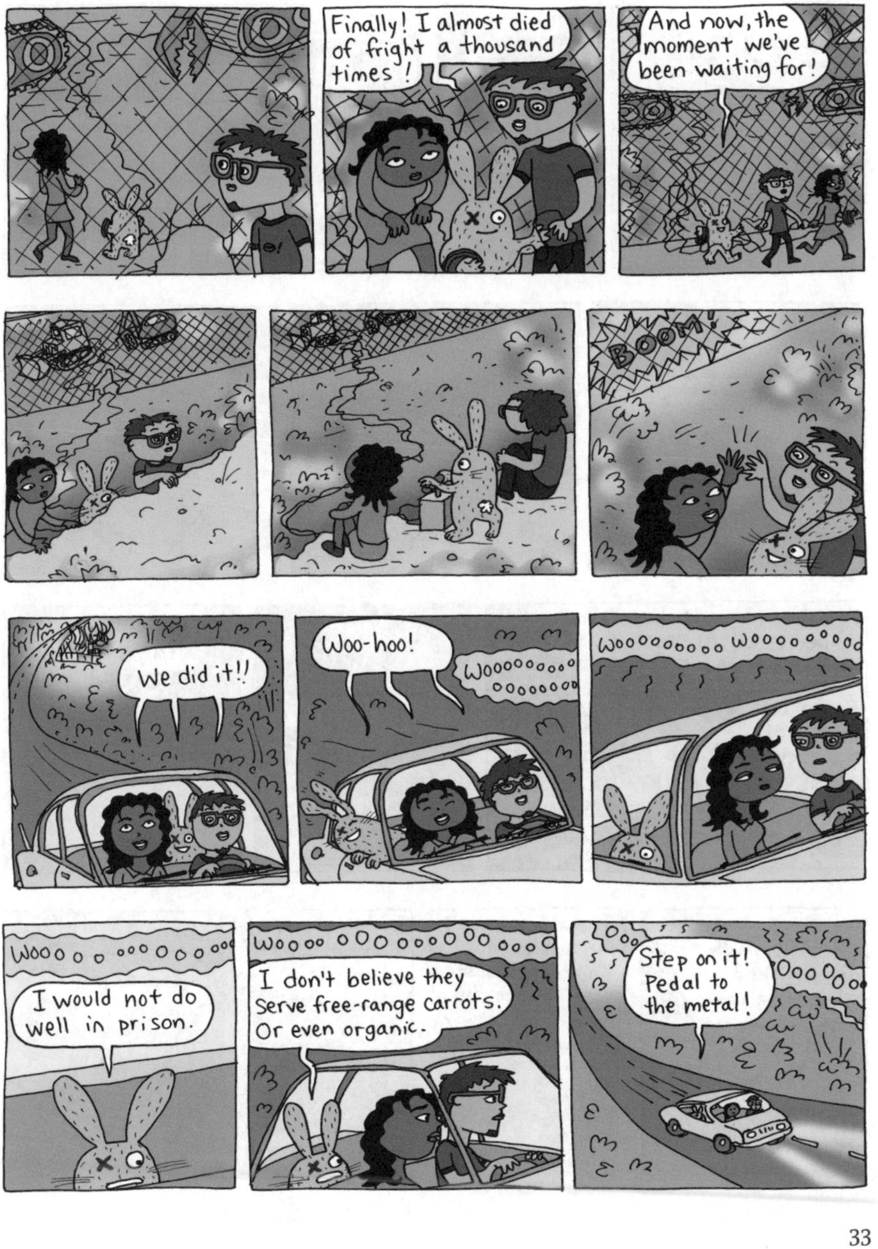
Finally! I almost died of fright a thousand times!
And now, the moment we've been waiting for!
BOOM!
We did it!!
Woo-hoo!
Wooooooooo
ooooooooo
Wooooooooo Wooooooooo
Wooo o o ooo ooo ooo
I would not do well in prison.
Woo oo ooo oooo ooo oooo
I don't believe they serve free-range carrots. Or even organic.
Step on it! Pedal to the metal!

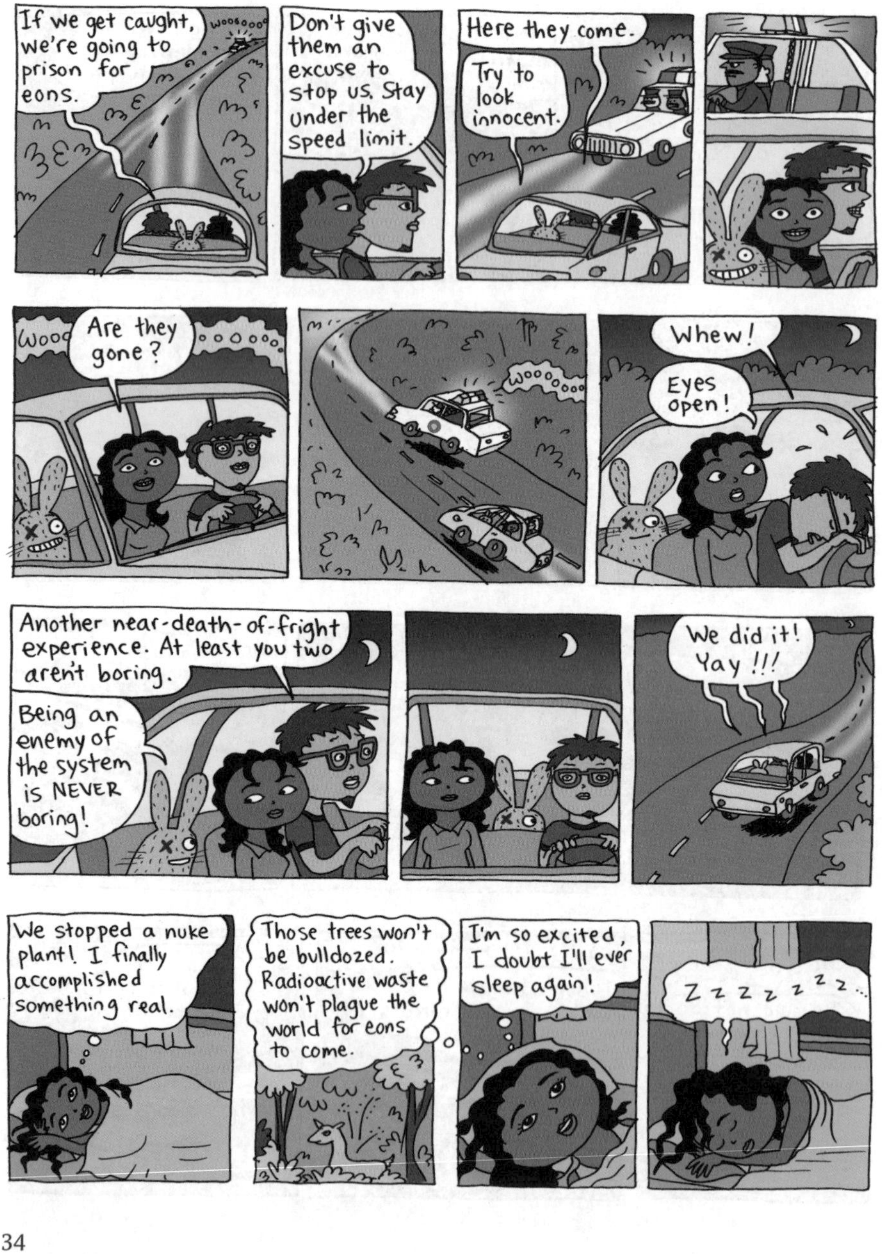
If we get caught, we're going to prison for eons.
WOOOOOOO
Don't give them an excuse to stop us. Stay under the speed limit.
Here they come.
Try to look innocent.
WOOO
Are they gone?
OOOOOOO
WOOOOOOO
Whew!
Eyes open!
Another near-death-of-fright experience. At least you two aren't boring.
Being an enemy of the system is NEVER boring!
We did it! Yay!!!
We stopped a nuke plant! I finally accomplished something real.
Those trees won't be bulldozed. Radioactive waste won't plague the world for eons to come.
I'm so excited, I doubt I'll ever sleep again!
Z z z z z z z...

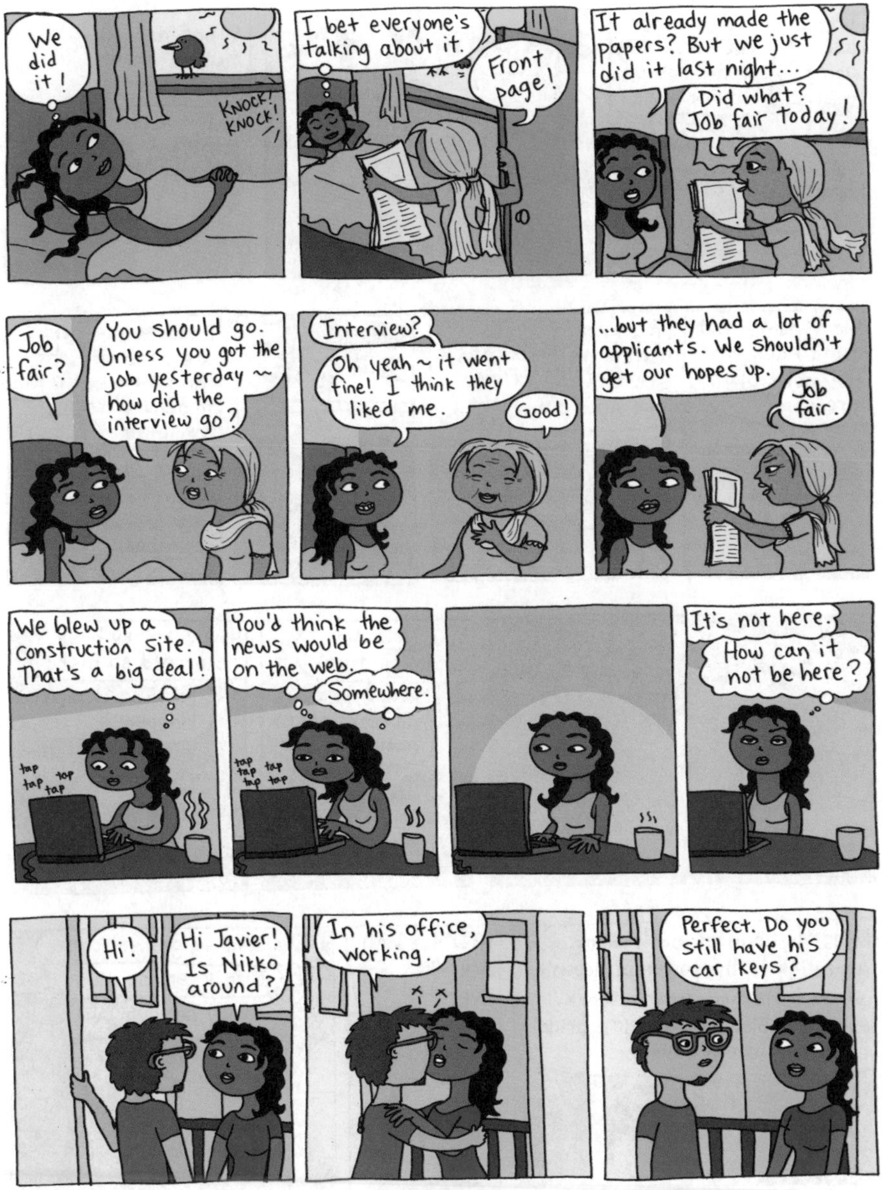
We did it!
KNOCK! KNOCK!
I bet everyone's talking about it.
Front page!
It already made the papers? But we just did it last night...
Did what? Job fair today!
Job fair?
You should go. Unless you got the job yesterday ~ how did the interview go?
Interview?
Oh yeah ~ it went fine! I think they liked me.
Good!
...but they had a lot of applicants. We shouldn't get our hopes up.
Job fair.
We blew up a construction site. That's a big deal!
tap tap tap tap
You'd think the news would be on the web.
Somewhere.
tap tap tap tap tap
It's not here.
How can it not be here?
Hi!
Hi Javier! Is Nikko around?
In his office, working.
Perfect. Do you still have his car keys?

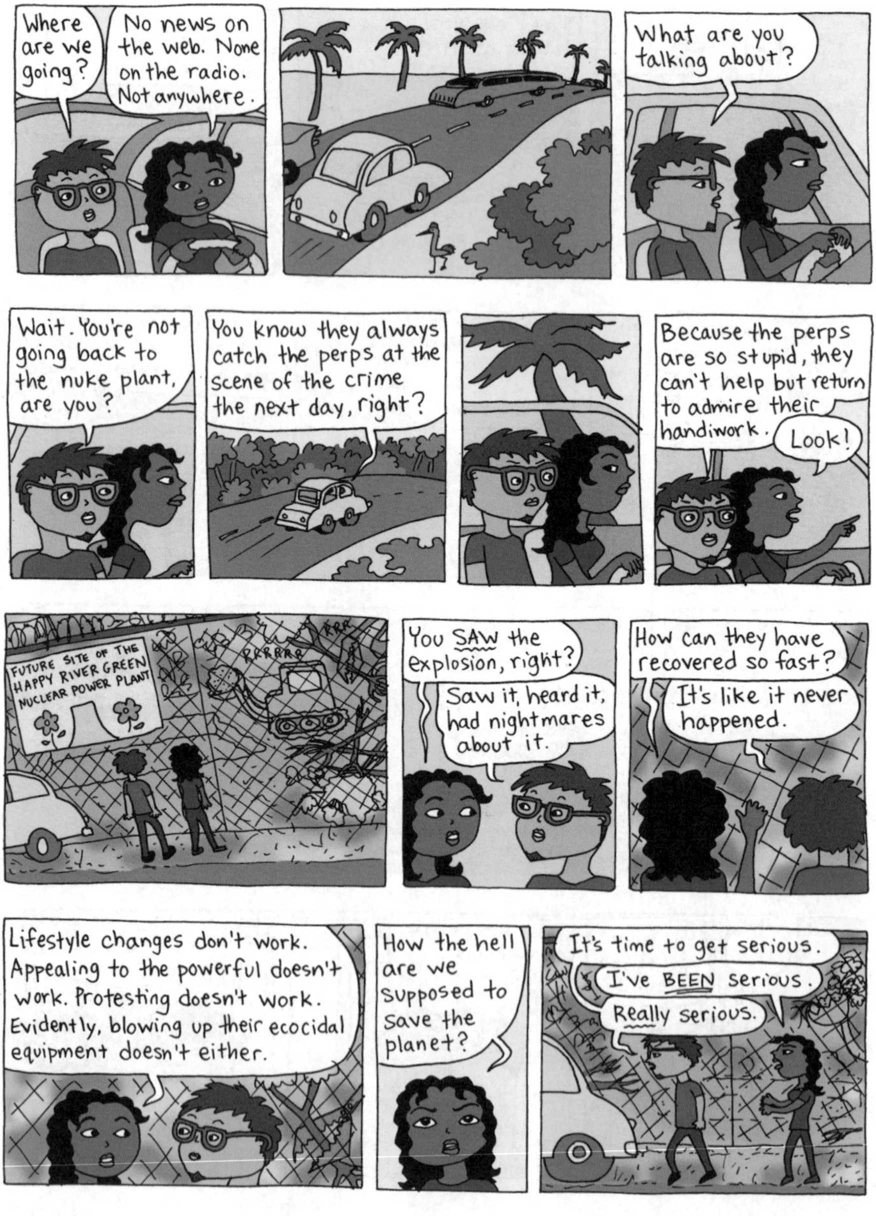
Where are we going?
No news on the web. None on the radio. Not anywhere.
What are you talking about?
Wait. You're not going back to the nuke plant, are you?
You know they always catch the perps at the scene of the crime the next day, right?
Because the perps are so stupid, they can't help but return to admire their handiwork.
Look!
FUTURE SITE OF THE HAPPY RIVER GREEN NUCLEAR POWER PLANT
You SAW the explosion, right?
Saw it, heard it, had nightmares about it.
How can they have recovered so fast?
It's like it never happened.
Lifestyle changes don't work. Appealing to the powerful doesn't work. Protesting doesn't work. Evidently, blowing up their ecocidal equipment doesn't either.
How the hell are we supposed to save the planet?
It's time to get serious.
I've BEEN serious.
Really serious.

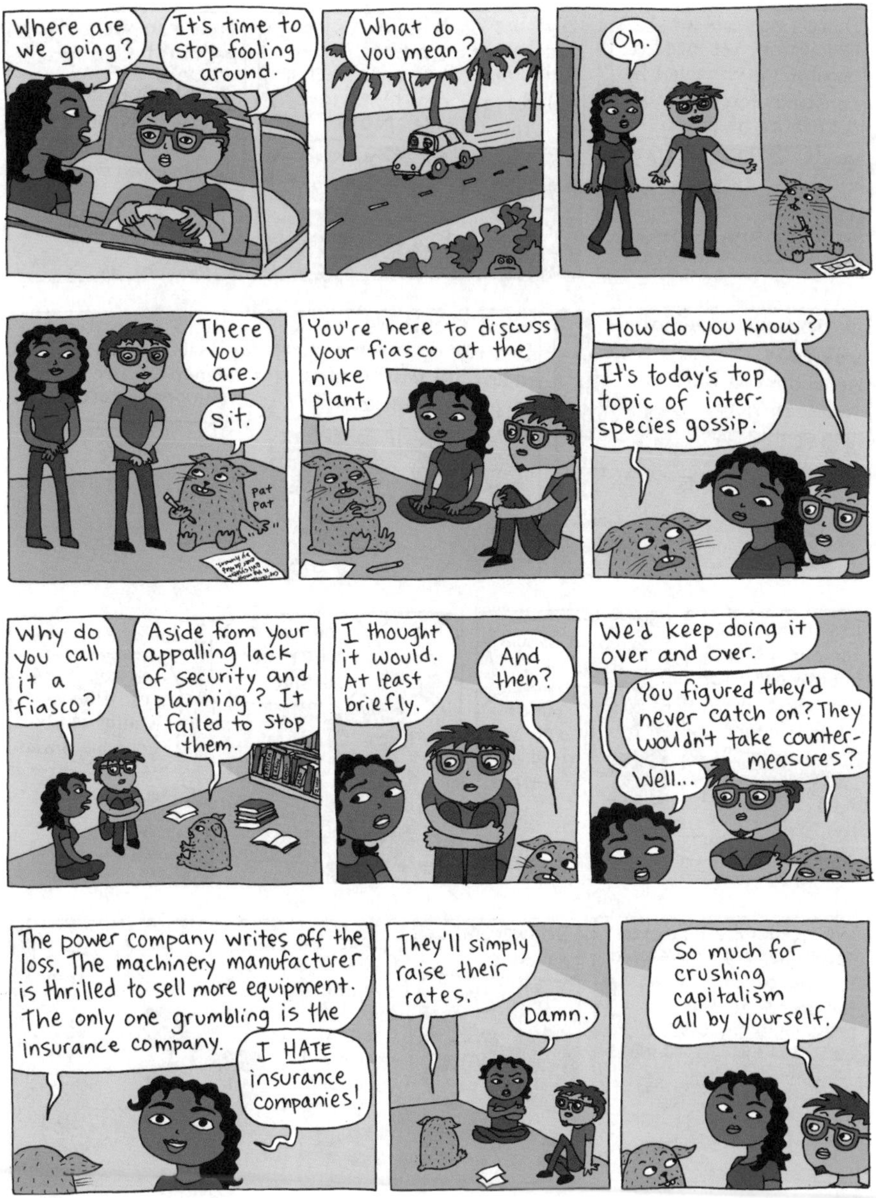
Where are we going?
It's time to stop fooling around.
What do you mean?
Oh.
There you are.
Sit.
Pat Pat
You're here to discuss your fiasco at the nuke plant.
How do you know?
It's today's top topic of inter-species gossip.
Why do you call it a fiasco?
Aside from your appalling lack of security and planning? It failed to stop them.
I thought it would. At least briefly.
And then?
We'd keep doing it over and over.
You figured they'd never catch on? They wouldn't take counter-measures?
Well...
The power company writes off the loss. The machinery manufacturer is thrilled to sell more equipment. The only one grumbling is the insurance company.
I HATE insurance companies!
They'll simply raise their rates.
Damn.
So much for crushing capitalism all by yourself.

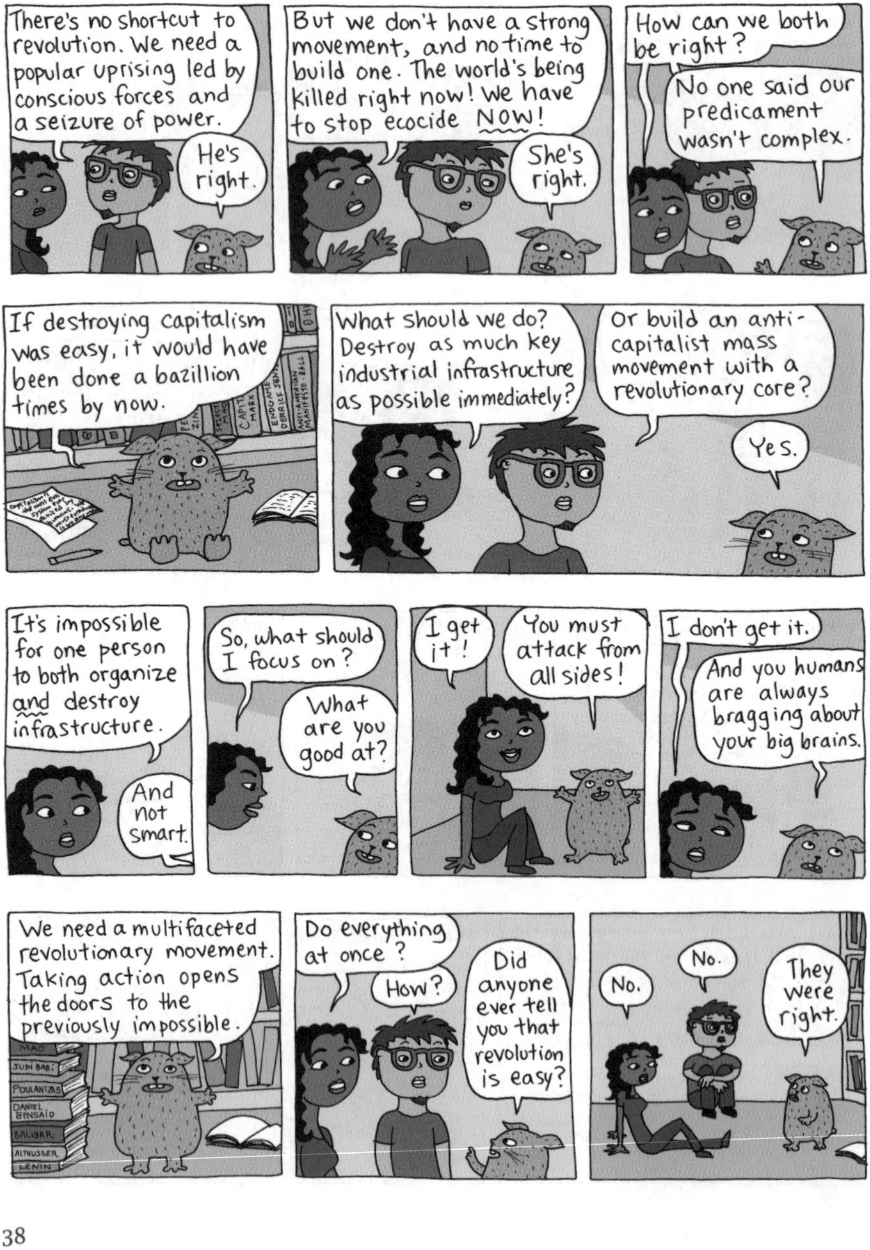
There's no shortcut to revolution. We need a popular uprising led by conscious forces and a seizure of power.
He's right.
But we don't have a strong movement, and no time to build one. The world's being killed right now! We have to stop ecocide NOW!
She's right.
How can we both be right?
No one said our predicament wasn't complex.
If destroying capitalism was easy, it would have been done a bazillion times by now.
What should we do? Destroy as much key industrial infrastructure as possible immediately?
Or build an anti-capitalist mass movement with a revolutionary core?
Yes.
It's impossible for one person to both organize and destroy infrastructure.
And not smart.
So, what should I focus on?
What are you good at?
I get it!
You must attack from all sides!
I don't get it.
And you humans are always bragging about your big brains.
We need a multifaceted revolutionary movement. Taking action opens the doors to the previously impossible.
MAO
JUDI BARI
POULANTZAS
DANIEL BENSAID
BALIBAR
ALTHUSSER
LENIN
Do everything at once?
How?
Did anyone ever tell you that revolution is easy?
No.
No.
They were right.

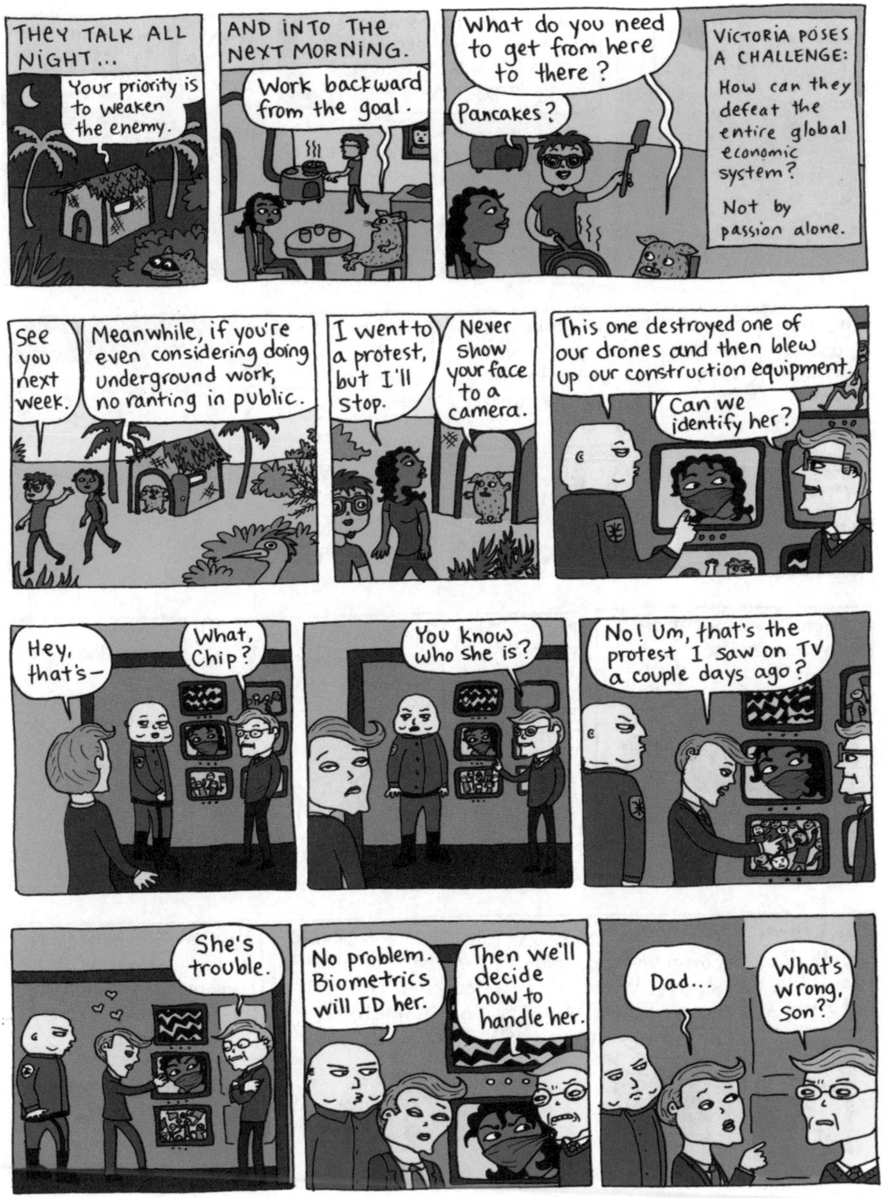
THEY TALK ALL NIGHT...
Your priority is to weaken the enemy.
AND INTO THE NEXT MORNING.
Work backward from the goal.
What do you need to get from here to there?
Pancakes?
VICTORIA POSES A CHALLENGE:
How can they defeat the entire global economic system?
Not by passion alone.
See you next week.
Meanwhile, if you're even considering doing underground work, no ranting in public.
I went to a protest, but I'll stop.
Never show your face to a camera.
This one destroyed one of our drones and then blew up our construction equipment.
Can we identify her?
Hey, that's—
What, Chip?
You know who she is?
No! Um, that's the protest I saw on TV a couple days ago?
She's trouble.
No problem. Biometrics will ID her.
Then we'll decide how to handle her.
Dad...
What's wrong, Son?

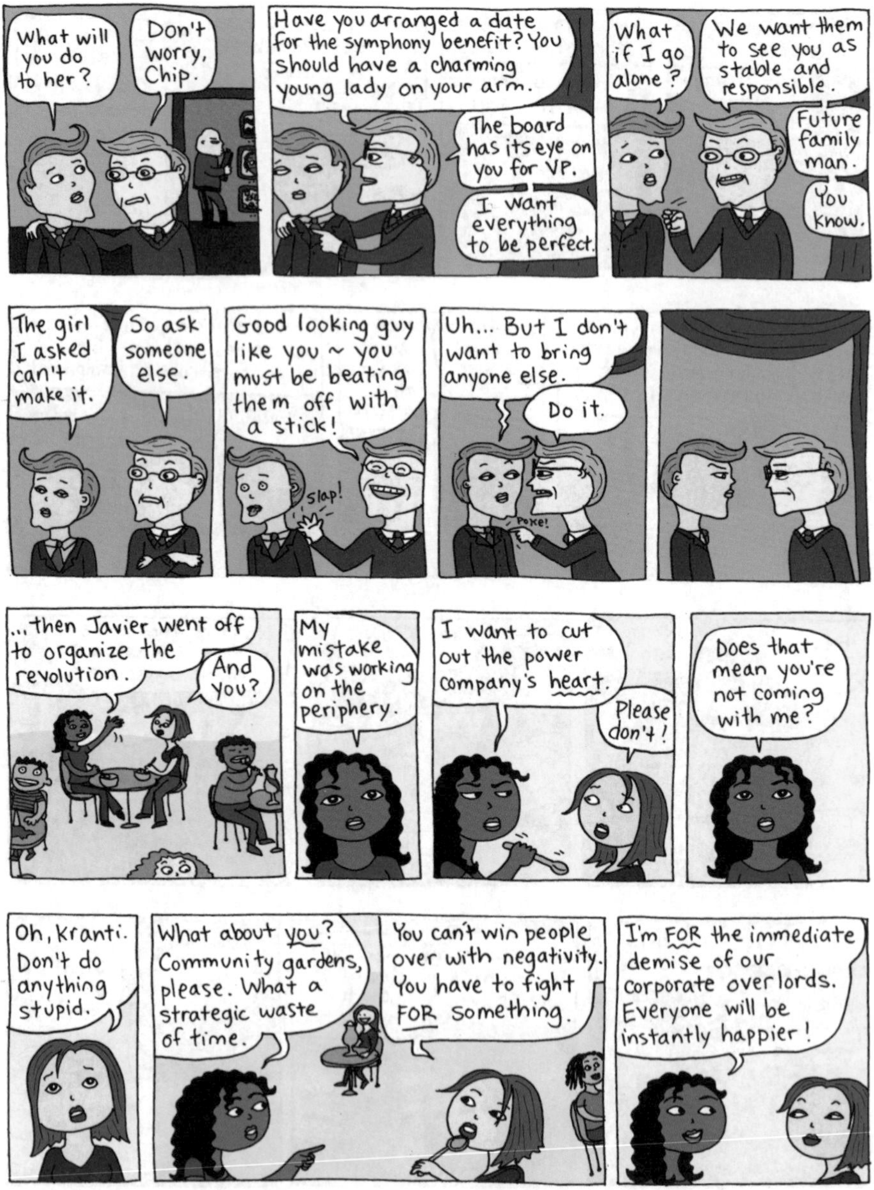
What will you do to her?
Don't worry, Chip.
Have you arranged a date for the symphony benefit? You should have a charming young lady on your arm.
The board has its eye on you for VP.
I want everything to be perfect.
What if I go alone?
We want them to see you as stable and responsible.
Future family man.
You know.
The girl I asked can't make it.
So ask someone else.
Good looking guy like you ~ you must be beating them off with a stick!
Slap!
Uh... But I don't want to bring anyone else.
Do it.
POKE!
...then Javier went off to organize the revolution.
And you?
My mistake was working on the periphery.
I want to cut out the power company's heart.
Please don't!
Does that mean you're not coming with me?
Oh, Kranti. Don't do anything stupid.
What about you? Community gardens, please. What a strategic waste of time.
You can't win people over with negativity. You have to fight FOR something.
I'm FOR the immediate demise of our corporate overlords. Everyone will be instantly happier!

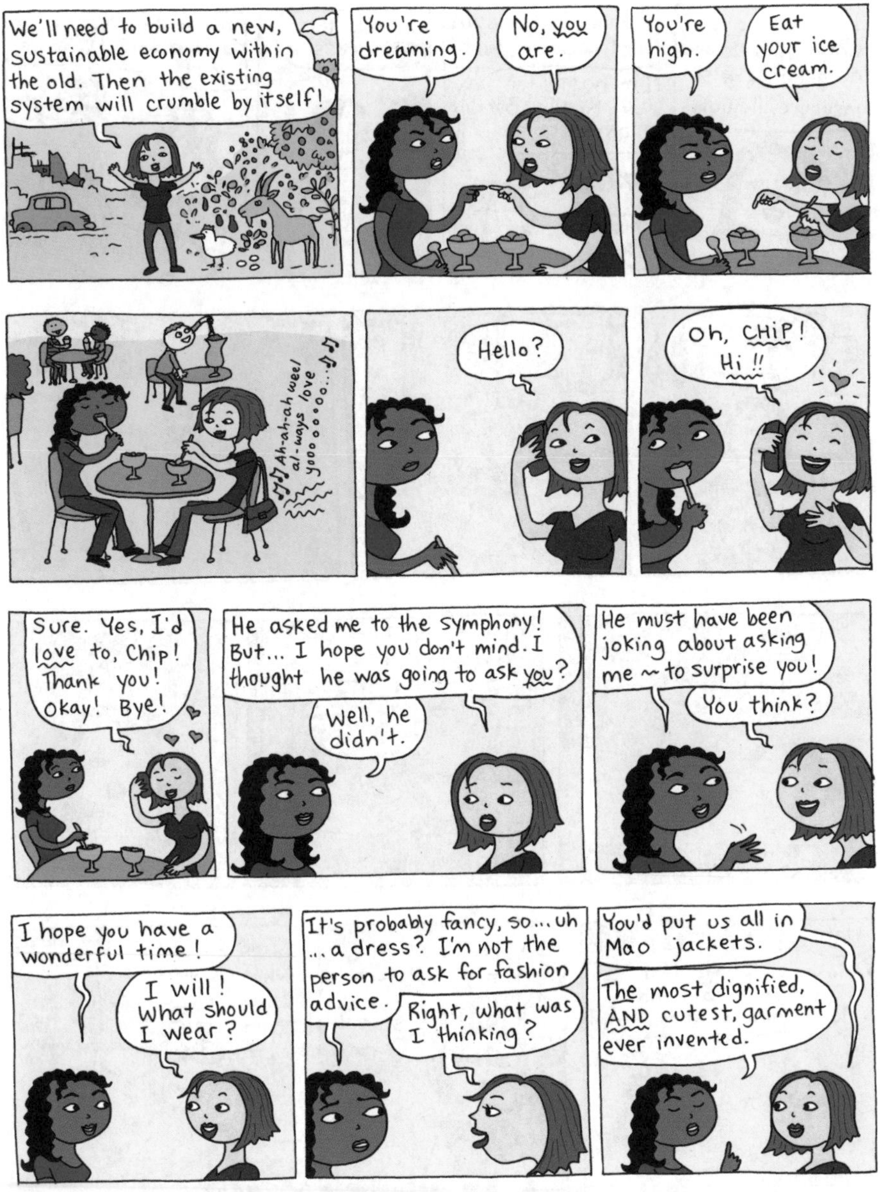
We'll need to build a new, sustainable economy within the old. Then the existing system will crumble by itself!
You're dreaming.
No, you are.
You're high.
Eat your ice cream.
Ah-ah-ah weel al-ways love yooo o o o o o o...
Hello?
Oh, CHIP! Hi !!
Sure. Yes, I'd love to, Chip! Thank you! Okay! Bye!
He asked me to the symphony! But... I hope you don't mind. I thought he was going to ask you?
Well, he didn't.
He must have been joking about asking me ~ to surprise you!
You think?
I hope you have a wonderful time!
I will! What should I wear?
It's probably fancy, so... uh ... a dress? I'm not the person to ask for fashion advice.
Right, what was I thinking?
You'd put us all in Mao jackets.
The most dignified, AND cutest, garment ever invented.

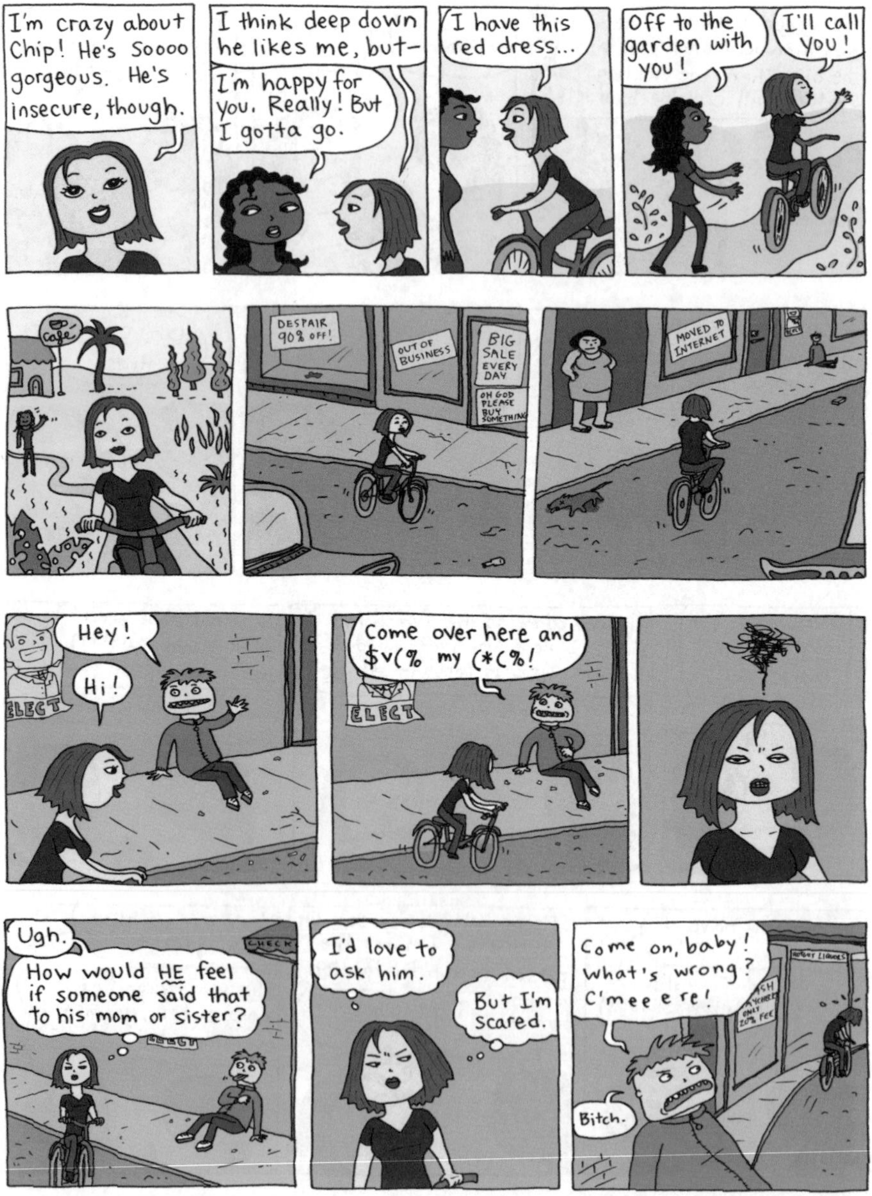
I'm crazy about Chip! He's Soooo gorgeous. He's insecure, though.
I think deep down he likes me, but-
I'm happy for you. Really! But I gotta go.
I have this red dress...
Off to the garden with you!
I'll call you!
Cafe
DESPAIR 90% OFF!
OUT OF BUSINESS
BIG SALE EVERY DAY
OH GOD PLEASE BUY SOMETHING
MOVED TO INTERNET
Hey!
Hi!
ELECT
Come over here and $v(% my (*(%!
ELECT
Ugh.
How would HE feel if someone said that to his mom or sister?
I'd love to ask him.
But I'm scared.
Come on, baby! What's wrong? C'mee e re!
Bitch.

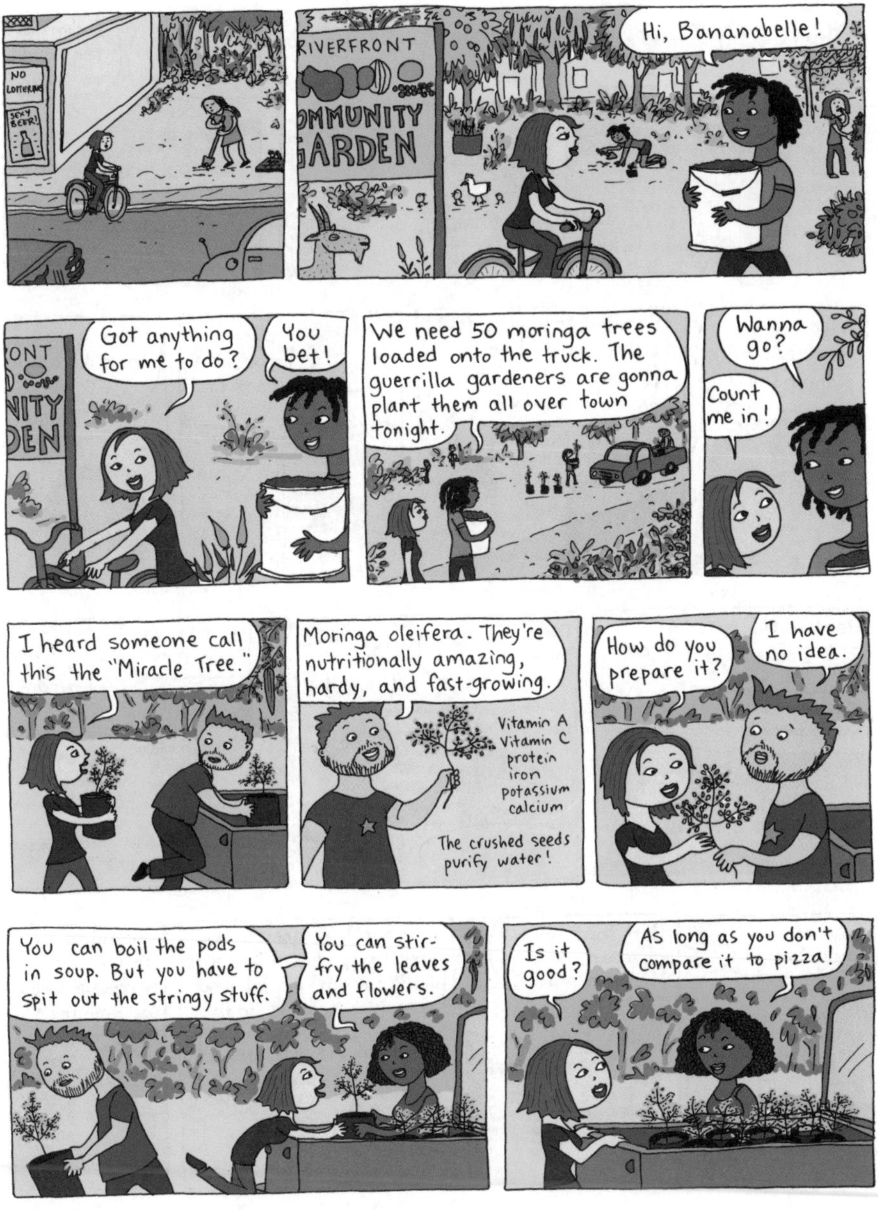
NO LOITERING
SEXY BEER!
RIVERFRONT COMMUNITY GARDEN
Hi, Bananabelle!
Got anything for me to do?
You bet!
We need 50 moringa trees loaded onto the truck. The guerrilla gardeners are gonna plant them all over town tonight.
Wanna go?
Count me in!
I heard someone call this the "Miracle Tree."
Moringa oleifera. They're nutritionally amazing, hardy, and fast-growing.
Vitamin A
Vitamin C
protein
iron
potassium
calcium
The crushed seeds purify water!
How do you prepare it?
I have no idea.
You can boil the pods in soup. But you have to spit out the stringy stuff.
You can stir-fry the leaves and flowers.
Is it good?
As long as you don't compare it to pizza!

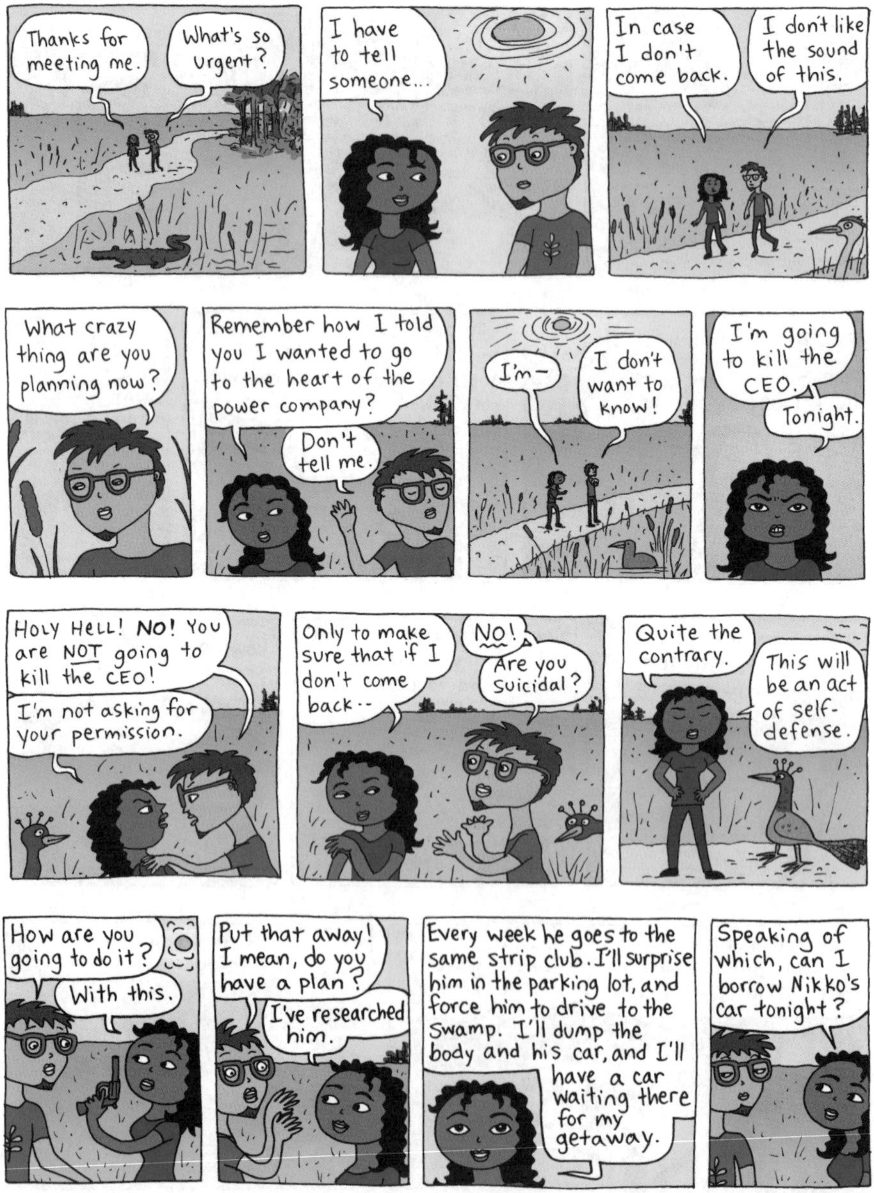
Thanks for meeting me.
What's so urgent?
I have to tell someone...
In case I don't come back.
I don't like the sound of this.
What crazy thing are you planning now?
Remember how I told you I wanted to go to the heart of the power company?
Don't tell me.
I'm–
I don't want to know!
I'm going to kill the CEO.
Tonight.
HOLY HELL! NO! You are NOT going to kill the CEO!
I'm not asking for your permission.
Only to make sure that if I don't come back..
NO!
Are you suicidal?
Quite the contrary.
This will be an act of self-defense.
How are you going to do it?
With this.
Put that away! I mean, do you have a plan?
I've researched him.
Every week he goes to the same strip club. I'll surprise him in the parking lot, and force him to drive to the swamp. I'll dump the body and his car, and I'll have a car waiting there for my getaway.
Speaking of which, can I borrow Nikko's car tonight?

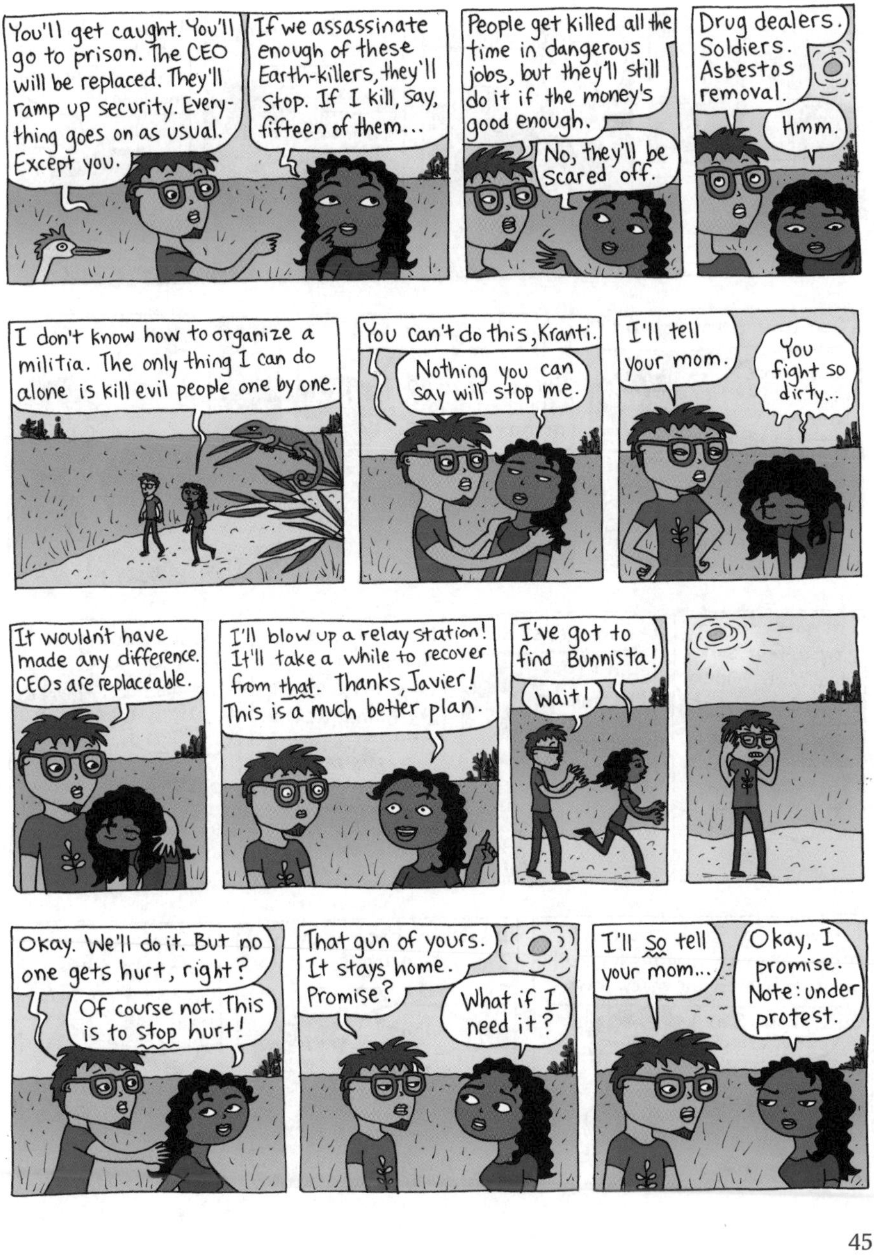

You'll get caught. You'll go to prison. The CEO will be replaced. They'll ramp up security. Everything goes on as usual. Except you.
If we assassinate enough of these Earth-killers, they'll stop. If I kill, say, fifteen of them...
People get killed all the time in dangerous jobs, but they'll still do it if the money's good enough.
No, they'll be scared off.
Drug dealers. Soldiers. Asbestos removal.
Hmm.
I don't know how to organize a militia. The only thing I can do alone is kill evil people one by one.
You can't do this, Kranti.
Nothing you can say will stop me.
I'll tell your mom.
You fight so dirty...
It wouldn't have made any difference. CEOs are replaceable.
I'll blow up a relay station! It'll take a while to recover from that. Thanks, Javier! This is a much better plan.
I've got to find Bunnista!
Wait!
Okay. We'll do it. But no one gets hurt, right?
Of course not. This is to stop hurt!
That gun of yours. It stays home. Promise?
What if I need it?
I'll so tell your mom...
Okay, I promise. Note: under protest.

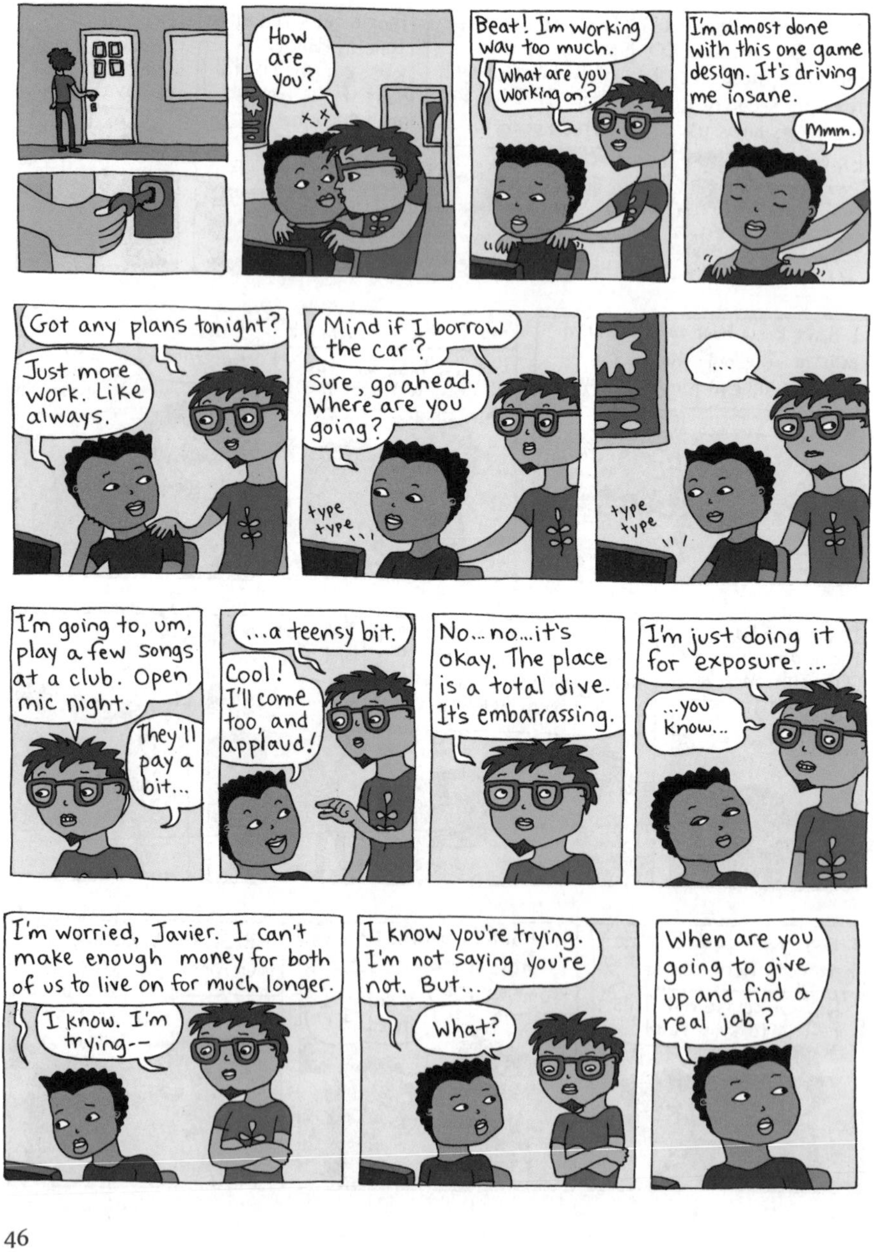
How are you?
Beat! I'm working way too much.
What are you working on?
I'm almost done with this one game design. It's driving me insane.
Mmm.
Got any plans tonight?
Just more work. Like always.
Mind if I borrow the car?
Sure, go ahead. Where are you going?
type type
...
type type
I'm going to, um, play a few songs at a club. Open mic night.
They'll pay a bit...
...a teensy bit.
Cool! I'll come too, and applaud!
No... no... it's okay. The place is a total dive. It's embarrassing.
I'm just doing it for exposure. ...
...you know...
I'm worried, Javier. I can't make enough money for both of us to live on for much longer.
I know. I'm trying--
I know you're trying. I'm not saying you're not. But...
What?
When are you going to give up and find a real job?

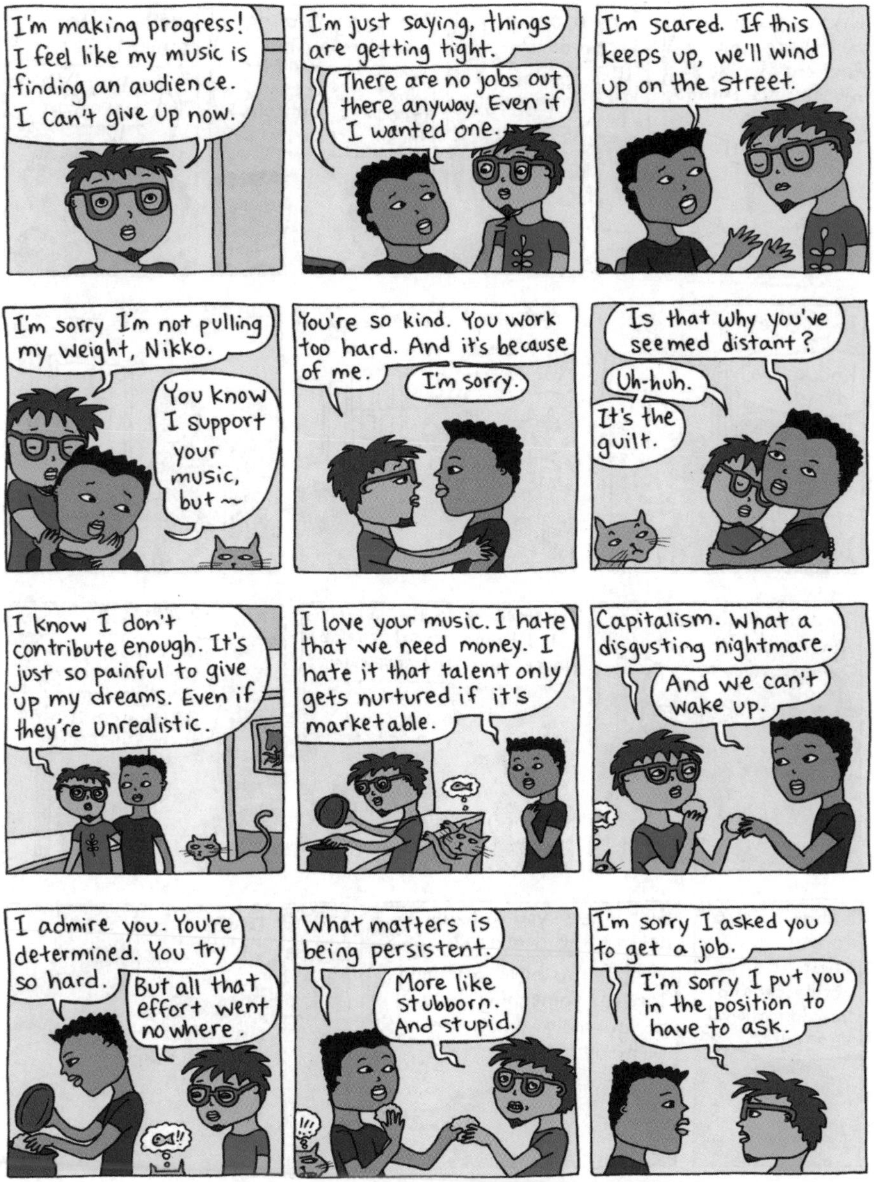
I'm making progress! I feel like my music is finding an audience. I can't give up now.
I'm just saying, things are getting tight.
There are no jobs out there anyway. Even if I wanted one.
I'm scared. If this keeps up, we'll wind up on the street.
I'm sorry I'm not pulling my weight, Nikko.
You know I support your music, but ~
You're so kind. You work too hard. And it's because of me.
I'm sorry.
Is that why you've seemed distant?
Uh-huh.
It's the guilt.
I know I don't contribute enough. It's just so painful to give up my dreams. Even if they're unrealistic.
I love your music. I hate that we need money. I hate it that talent only gets nurtured if it's marketable.
Capitalism. What a disgusting nightmare.
And we can't wake up.
I admire you. You're determined. You try so hard.
But all that effort went nowhere.
What matters is being persistent.
More like stubborn. And stupid.
I'm sorry I asked you to get a job.
I'm sorry I put you in the position to have to ask.

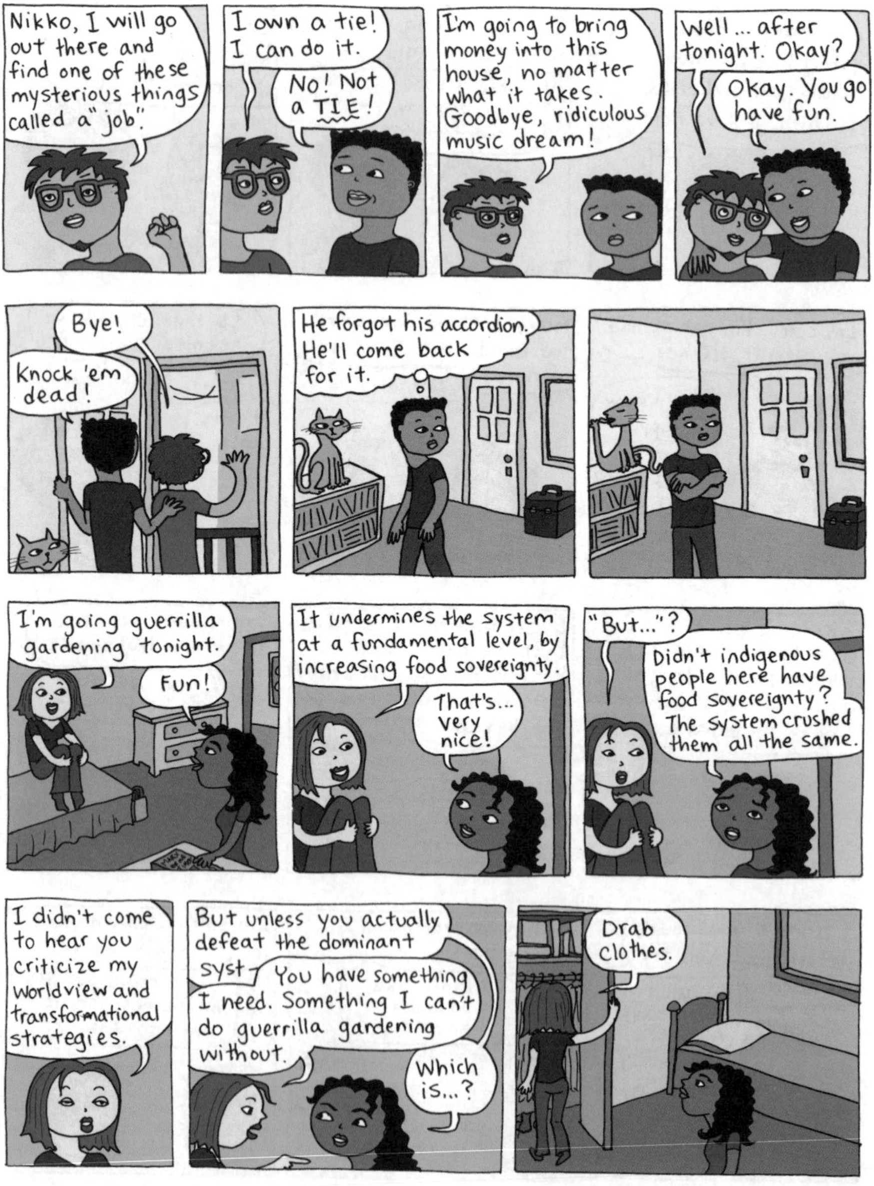
Nikko, I will go out there and find one of these mysterious things called a "job".
I own a tie! I can do it.
No! Not a TIE!
I'm going to bring money into this house, no matter what it takes. Goodbye, ridiculous music dream!
Well ... after tonight. Okay?
Okay. You go have fun.
Bye!
Knock 'em dead!
He forgot his accordion. He'll come back for it.
I'm going guerrilla gardening tonight.
Fun!
It undermines the system at a fundamental level, by increasing food sovereignty.
That's... very nice!
"But..."?
Didn't indigenous people here have food sovereignty? The system crushed them all the same.
I didn't come to hear you criticize my worldview and transformational strategies.
But unless you actually defeat the dominant syst-
You have something I need. Something I can't do guerrilla gardening without.
Which is...?
Drab clothes.

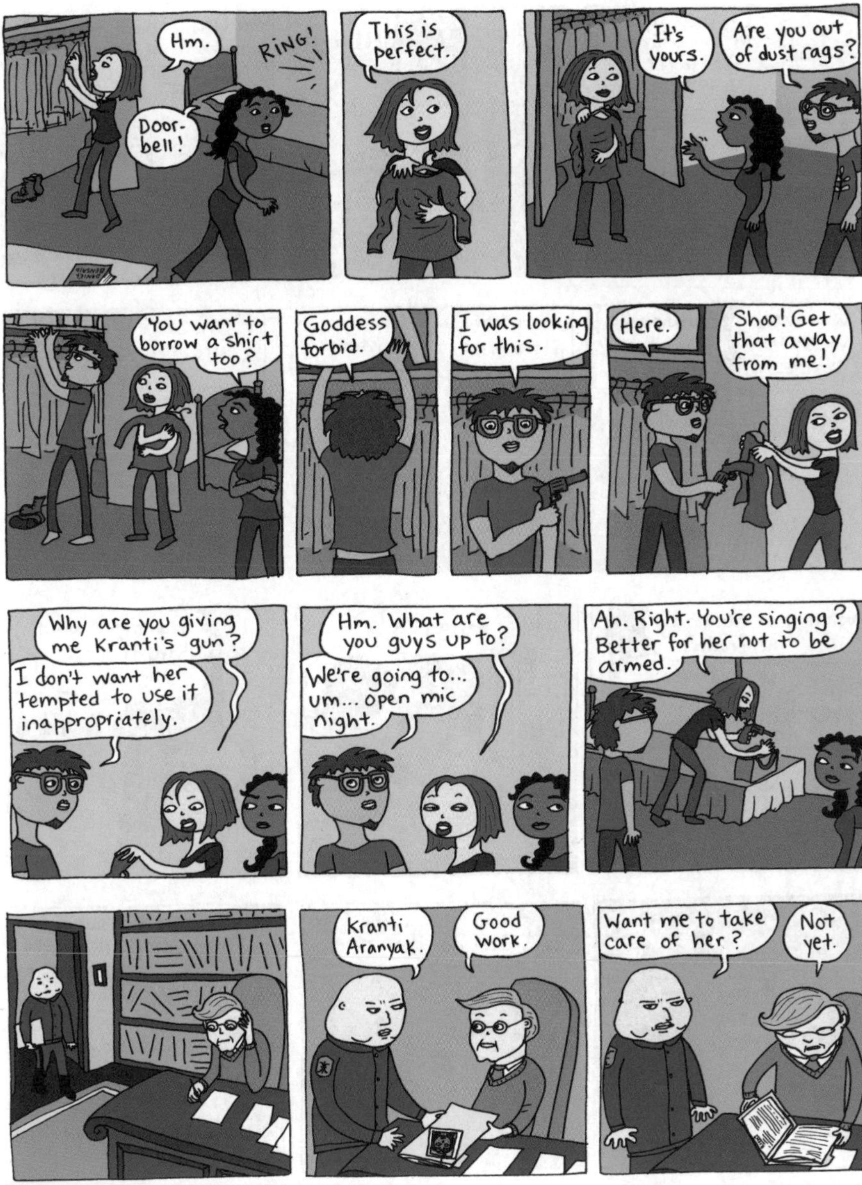
Hm.
RING!
Door-bell!
This is perfect.
It's yours.
Are you out of dust rags?
You want to borrow a shirt too?
Goddess forbid.
I was looking for this.
Here.
Shoo! Get that away from me!
Why are you giving me Kranti's gun?
I don't want her tempted to use it inappropriately.
Hm. What are you guys up to?
We're going to... um... open mic night.
Ah. Right. You're singing? Better for her not to be armed.
Kranti Aranyak.
Good work.
Want me to take care of her?
Not yet.

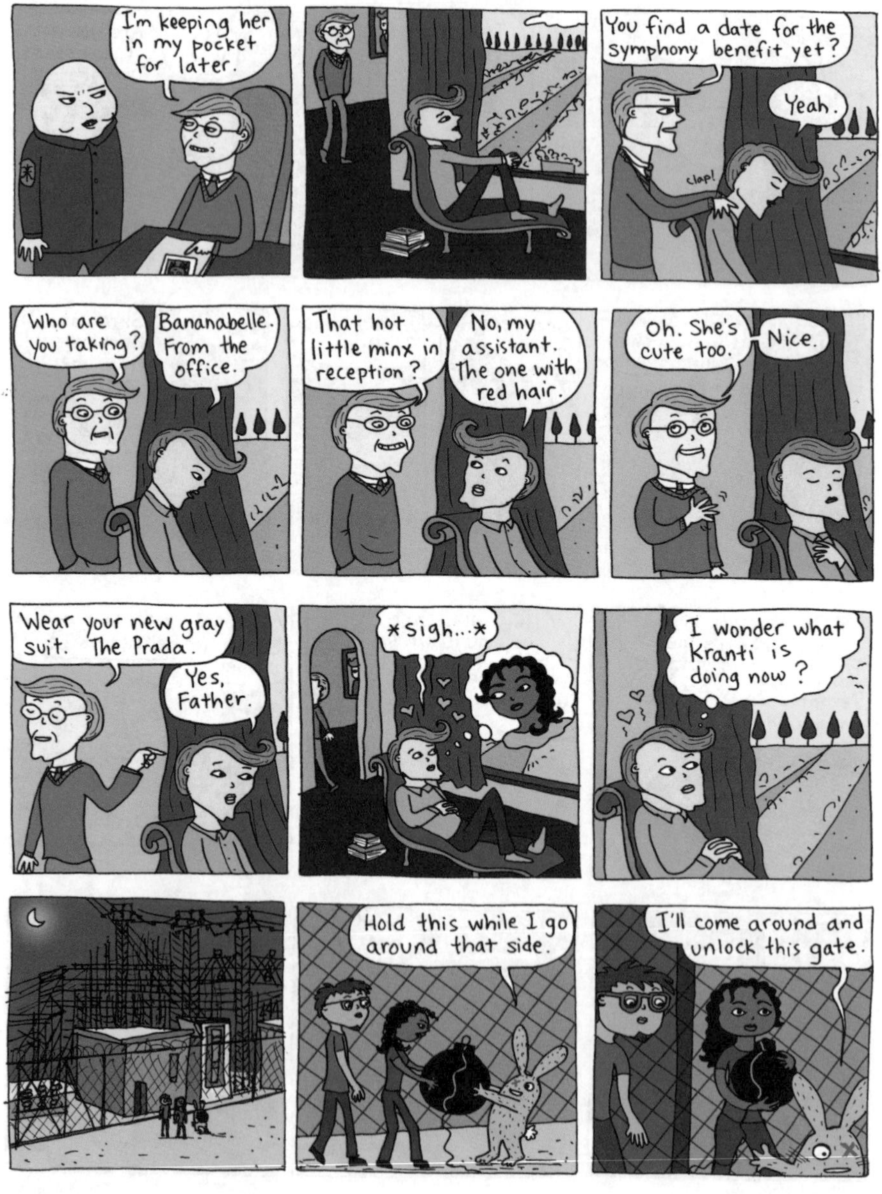
I'm keeping her in my pocket for later.
You find a date for the symphony benefit yet?
Yeah.
clap!
Who are you taking?
Bananabelle. From the office.
That hot little minx in reception?
No, my assistant. The one with red hair.
Oh. She's cute too.
Nice.
Wear your new gray suit. The Prada.
Yes, Father.
sigh...
I wonder what Kranti is doing now?
Hold this while I go around that side.
I'll come around and unlock this gate.

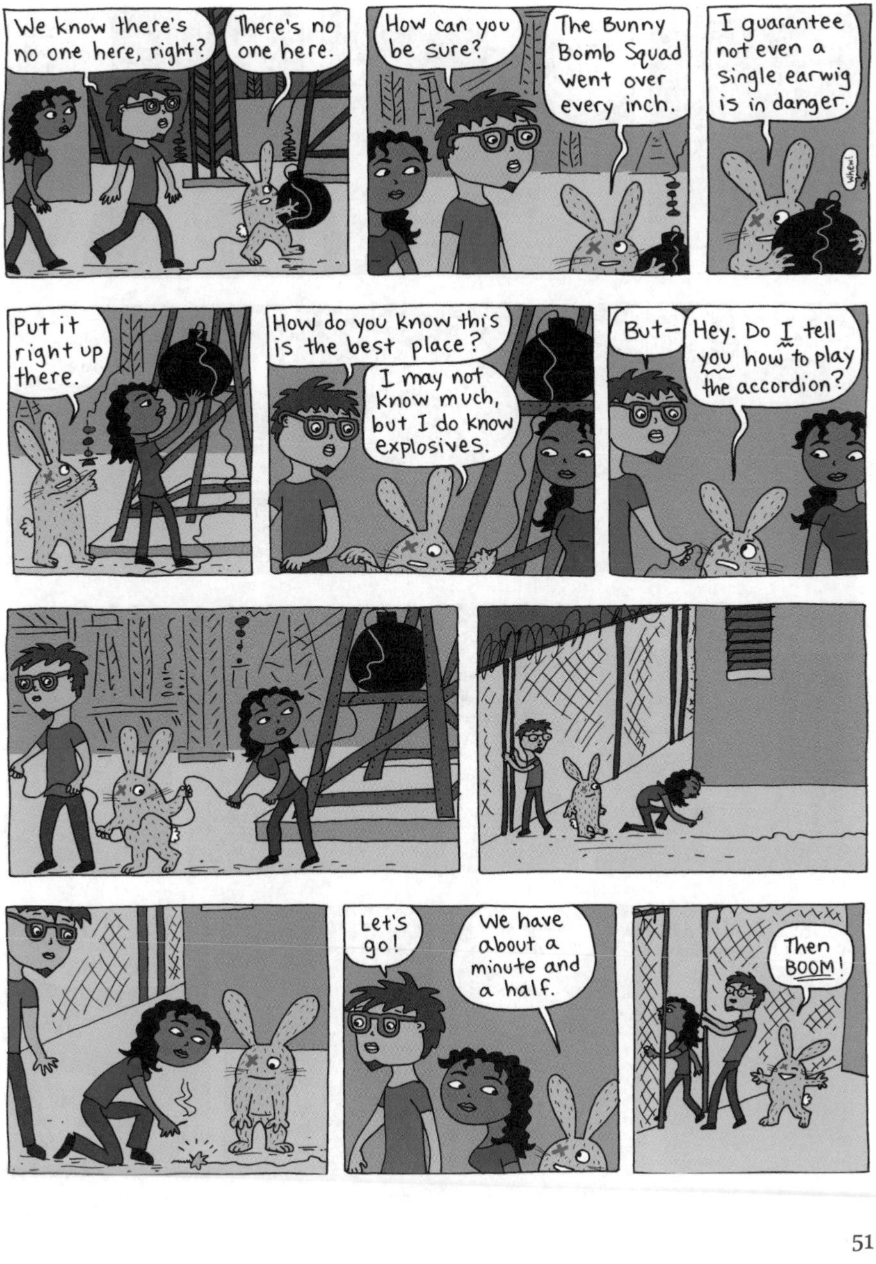
We know there's no one here, right?
There's no one here.
How can you be sure?
The Bunny Bomb Squad went over every inch.
I guarantee not even a single earwig is in danger.
Whew!
Put it right up there.
How do you know this is the best place?
I may not know much, but I do know explosives.
But—
Hey. Do I tell you how to play the accordion?
Let's go!
We have about a minute and a half.
Then BOOM!

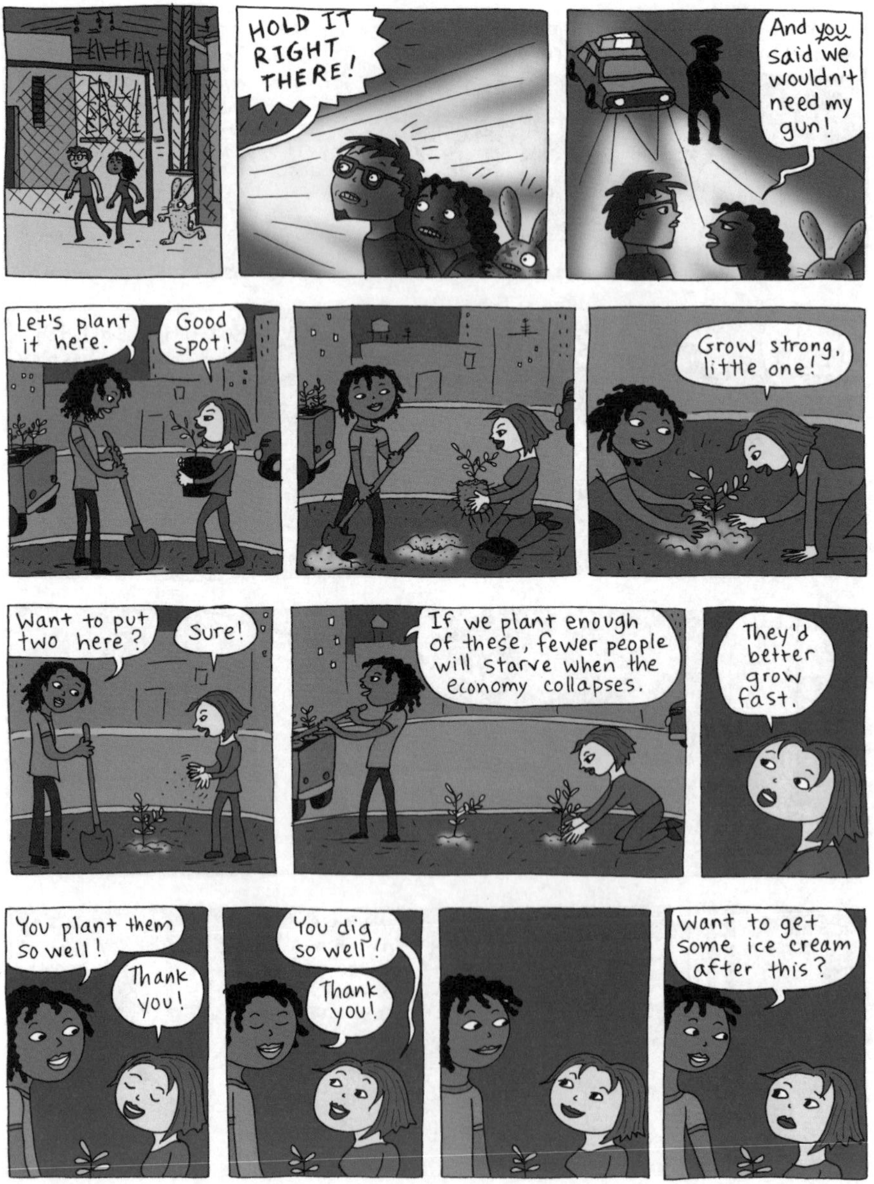
HOLD IT RIGHT THERE!
And you said we wouldn't need my gun!
Let's plant it here.
Good spot!
Grow strong, little one!
Want to put two here?
Sure!
If we plant enough of these, fewer people will starve when the economy collapses.
They'd better grow fast.
You plant them so well!
Thank you!
You dig so well!
Thank you!
Want to get some ice cream after this?

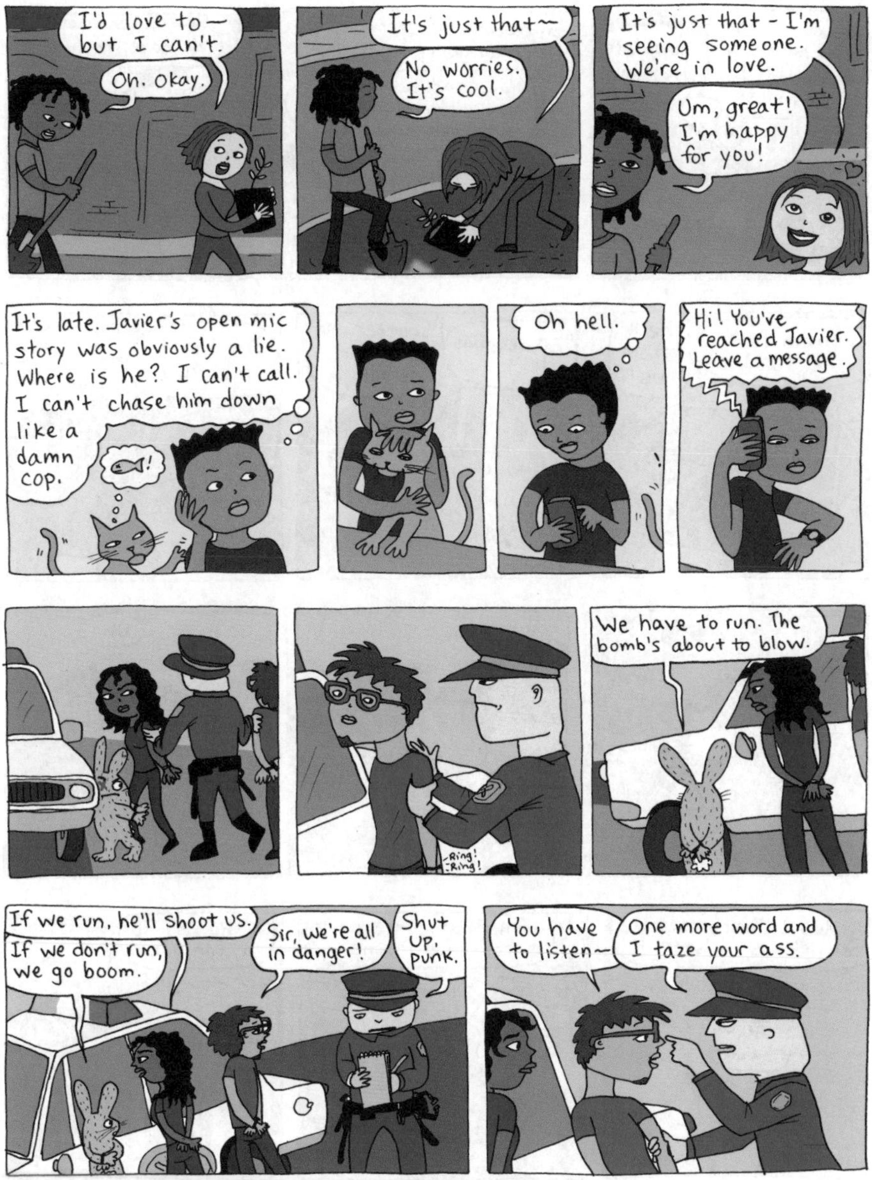

I'd love to— but I can't.
Oh. Okay.
It's just that~
No worries. It's cool.
It's just that - I'm seeing someone. We're in love.
Um, great! I'm happy for you!
It's late. Javier's open mic story was obviously a lie. Where is he? I can't call. I can't chase him down like a damn cop.
!
Oh hell.
!
Hi! You've reached Javier. Leave a message.
Ring! Ring!
We have to run. The bomb's about to blow.
If we run, he'll shoot us.
If we don't run, we go boom.
Sir, we're all in danger!
Shut up, punk.
You have to listen~
One more word and I taze your ass.

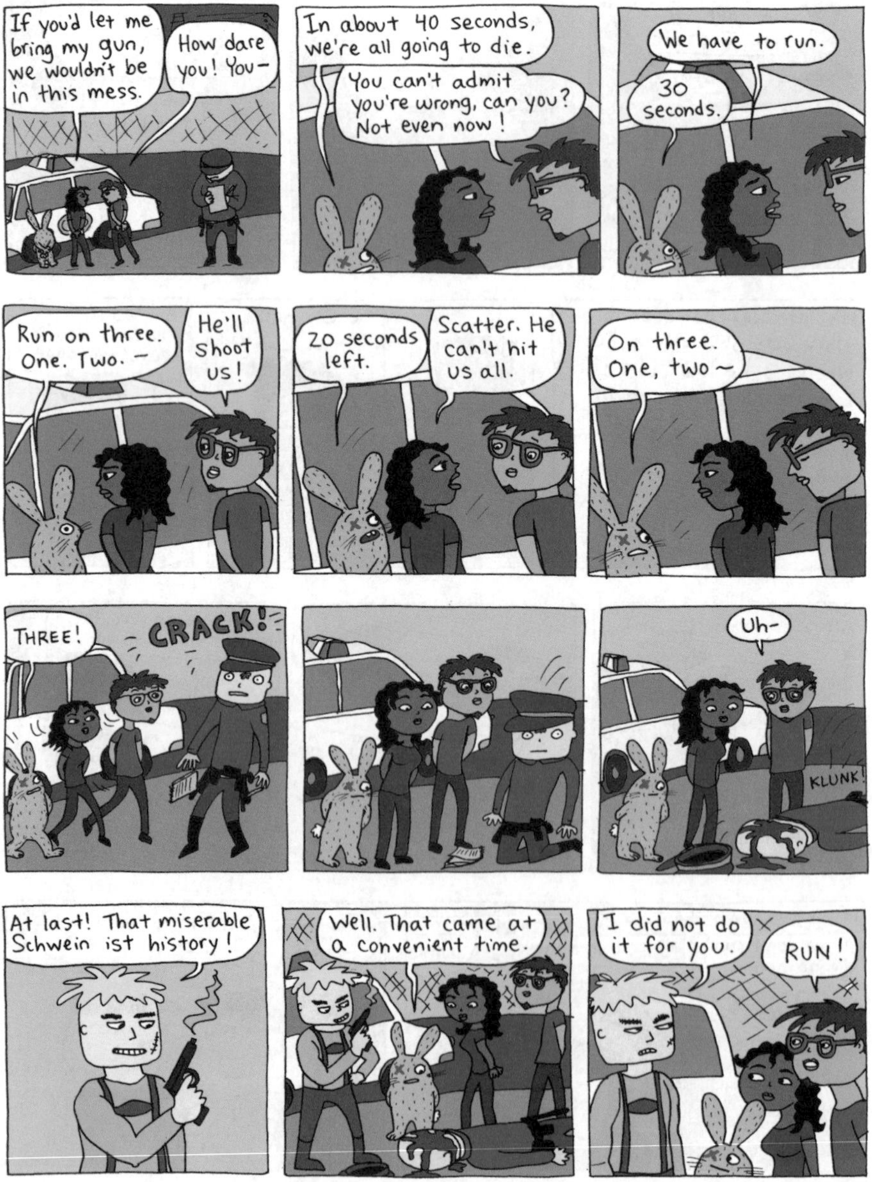
If you'd let me bring my gun, we wouldn't be in this mess.
How dare you! You—
In about 40 seconds, we're all going to die.
You can't admit you're wrong, can you? Not even now!
We have to run.
30 seconds.
Run on three. One. Two. —
He'll shoot us!
20 seconds left.
Scatter. He can't hit us all.
On three. One, two ~
THREE!
CRACK!
Uh-
KLUNK!
At last! That miserable Schwein ist history!
Well. That came at a convenient time.
I did not do it for you.
RUN!

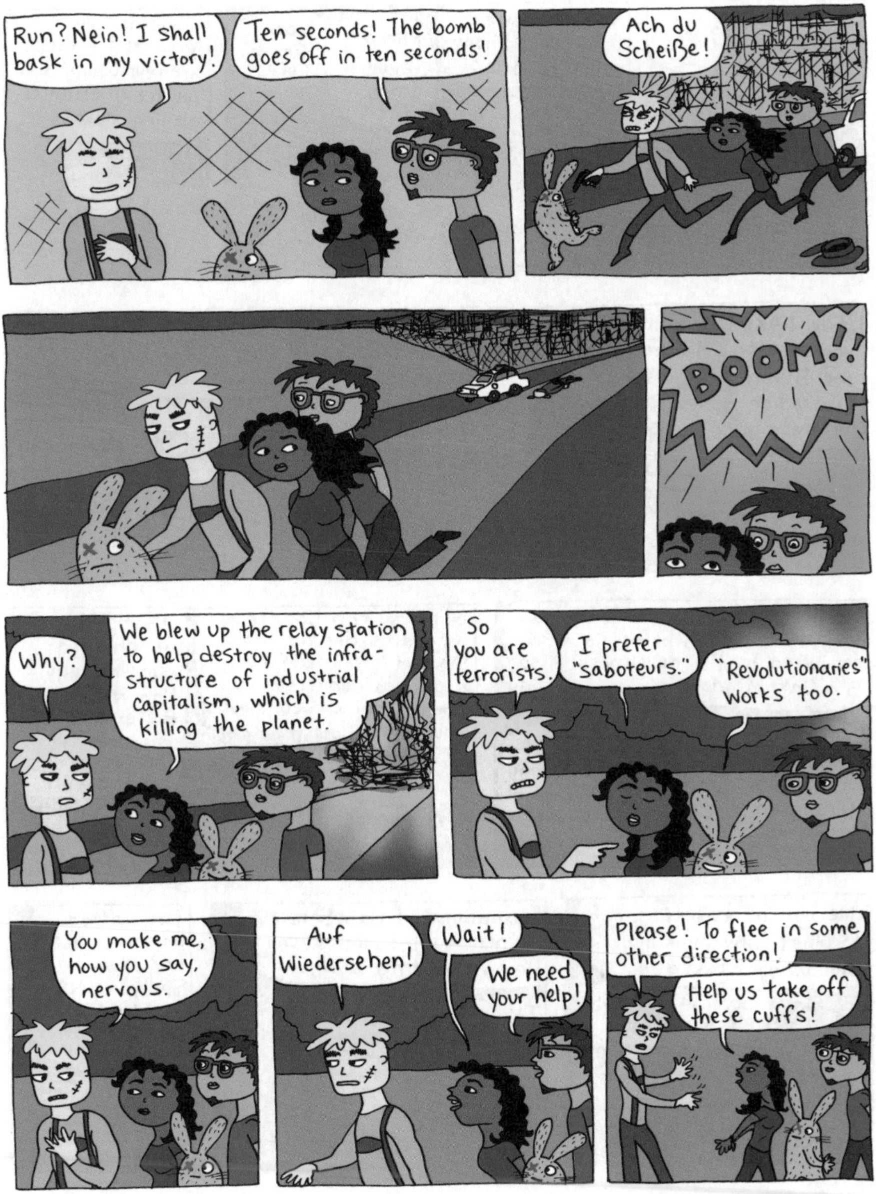
Run? Nein! I shall bask in my victory!
Ten seconds! The bomb goes off in ten seconds!
Ach du Scheiße!
BOOM!!
Why?
We blew up the relay station to help destroy the infra-structure of industrial capitalism, which is killing the planet.
So you are terrorists.
I prefer "saboteurs."
"Revolutionaries" works too.
You make me, how you say, nervous.
Auf Wiedersehen!
Wait!
We need your help!
Please! To flee in some other direction!
Help us take off these cuffs!

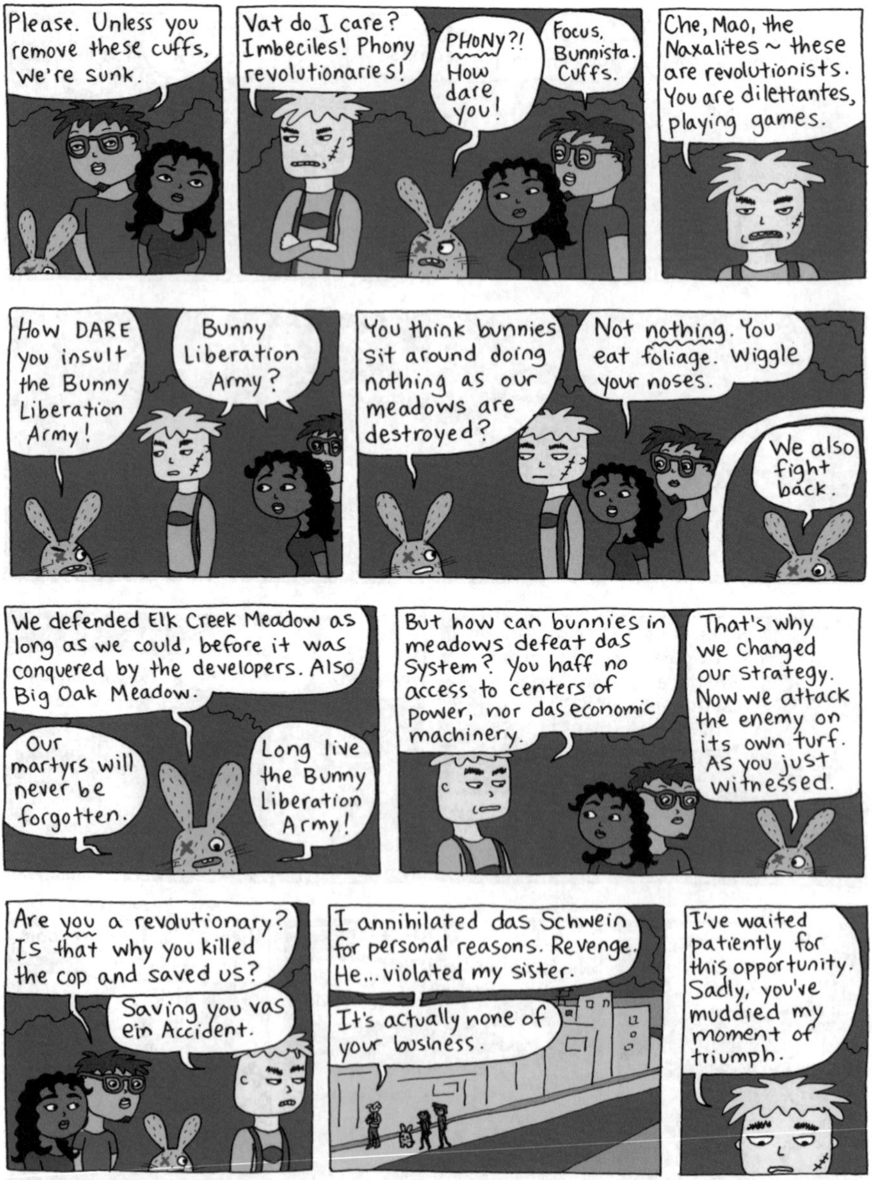
Please. Unless you remove these cuffs, we're sunk.
Vat do I care? Imbeciles! Phony revolutionaries!
PHONY?! How dare you!
Focus, Bunnista. Cuffs.
Che, Mao, the Naxalites ~ these are revolutionists. You are dilettantes, playing games.
How DARE you insult the Bunny Liberation Army!
Bunny Liberation Army?
You think bunnies sit around doing nothing as our meadows are destroyed?
Not nothing. You eat foliage. Wiggle your noses.
We also fight back.
We defended Elk Creek Meadow as long as we could, before it was conquered by the developers. Also Big Oak Meadow.
Our martyrs will never be forgotten.
Long live the Bunny Liberation Army!
But how can bunnies in meadows defeat das System? You haff no access to centers of power, nor das economic machinery.
That's why we changed our strategy. Now we attack the enemy on its own turf. As you just witnessed.
Are you a revolutionary? Is that why you killed the cop and saved us?
Saving you vas ein Accident.
I annihilated das Schwein for personal reasons. Revenge. He... violated my sister.
It's actually none of your business.
I've waited patiently for this opportunity. Sadly, you've muddied my moment of triumph.

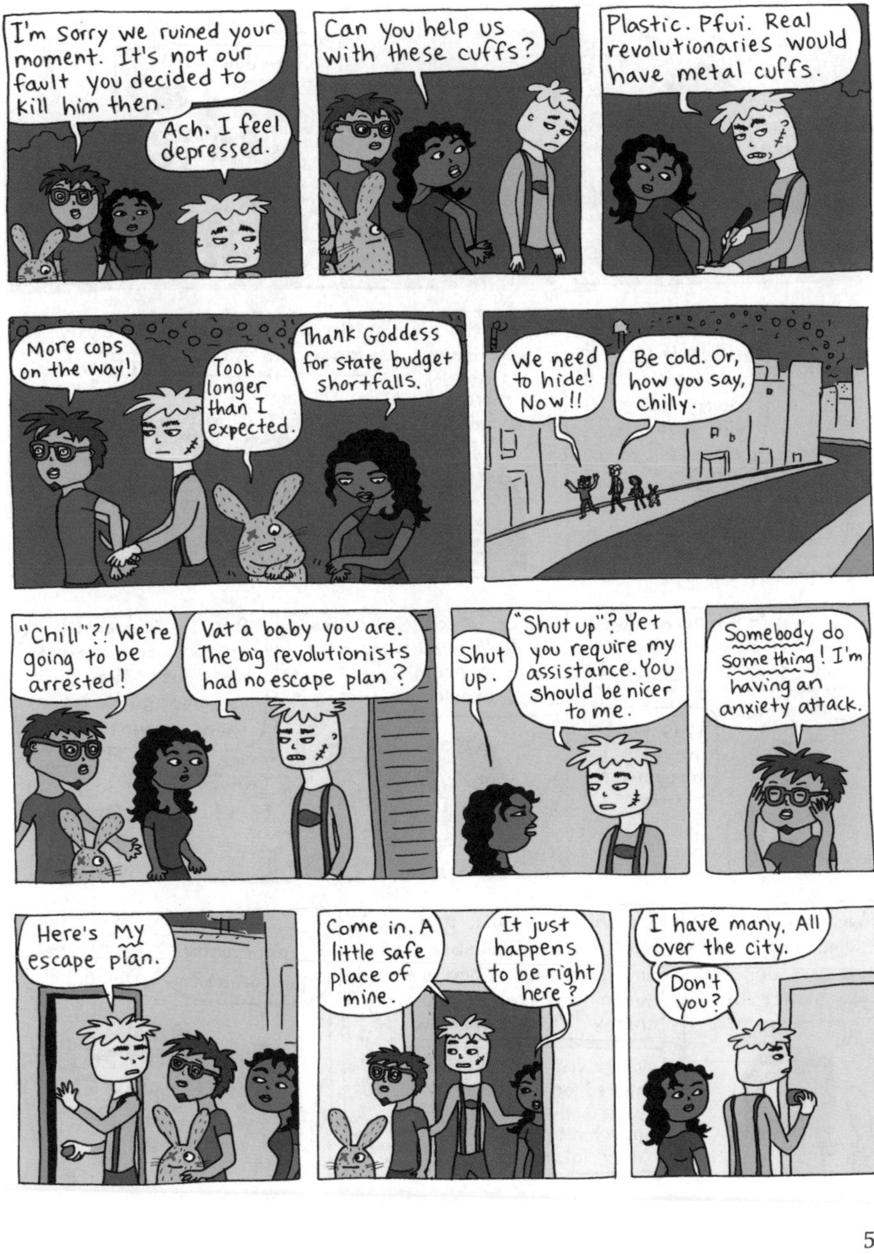
I'm sorry we ruined your moment. It's not our fault you decided to kill him then.
Ach. I feel depressed.
Can you help us with these cuffs?
Plastic. Pfui. Real revolutionaries would have metal cuffs.
More cops on the way!
Took longer than I expected.
Thank Goddess for state budget shortfalls.
We need to hide! Now!!
Be cold. Or, how you say, chilly.
"Chill"?! We're going to be arrested!
Vat a baby you are. The big revolutionists had no escape plan?
Shut up.
"Shut up"? Yet you require my assistance. You should be nicer to me.
Somebody do something! I'm having an anxiety attack.
Here's My escape plan.
Come in. A little safe place of mine.
It just happens to be right here?
I have many. All over the city.
Don't you?

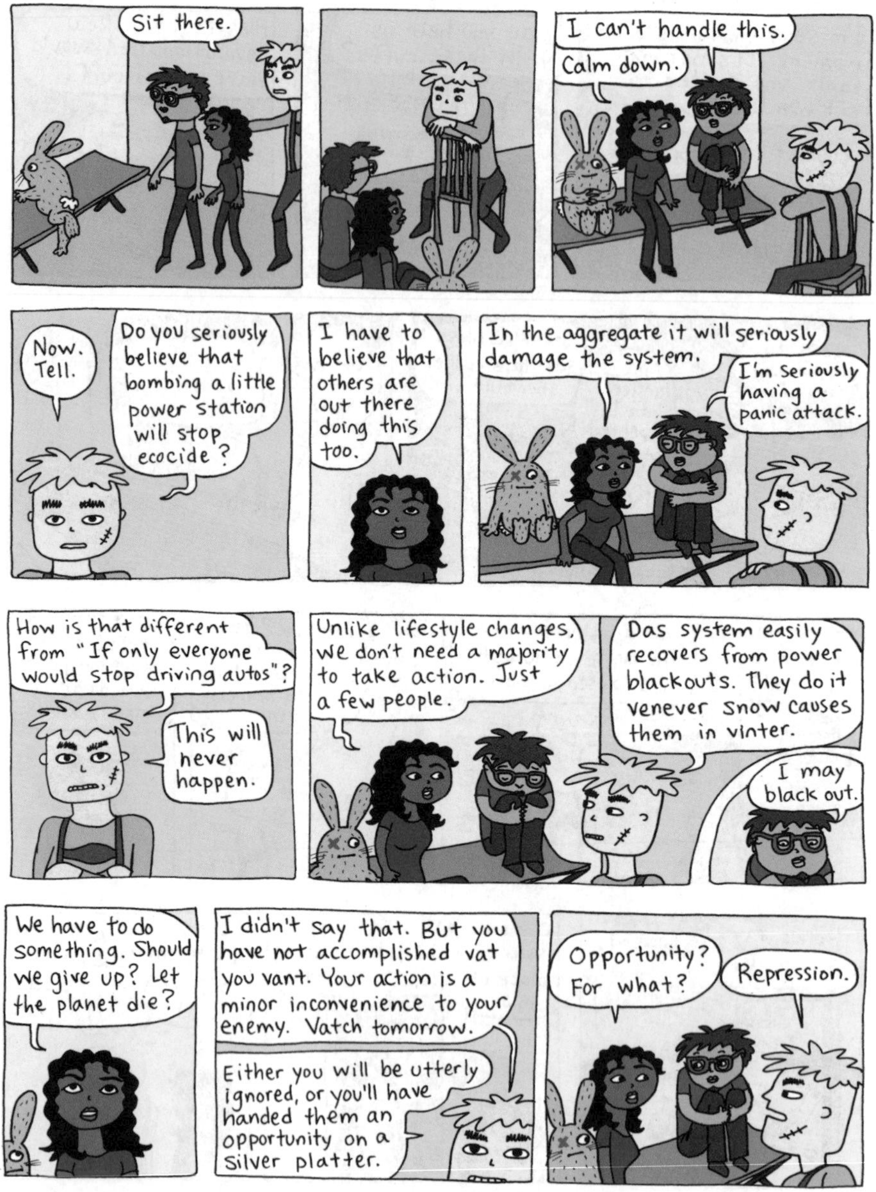
Sit there.
I can't handle this.
Calm down.
Now. Tell.
Do you seriously believe that bombing a little power station will stop ecocide?
I have to believe that others are out there doing this too.
In the aggregate it will seriously damage the system.
I'm seriously having a panic attack.
How is that different from "If only everyone would stop driving autos"?
This will never happen.
Unlike lifestyle changes, we don't need a majority to take action. Just a few people.
Das system easily recovers from power blackouts. They do it venever snow causes them in vinter.
I may black out.
We have to do something. Should we give up? Let the planet die?
I didn't say that. But you have not accomplished vat you vant. Your action is a minor inconvenience to your enemy. Vatch tomorrow.
Either you will be utterly ignored, or you'll have handed them an opportunity on a silver platter.
Opportunity? For what?
Repression.

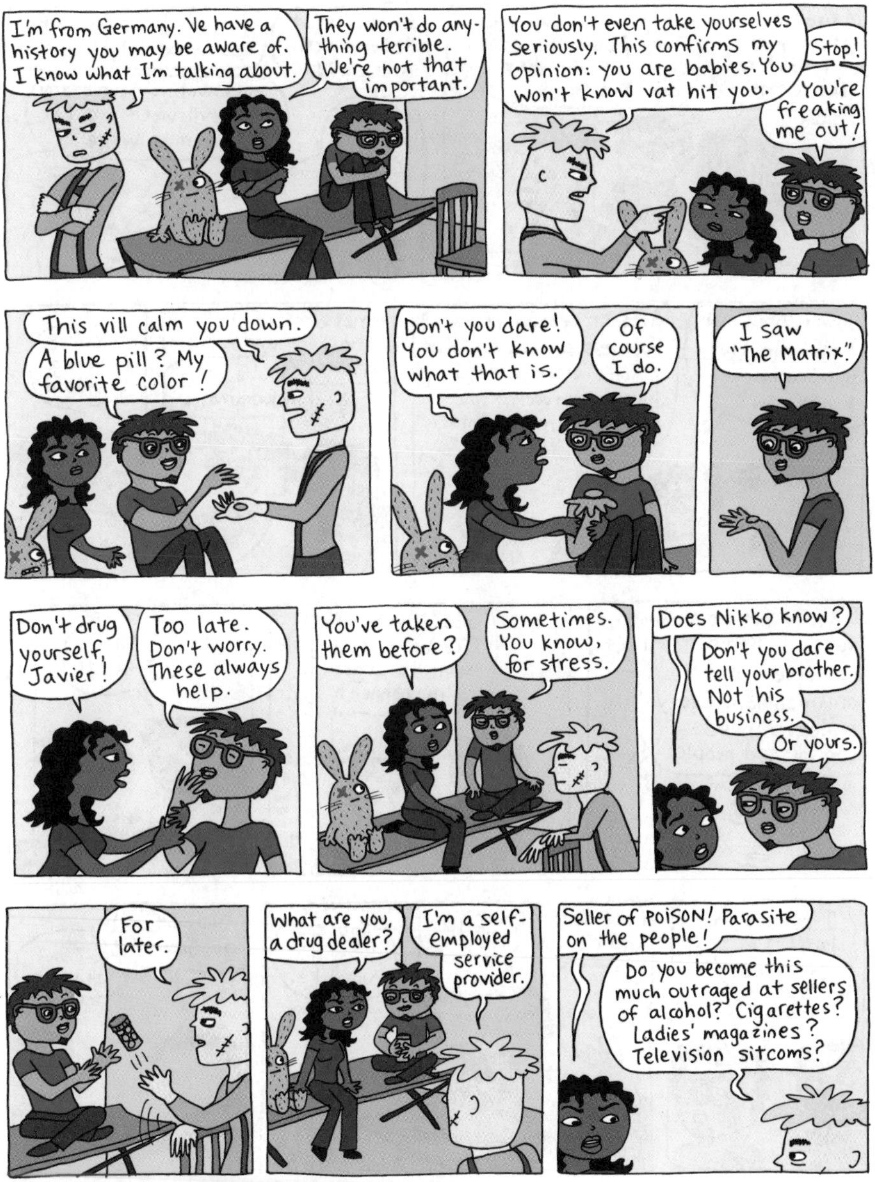

I'm from Germany. Ve have a history you may be aware of. I know what I'm talking about.
They won't do anything terrible. We're not that important.
You don't even take yourselves seriously. This confirms my opinion: you are babies. You won't know vat hit you.
Stop!
You're freaking me out!
This vill calm you down.
A blue pill? My favorite color!
Don't you dare! You don't know what that is.
Of course I do.
I saw "The Matrix."
Don't drug yourself, Javier!
Too late. Don't worry. These always help.
You've taken them before?
Sometimes. You know, for stress.
Does Nikko know?
Don't you dare tell your brother. Not his business.
Or yours.
For later.
What are you, a drug dealer?
I'm a self-employed service provider.
Seller of POISON! Parasite on the people!
Do you become this much outraged at sellers of alcohol? Cigarettes? Ladies' magazines? Television sitcoms?

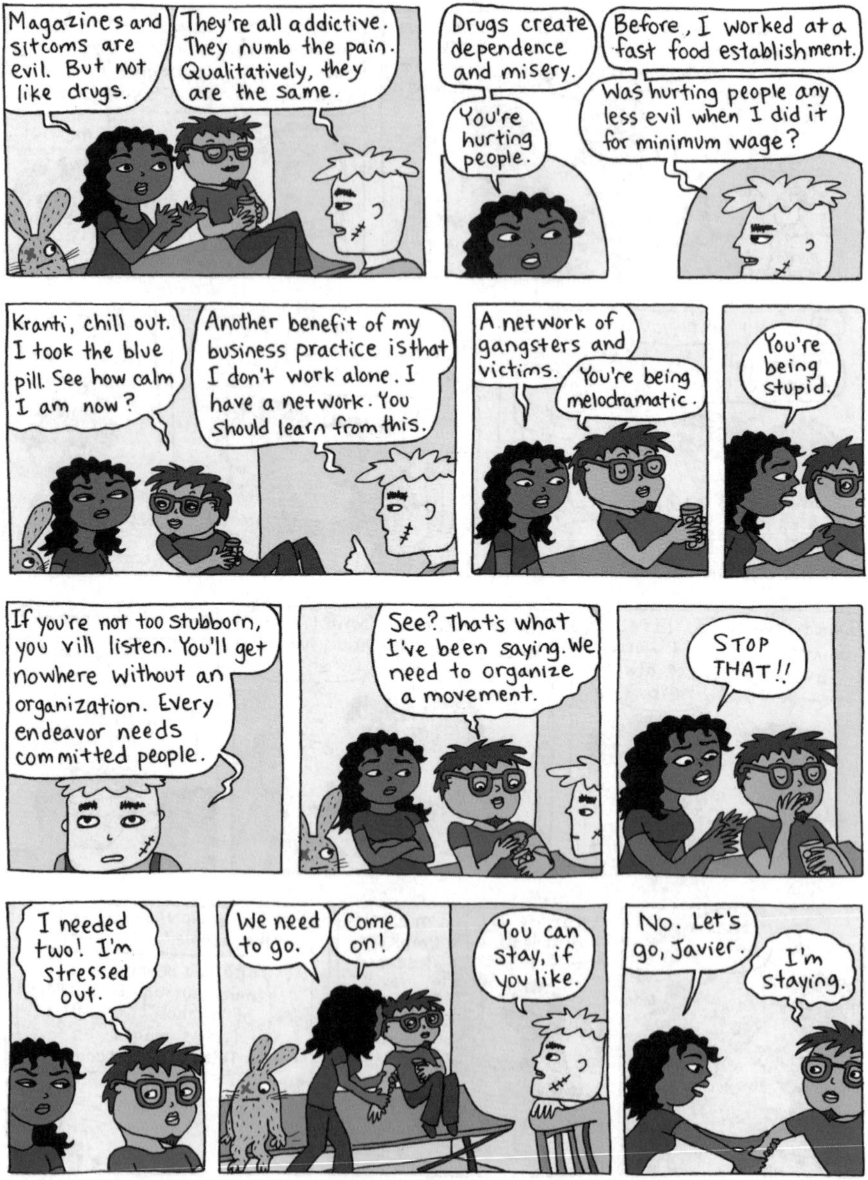
Magazines and sitcoms are evil. But not like drugs.
They're all addictive. They numb the pain. Qualitatively, they are the same.
Drugs create dependence and misery.
You're hurting people.
Before, I worked at a fast food establishment.
Was hurting people any less evil when I did it for minimum wage?
Kranti, chill out. I took the blue pill. See how calm I am now?
Another benefit of my business practice is that I don't work alone. I have a network. You should learn from this.
A network of gangsters and victims.
You're being melodramatic.
You're being stupid.
If you're not too stubborn, you vill listen. You'll get nowhere without an organization. Every endeavor needs committed people.
See? That's what I've been saying. We need to organize a movement.
STOP THAT!!
I needed two! I'm stressed out.
We need to go.
Come on!
You can stay, if you like.
No. Let's go, Javier.
I'm staying.

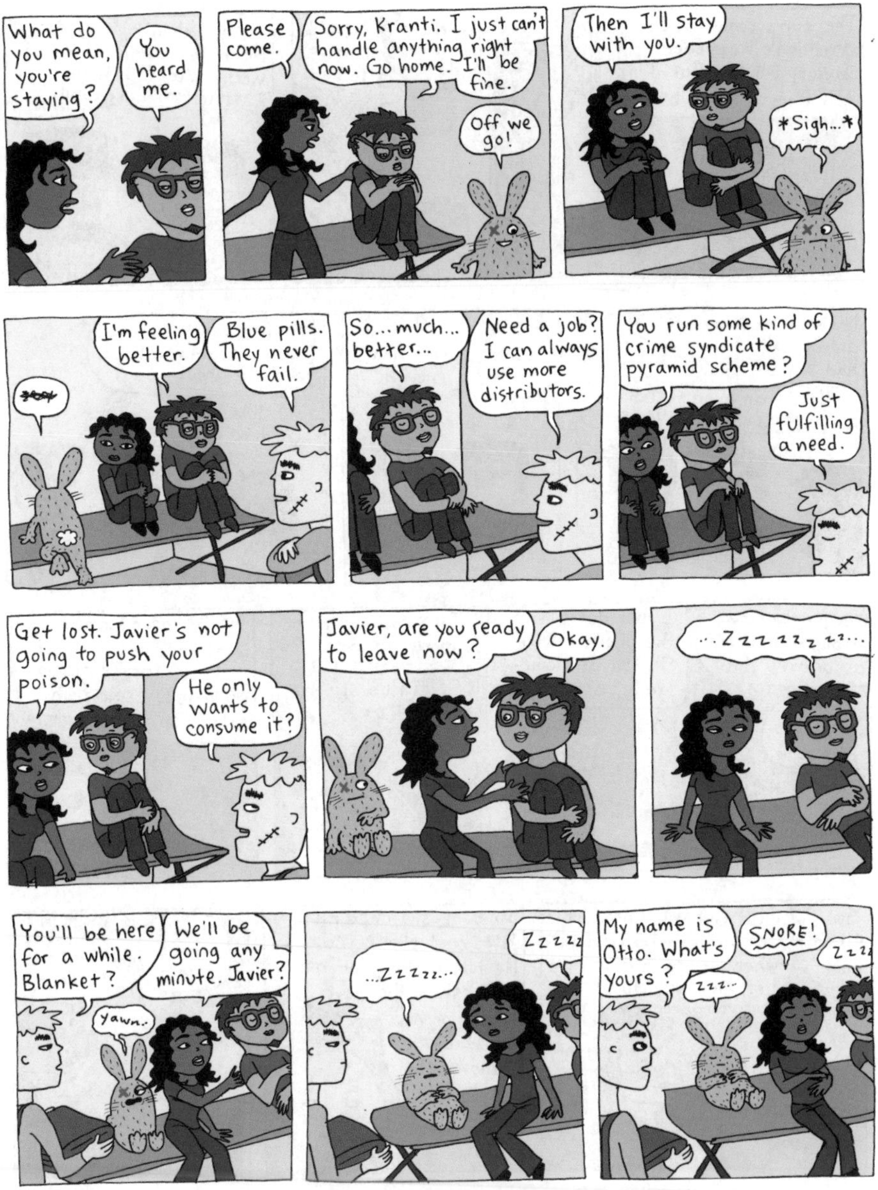
What do you mean, you're staying?
You heard me.
Please come.
Sorry, Kranti. I just can't handle anything right now. Go home. I'll be fine.
Off we go!
Then I'll stay with you.
Sigh...
I'm feeling better.
Blue pills. They never fail.
So... much... better...
Need a job? I can always use more distributors.
You run some kind of crime syndicate pyramid scheme?
Just fulfilling a need.
Get lost. Javier's not going to push your poison.
He only wants to consume it?
Javier, are you ready to leave now?
Okay.
...Zzzzzzzz...
You'll be here for a while. Blanket?
We'll be going any minute. Javier?
yawn..
Zzzzz
...Zzzzz...
My name is Otto. What's yours?
SNORE!
zzz..
Zzz

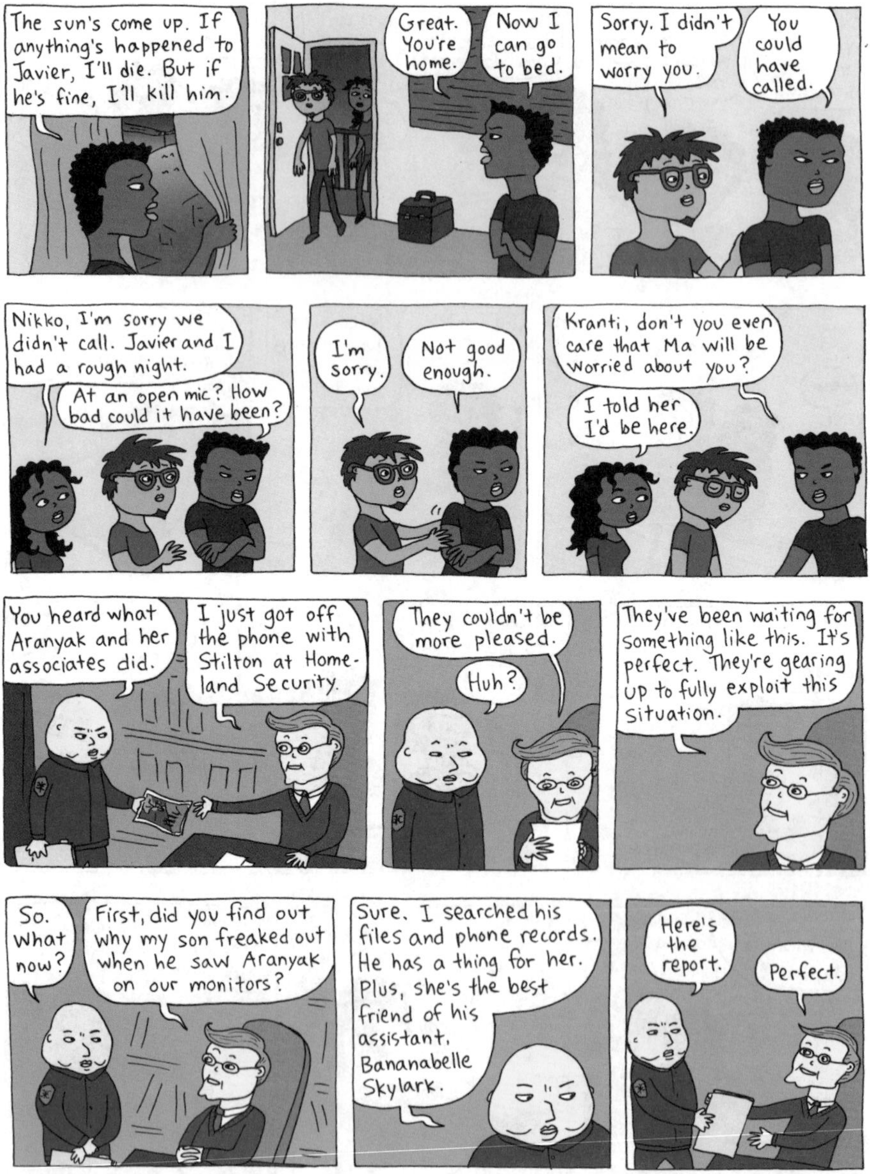

The sun's come up. If anything's happened to Javier, I'll die. But if he's fine, I'll kill him.
Great. You're home.
Now I can go to bed.
Sorry. I didn't mean to worry you.
You could have called.
Nikko, I'm sorry we didn't call. Javier and I had a rough night.
At an open mic? How bad could it have been?
I'm sorry.
Not good enough.
Kranti, don't you even care that Ma will be worried about you?
I told her I'd be here.
You heard what Aranyak and her associates did.
I just got off the phone with Stilton at Homeland Security.
They couldn't be more pleased.
Huh?
They've been waiting for something like this. It's perfect. They're gearing up to fully exploit this situation.
So. What now?
First, did you find out why my son freaked out when he saw Aranyak on our monitors?
Sure. I searched his files and phone records. He has a thing for her. Plus, she's the best friend of his assistant, Bananabelle Skylark.
Here's the report.
Perfect.

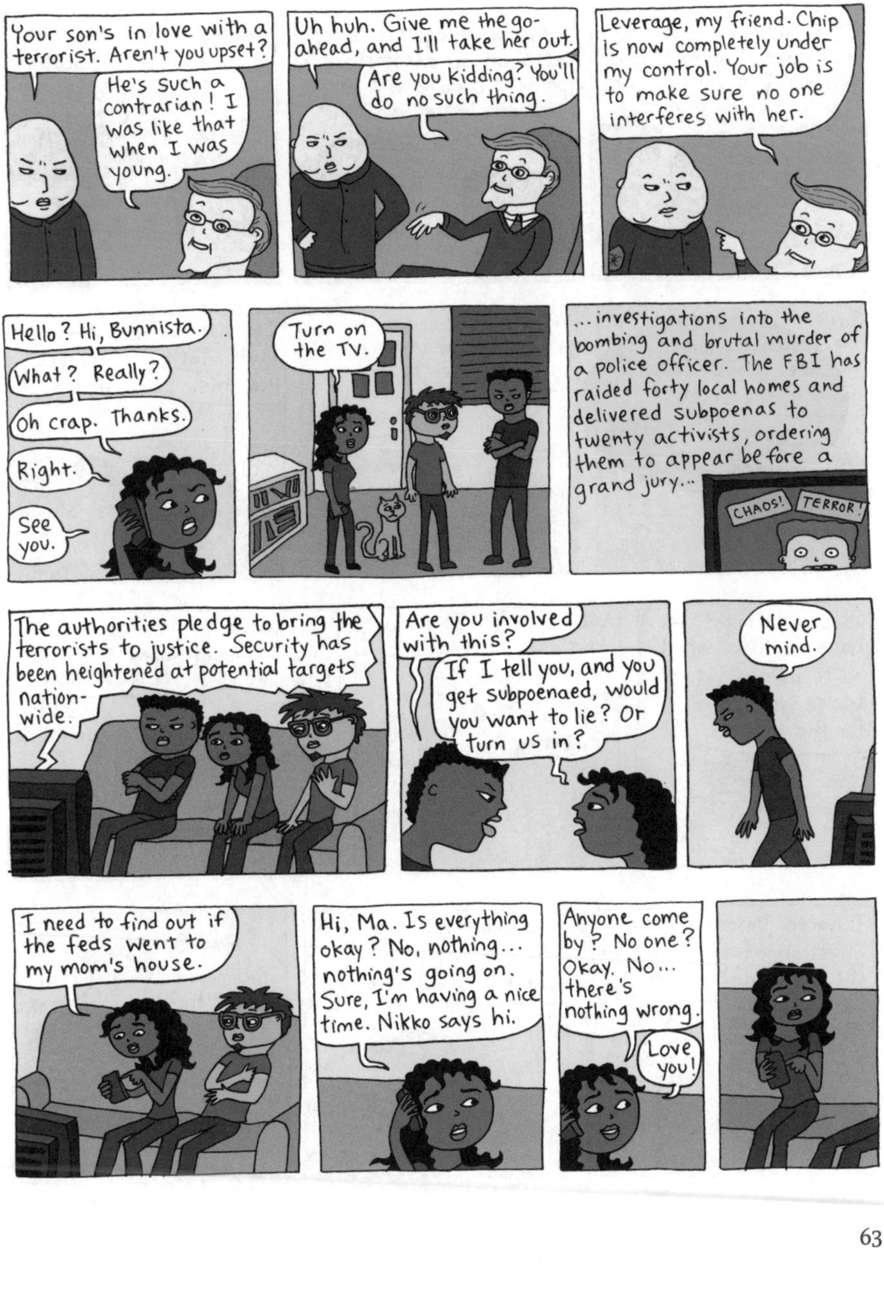

Your son's in love with a terrorist. Aren't you upset?
He's such a contrarian! I was like that when I was young.
Uh huh. Give me the go-ahead, and I'll take her out.
Are you kidding? You'll do no such thing.
Leverage, my friend. Chip is now completely under my control. Your job is to make sure no one interferes with her.
Hello? Hi, Bunnista.
What? Really?
Oh crap. Thanks.
Right.
See you.
Turn on the TV.
...investigations into the bombing and brutal murder of a police officer. The FBI has raided forty local homes and delivered subpoenas to twenty activists, ordering them to appear before a grand jury...
CHAOS!
TERROR!
The authorities pledge to bring the terrorists to justice. Security has been heightened at potential targets nation-wide.
Are you involved with this?
If I tell you, and you get subpoenaed, would you want to lie? Or turn us in?
Never mind.
I need to find out if the feds went to my mom's house.
Hi, Ma. Is everything okay? No, nothing... nothing's going on. Sure, I'm having a nice time. Nikko says hi.
Anyone come by? No one? Okay. No... there's nothing wrong.
Love you!

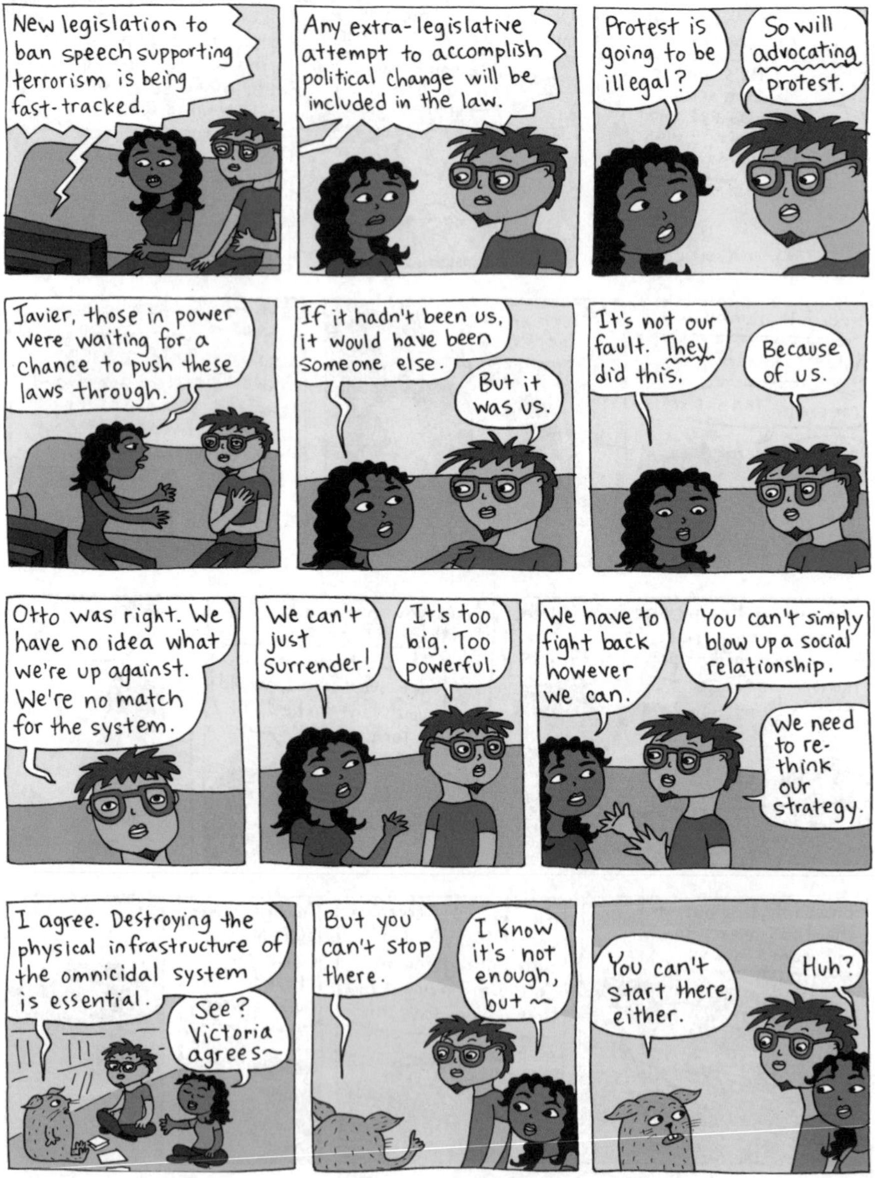
New legislation to ban speech supporting terrorism is being fast-tracked.
Any extra-legislative attempt to accomplish political change will be included in the law.
Protest is going to be illegal?
So will advocating protest.
Javier, those in power were waiting for a chance to push these laws through.
If it hadn't been us, it would have been someone else.
But it was us.
It's not our fault. They did this.
Because of us.
Otto was right. We have no idea what we're up against. We're no match for the system.
We can't just surrender!
It's too big. Too powerful.
We have to fight back however we can.
You can't simply blow up a social relationship.
We need to re-think our strategy.
I agree. Destroying the physical infrastructure of the omnicidal system is essential.
See? Victoria agrees~
But you can't stop there.
I know it's not enough, but ~
You can't start there, either.
Huh?

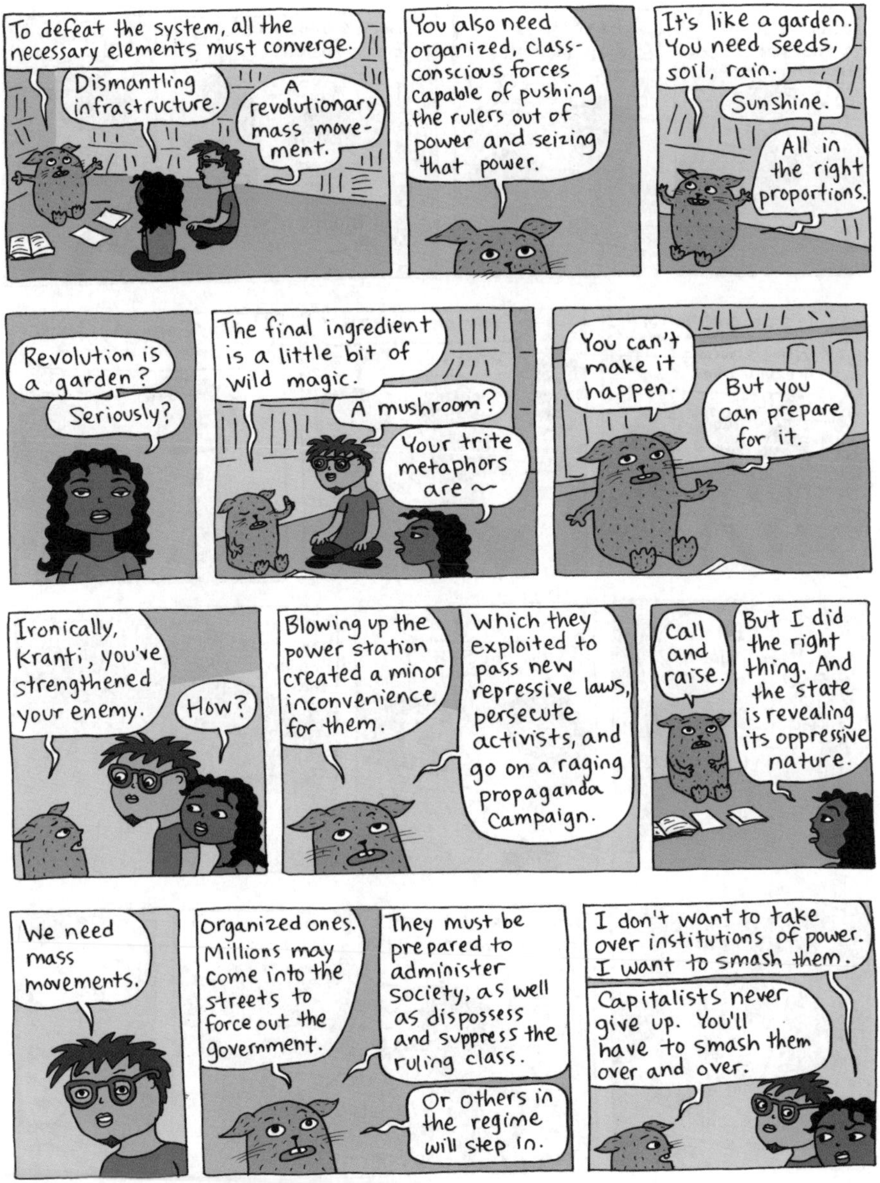

To defeat the system, all the necessary elements must converge.
Dismantling infrastructure.
A revolutionary mass movement.
You also need organized, class-conscious forces capable of pushing the rulers out of power and seizing that power.
It's like a garden. You need seeds, soil, rain.
Sunshine.
All in the right proportions.
Revolution is a garden?
Seriously?
The final ingredient is a little bit of wild magic.
A mushroom?
Your trite metaphors are ~
You can't make it happen.
But you can prepare for it.
Ironically, Kranti, you've strengthened your enemy.
How?
Blowing up the power station created a minor inconvenience for them.
Which they exploited to pass new repressive laws, persecute activists, and go on a raging propaganda campaign.
Call and raise.
But I did the right thing. And the state is revealing its oppressive nature.
We need mass movements.
Organized ones. Millions may come into the streets to force out the government.
They must be prepared to administer society, as well as dispossess and suppress the ruling class.
Or others in the regime will step in.
I don't want to take over institutions of power. I want to smash them.
Capitalists never give up. You'll have to smash them over and over.

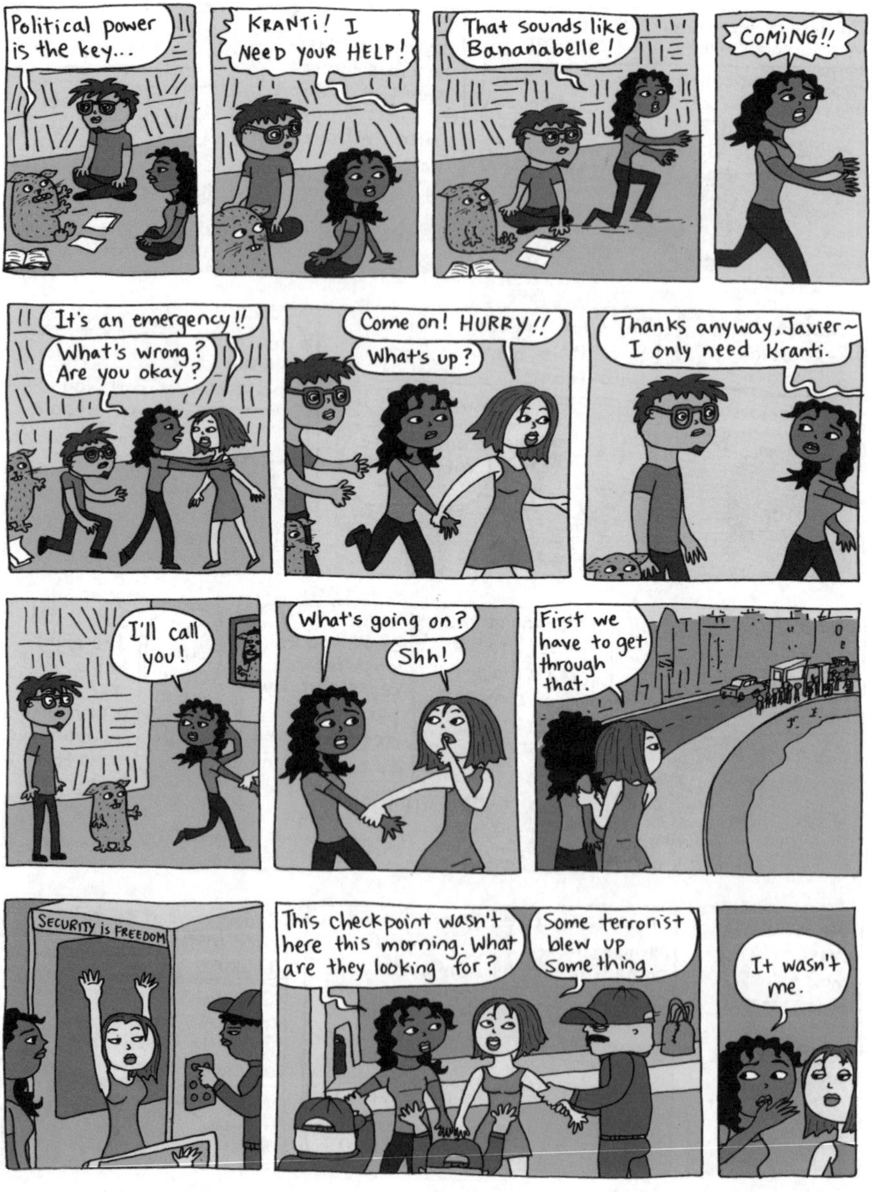

Political power is the key...
KRANTI! I NEED YOUR HELP!
That sounds like Bananabelle!
COMING!!
It's an emergency!!
What's wrong? Are you okay?
Come on! HURRY!!
What's up?
Thanks anyway, Javier~ I only need Kranti.
I'll call you!
What's going on?
Shh!
First we have to get through that.
SECURITY is FREEDOM
This checkpoint wasn't here this morning. What are they looking for?
Some terrorist blew up some thing.
It wasn't me.

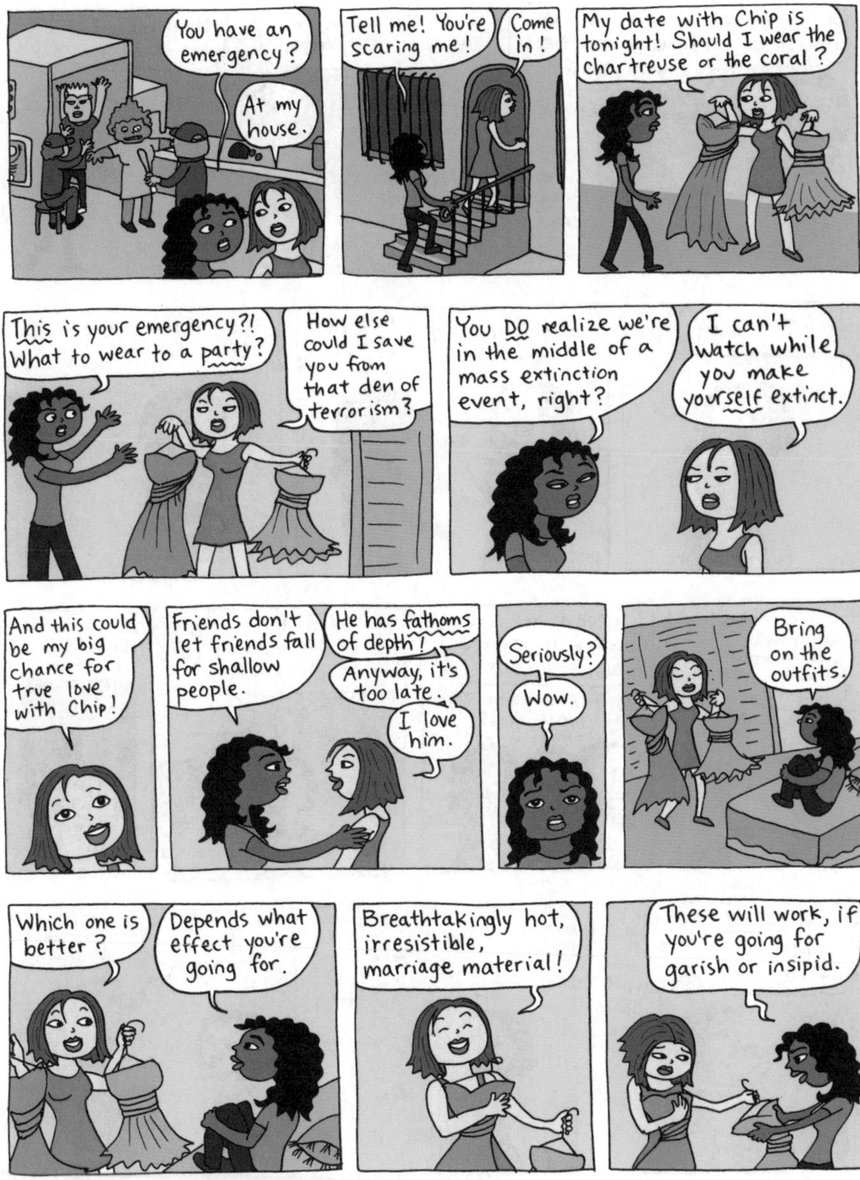
You have an emergency?
At my house.
Tell me! You're scaring me!
Come in!
My date with Chip is tonight! Should I wear the chartreuse or the coral?
This is your emergency?! What to wear to a party?
How else could I save you from that den of terrorism?
You DO realize we're in the middle of a mass extinction event, right?
I can't watch while you make yourself extinct.
And this could be my big chance for true love with Chip!
Friends don't let friends fall for shallow people.
He has fathoms of depth!
Anyway, it's too late.
I love him.
Seriously?
Wow.
Bring on the outfits.
Which one is better?
Depends what effect you're going for.
Breathtakingly hot, irresistible, marriage material!
These will work, if you're going for garish or insipid.

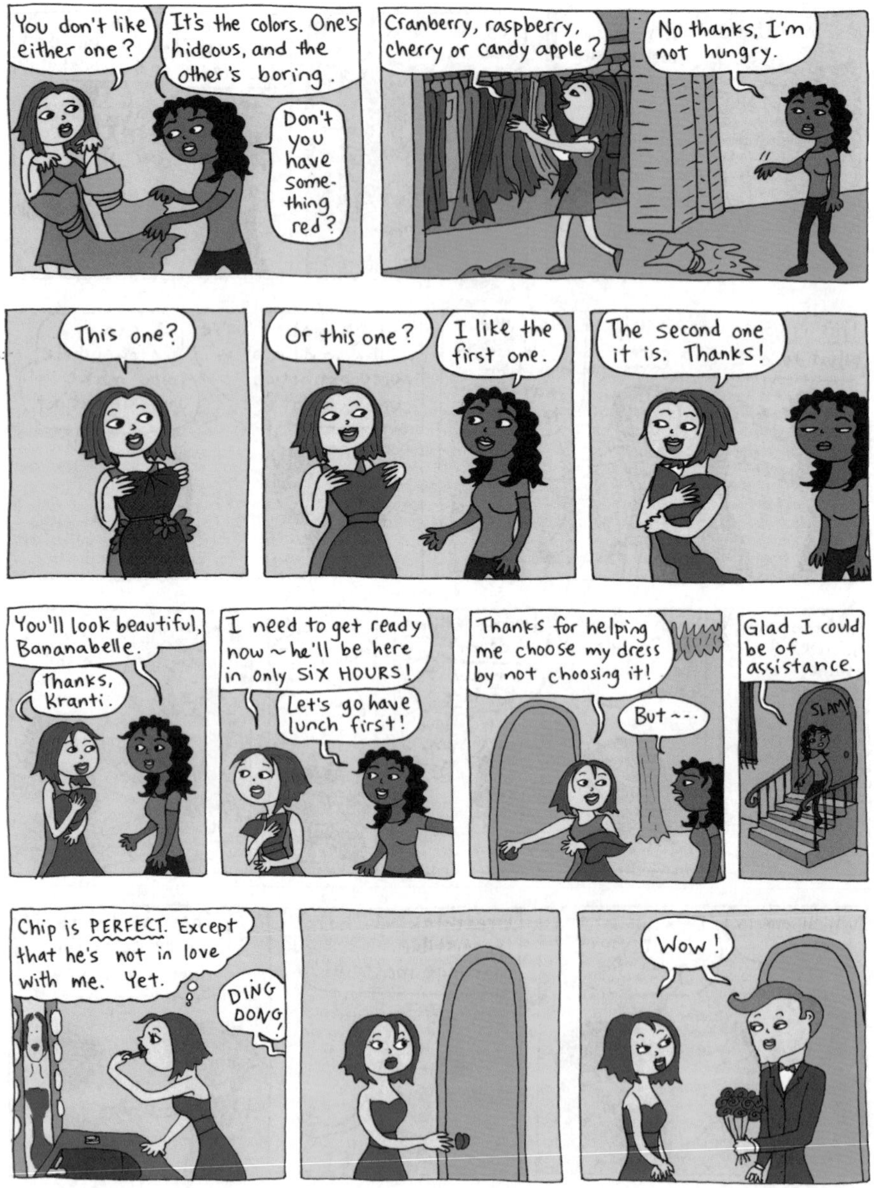
You don't like either one?
It's the colors. One's hideous, and the other's boring.
Don't you have something red?
Cranberry, raspberry, cherry or candy apple?
No thanks, I'm not hungry.
This one?
Or this one?
I like the first one.
The second one it is. Thanks!
You'll look beautiful, Bananabelle.
Thanks, Kranti.
I need to get ready now ~ he'll be here in only SIX HOURS!
Let's go have lunch first!
Thanks for helping me choose my dress by not choosing it!
But ~ . .
Glad I could be of assistance.
SLAM!
Chip is PERFECT. Except that he's not in love with me. Yet.
DING DONG!
Wow!

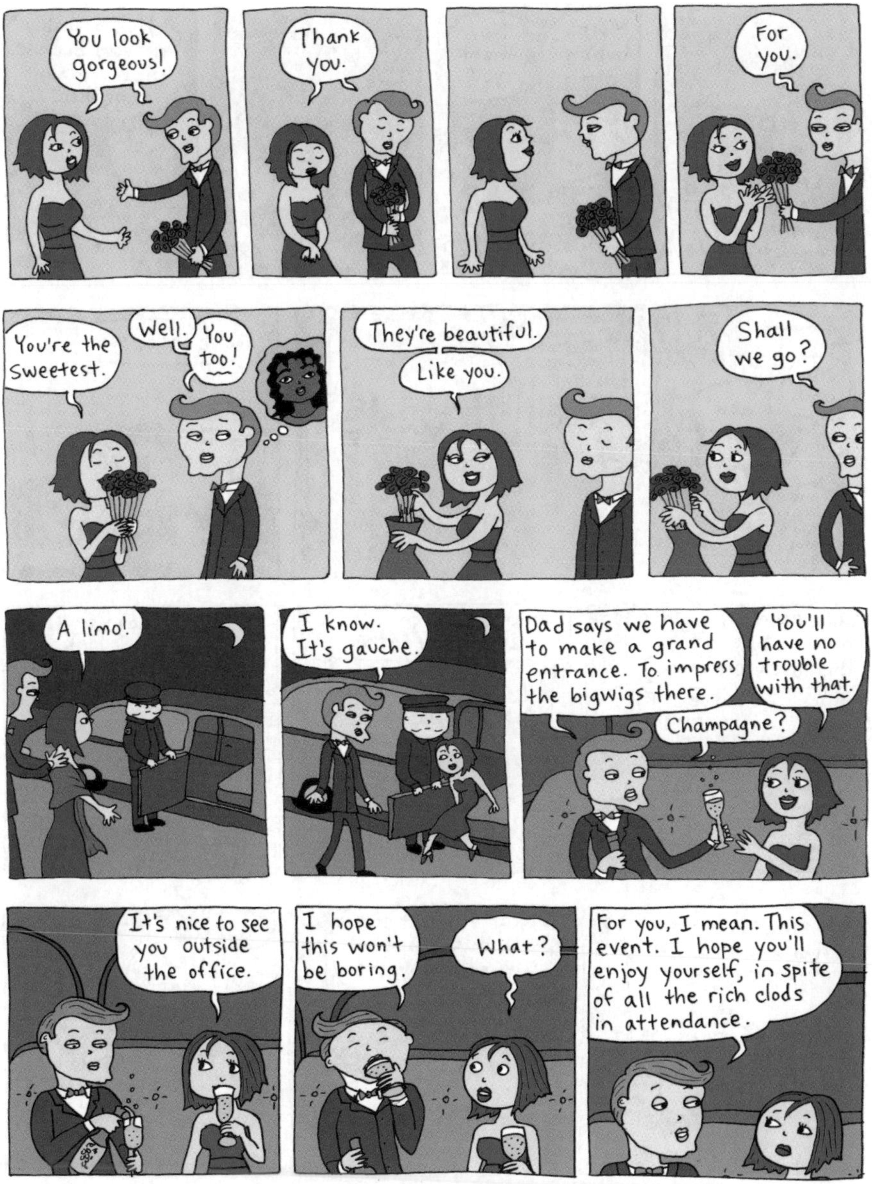

You look gorgeous!
Thank you.
For you.
You're the sweetest.
Well.
You too!
They're beautiful.
Like you.
Shall we go?
A limo!
I know. It's gauche.
Dad says we have to make a grand entrance. To impress the bigwigs there.
You'll have no trouble with that.
Champagne?
It's nice to see you outside the office.
I hope this won't be boring.
What?
For you, I mean. This event. I hope you'll enjoy yourself, in spite of all the rich clods in attendance.

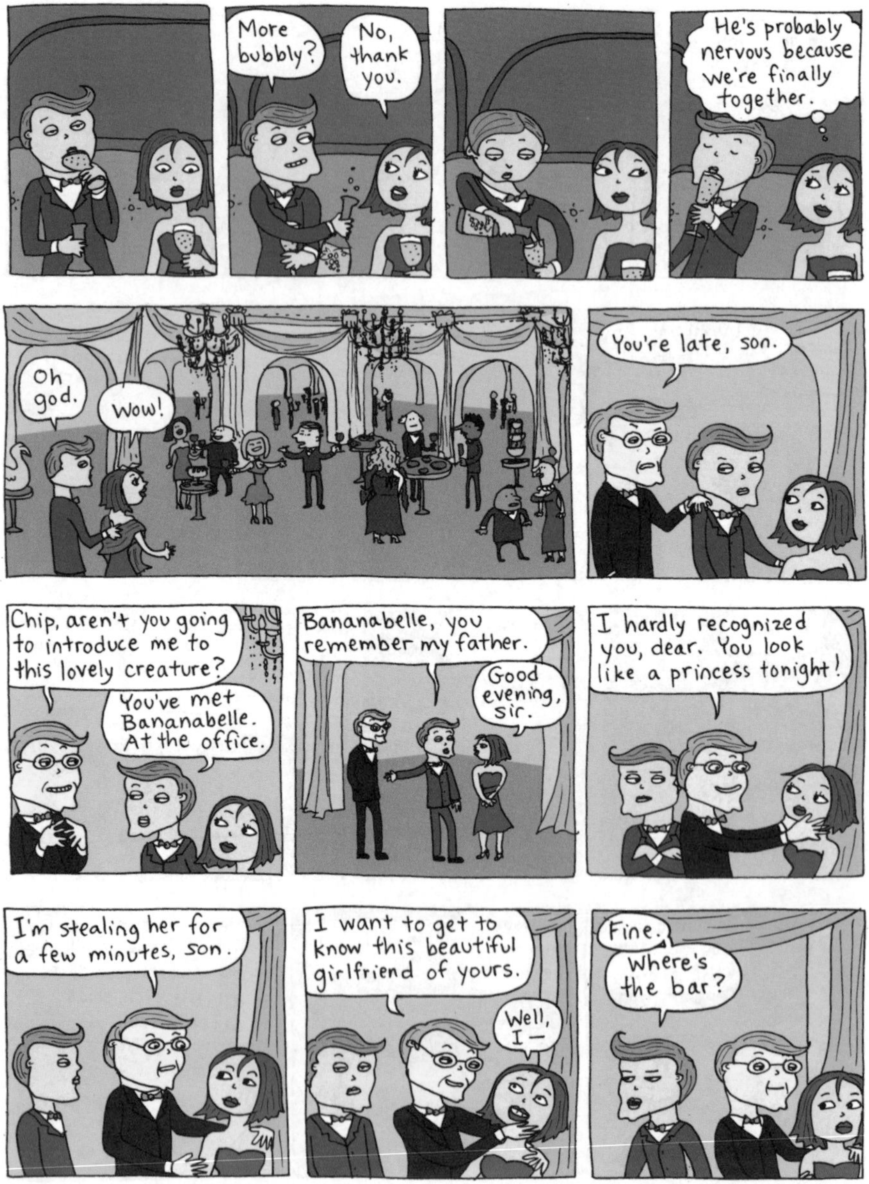
More bubbly?
No, thank you.
He's probably nervous because we're finally together.
Oh god.
Wow!
You're late, son.
Chip, aren't you going to introduce me to this lovely creature?
You've met Bananabelle. At the office.
Bananabelle, you remember my father.
Good evening, sir.
I hardly recognized you, dear. You look like a princess tonight!
I'm stealing her for a few minutes, son.
I want to get to know this beautiful girlfriend of yours.
Well, I—
Fine.
Where's the bar?

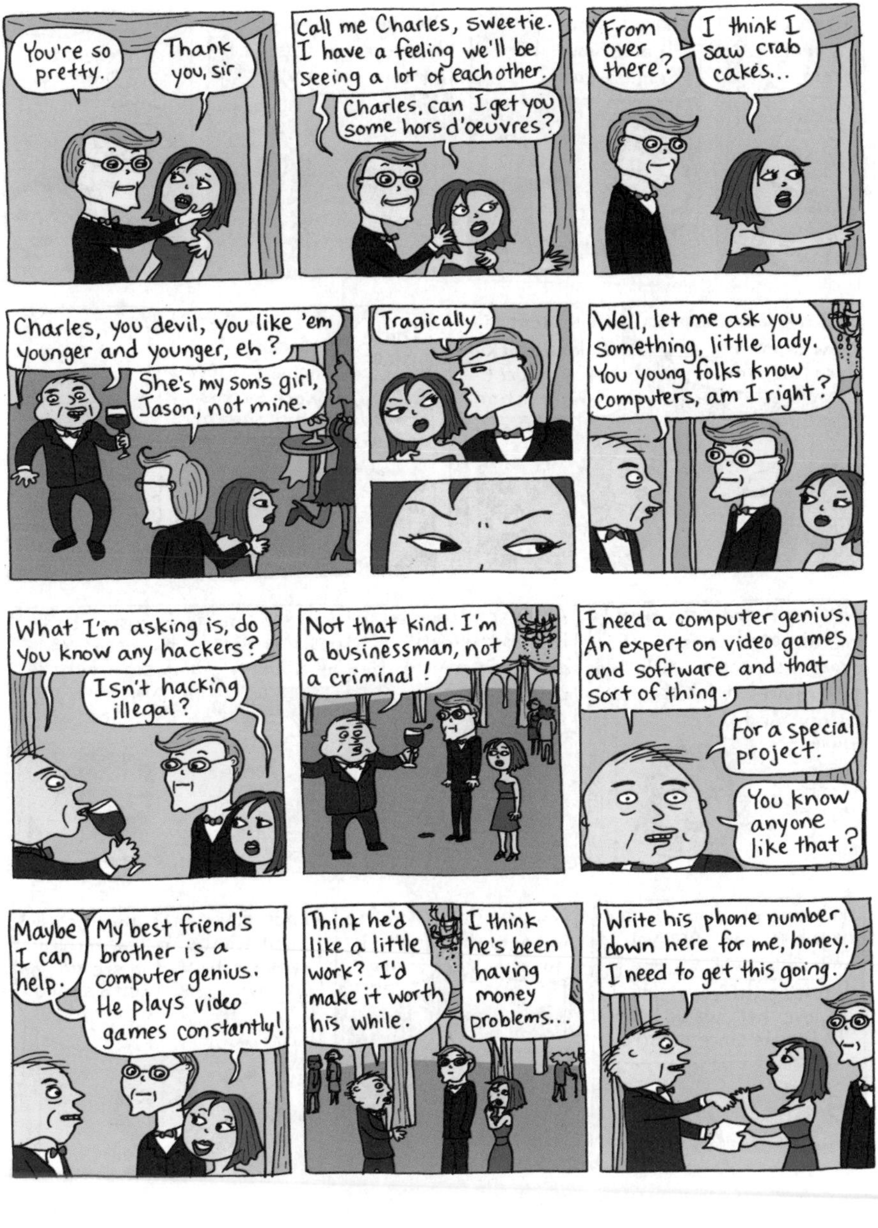
You're so pretty.
Thank you, sir.
Call me Charles, sweetie. I have a feeling we'll be seeing a lot of each other.
Charles, can I get you some hors d'oeuvres?
From over there?
I think I saw crab cakes...
Charles, you devil, you like 'em younger and younger, eh?
She's my son's girl, Jason, not mine.
Tragically.
Well, let me ask you something, little lady. You young folks know computers, am I right?
What I'm asking is, do you know any hackers?
Isn't hacking illegal?
Not that kind. I'm a businessman, not a criminal!
I need a computer genius. An expert on video games and software and that sort of thing.
For a special project.
You know anyone like that?
Maybe I can help.
My best friend's brother is a computer genius. He plays video games constantly!
Think he'd like a little work? I'd make it worth his while.
I think he's been having money problems...
Write his phone number down here for me, honey. I need to get this going.

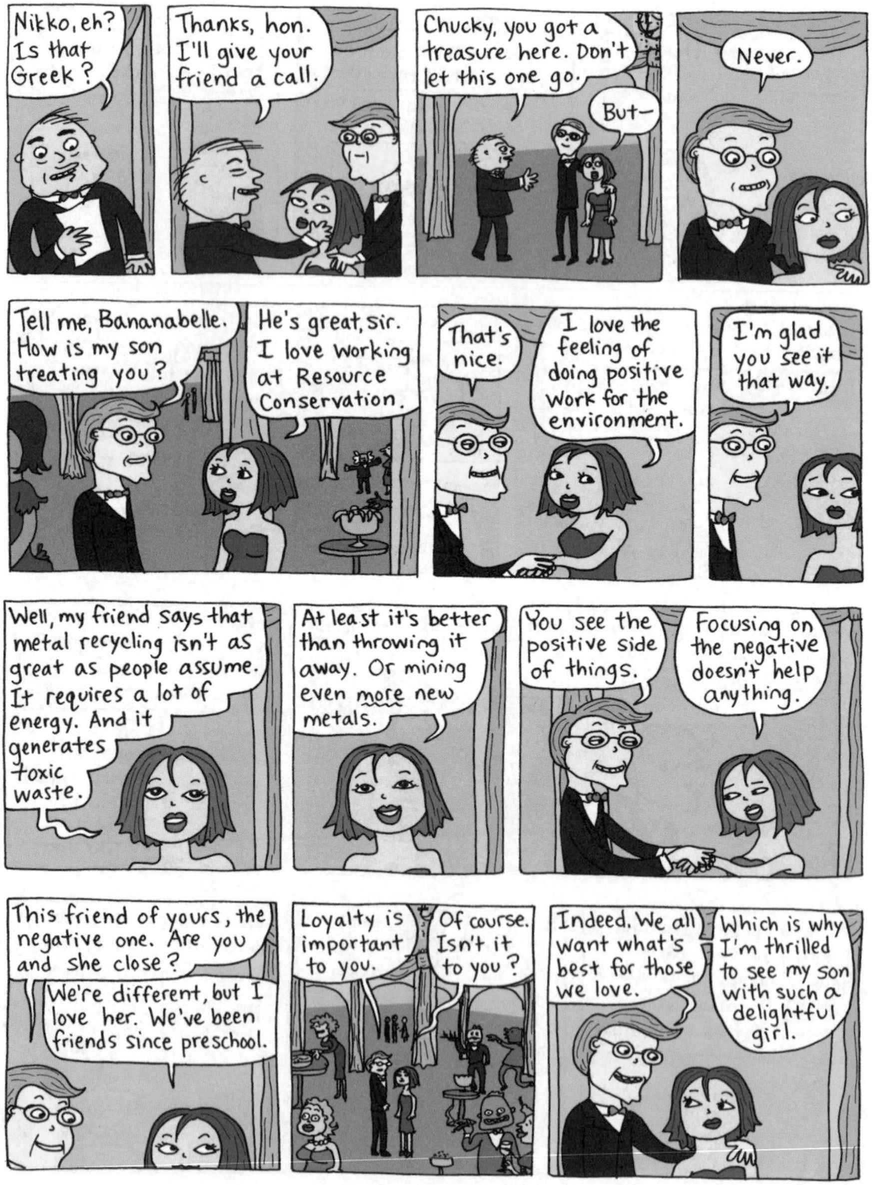
Nikko, eh? Is that Greek?
Thanks, hon. I'll give your friend a call.
Chucky, you got a treasure here. Don't let this one go.
But—
Never.
Tell me, Bananabelle. How is my son treating you?
He's great, sir. I love working at Resource Conservation.
That's nice.
I love the feeling of doing positive work for the environment.
I'm glad you see it that way.
Well, my friend says that metal recycling isn't as great as people assume. It requires a lot of energy. And it generates toxic waste.
At least it's better than throwing it away. Or mining even more new metals.
You see the positive side of things.
Focusing on the negative doesn't help anything.
This friend of yours, the negative one. Are you and she close?
We're different, but I love her. We've been friends since preschool.
Loyalty is important to you.
Of course. Isn't it to you?
Indeed. We all want what's best for those we love.
Which is why I'm thrilled to see my son with such a delightful girl.

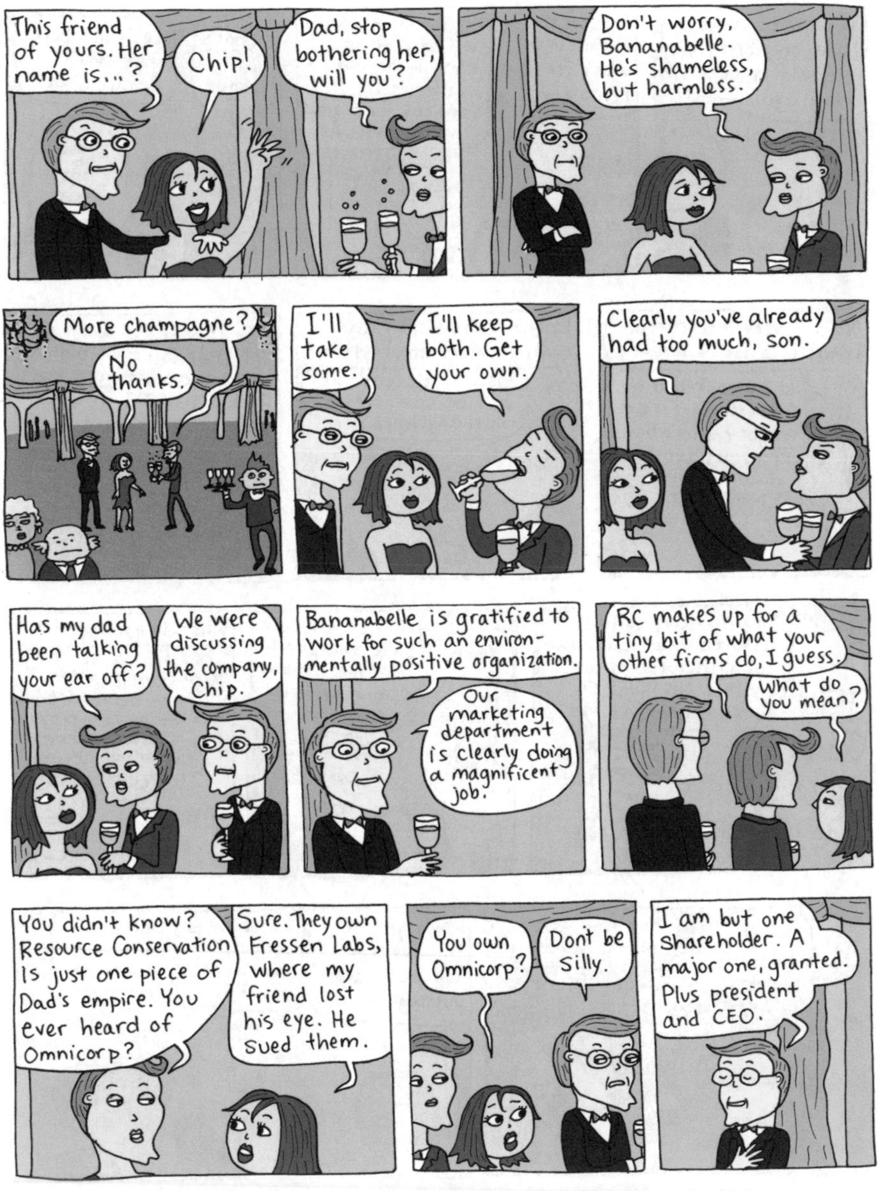
This friend of yours. Her name is...?
Chip!
Dad, stop bothering her, will you?
Don't worry, Bananabelle. He's shameless, but harmless.
More champagne?
No thanks.
I'll take some.
I'll keep both. Get your own.
Clearly you've already had too much, son.
Has my dad been talking your ear off?
We were discussing the company, Chip.
Bananabelle is gratified to work for such an environmentally positive organization.
Our marketing department is clearly doing a magnificent job.
RC makes up for a tiny bit of what your other firms do, I guess.
What do you mean?
You didn't know? Resource Conservation is just one piece of Dad's empire. You ever heard of Omnicorp?
Sure. They own Fressen Labs, where my friend lost his eye. He sued them.
You own Omnicorp?
Don't be silly.
I am but one shareholder. A major one, granted. Plus president and CEO.

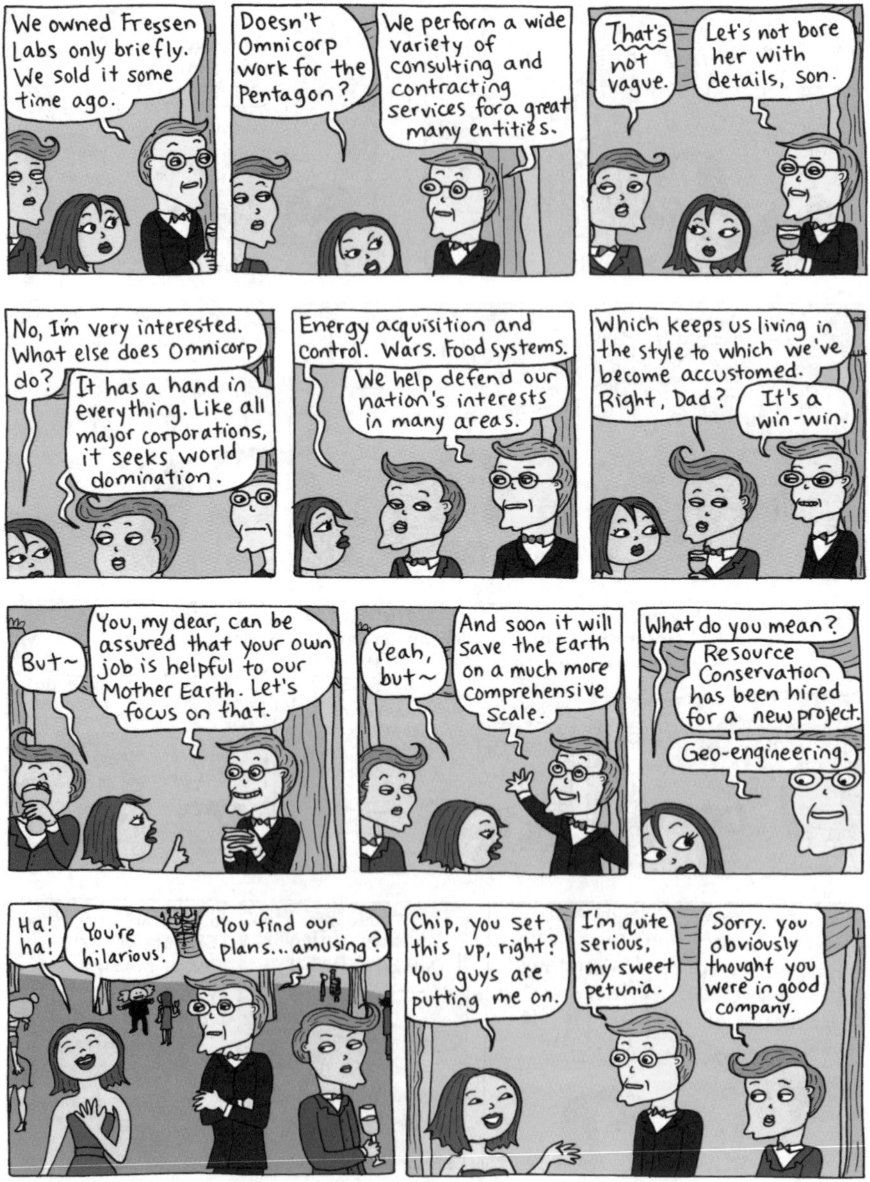
We owned Fressen Labs only briefly. We sold it some time ago.
Doesn't Omnicorp work for the Pentagon?
We perform a wide variety of consulting and contracting services for a great many entities.
That's not vague.
Let's not bore her with details, son.
No, I'm very interested. What else does Omnicorp do?
It has a hand in everything. Like all major corporations, it seeks world domination.
Energy acquisition and control. Wars. Food systems.
We help defend our nation's interests in many areas.
Which keeps us living in the style to which we've become accustomed. Right, Dad?
It's a win-win.
But~
You, my dear, can be assured that your own job is helpful to our Mother Earth. Let's focus on that.
Yeah, but~
And soon it will save the Earth on a much more comprehensive scale.
What do you mean?
Resource Conservation has been hired for a new project.
Geo-engineering.
Ha! ha!
You're hilarious!
You find our plans... amusing?
Chip, you set this up, right? You guys are putting me on.
I'm quite serious, my sweet petunia.
Sorry. you obviously thought you were in good company.

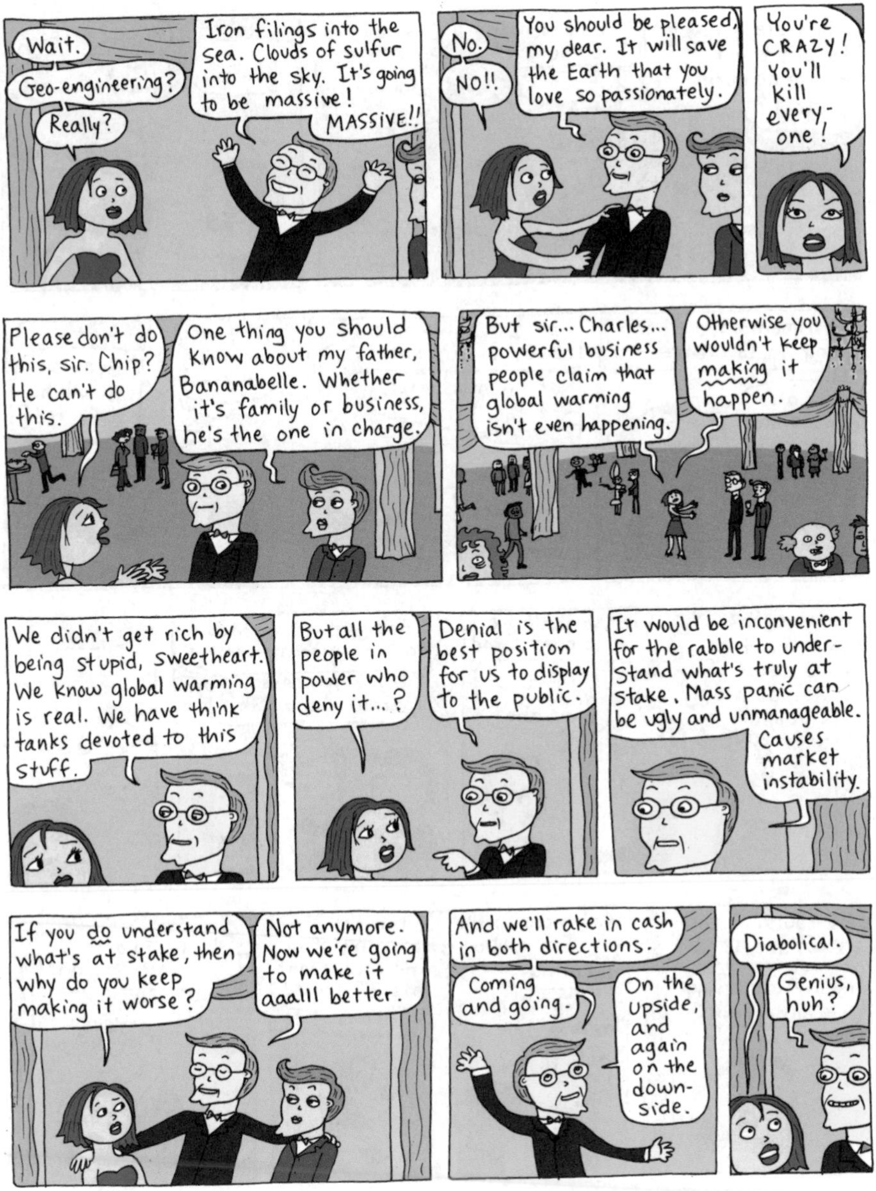
Wait.
Geo-engineering?
Really?
Iron filings into the sea. Clouds of sulfur into the sky. It's going to be massive!
MASSIVE!!
No.
NO!!
You should be pleased, my dear. It will save the Earth that you love so passionately.
You're CRAZY! You'll kill every-one!
Please don't do this, sir. Chip? He can't do this.
One thing you should know about my father, Bananabelle. Whether it's family or business, he's the one in charge.
But sir... Charles... powerful business people claim that global warming isn't even happening.
Otherwise you wouldn't keep making it happen.
We didn't get rich by being stupid, sweetheart. We know global warming is real. We have think tanks devoted to this stuff.
But all the people in power who deny it...?
Denial is the best position for us to display to the public.
It would be inconvenient for the rabble to under-stand what's truly at stake. Mass panic can be ugly and unmanageable.
Causes market instability.
If you do understand what's at stake, then why do you keep making it worse?
Not anymore. Now we're going to make it aaalll better.
And we'll rake in cash in both directions.
Coming and going.
On the upside, and again on the down-side.
Diabolical.
Genius, huh?

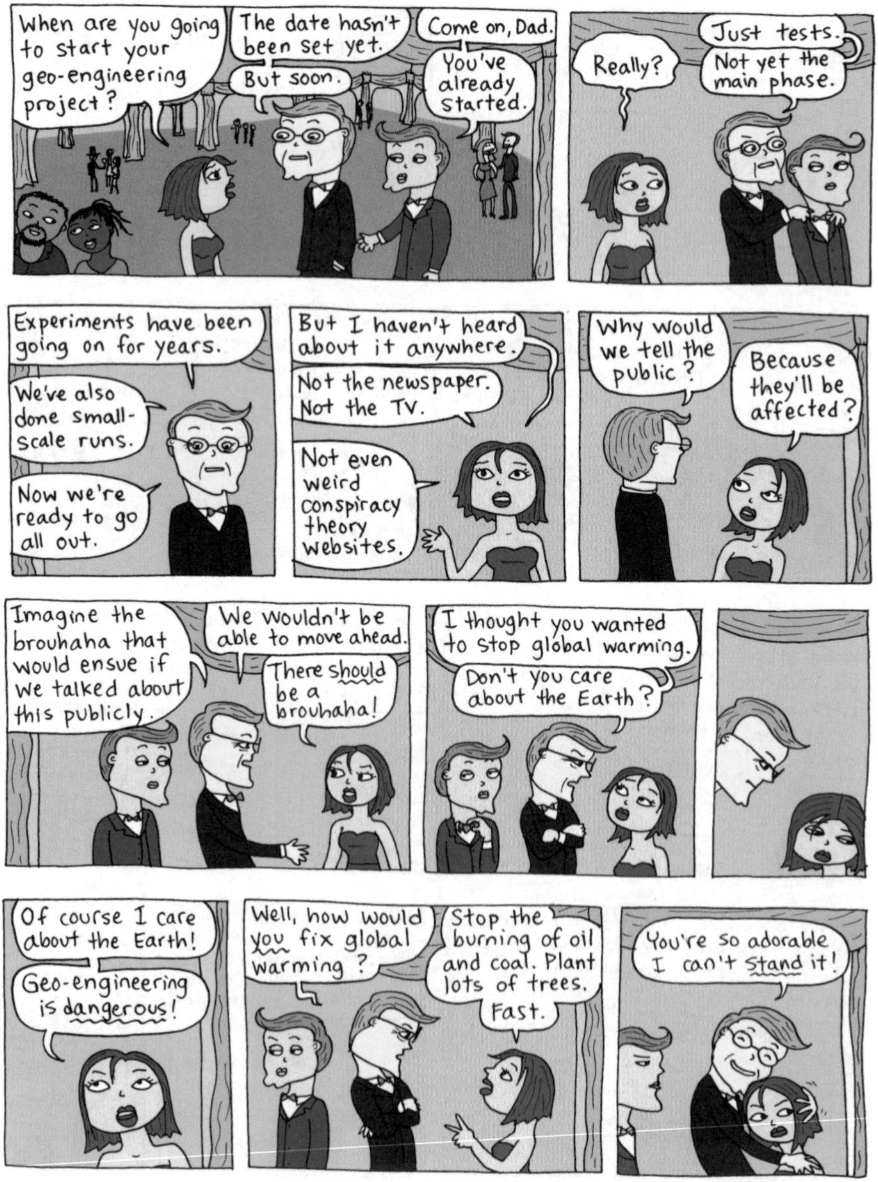

When are you going to start your geo-engineering project?
The date hasn't been set yet.
But soon.
Come on, Dad.
You've already started.
Really?
Just tests.
Not yet the main phase.
Experiments have been going on for years.
We've also done small-scale runs.
Now we're ready to go all out.
But I haven't heard about it anywhere.
Not the newspaper. Not the TV.
Not even weird conspiracy theory websites.
Why would we tell the public?
Because they'll be affected?
Imagine the brouhaha that would ensue if we talked about this publicly.
We wouldn't be able to move ahead.
There should be a brouhaha!
I thought you wanted to stop global warming.
Don't you care about the Earth?
Of course I care about the Earth!
Geo-engineering is dangerous!
Well, how would you fix global warming?
Stop the burning of oil and coal. Plant lots of trees.
Fast.
You're so adorable I can't stand it!

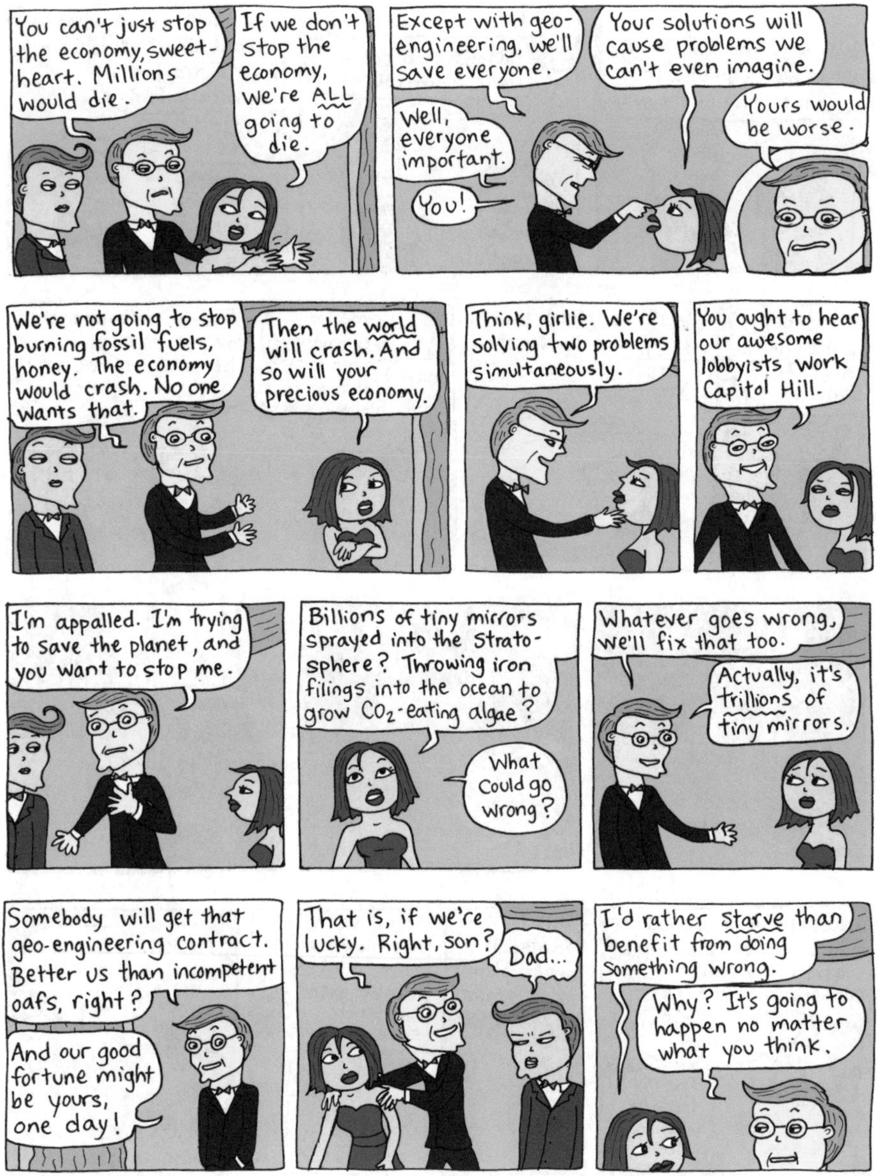
You can't just stop the economy, sweetheart. Millions would die.
If we don't stop the economy, we're ALL going to die.
Except with geo-engineering, we'll save everyone.
Well, everyone important.
You!
Your solutions will cause problems we can't even imagine.
Yours would be worse.
We're not going to stop burning fossil fuels, honey. The economy would crash. No one wants that.
Then the world will crash. And so will your precious economy.
Think, girlie. We're solving two problems simultaneously.
You ought to hear our awesome lobbyists work Capitol Hill.
I'm appalled. I'm trying to save the planet, and you want to stop me.
Billions of tiny mirrors sprayed into the Stratosphere? Throwing iron filings into the ocean to grow CO2-eating algae?
What could go wrong?
Whatever goes wrong, we'll fix that too.
Actually, it's trillions of tiny mirrors.
Somebody will get that geo-engineering contract. Better us than incompetent oafs, right?
And our good fortune might be yours, one day!
That is, if we're lucky. Right, son?
Dad...
I'd rather starve than benefit from doing something wrong.
Why? It's going to happen no matter what you think.

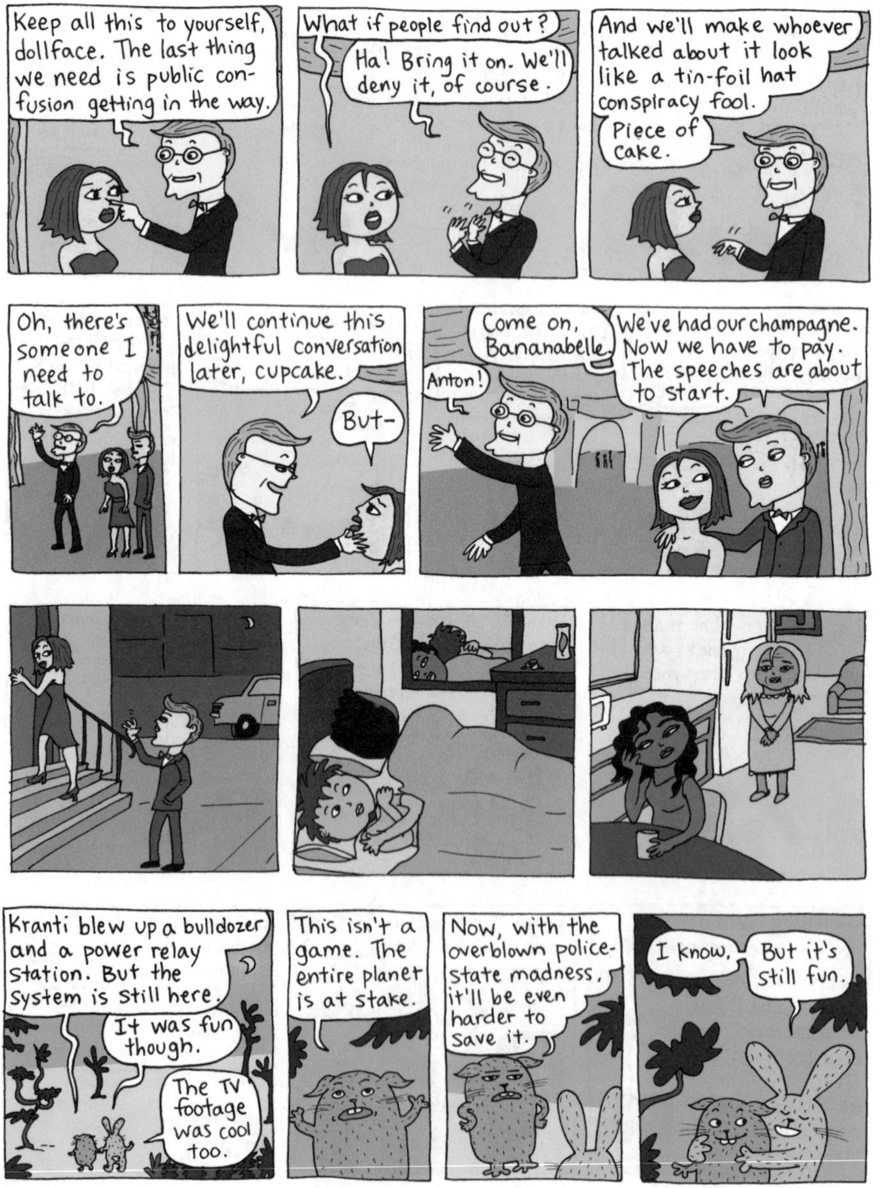
Keep all this to yourself, dollface. The last thing we need is public confusion getting in the way.
What if people find out?
Ha! Bring it on. We'll deny it, of course.
And we'll make whoever talked about it look like a tin-foil hat conspiracy fool.
Piece of cake.
Oh, there's someone I need to talk to.
We'll continue this delightful conversation later, cupcake.
But-
Anton!
Come on, Bananabelle.
We've had our champagne. Now we have to pay. The speeches are about to start.
Kranti blew up a bulldozer and a power relay station. But the system is still here.
It was fun though.
The TV footage was cool too.
This isn't a game. The entire planet is at stake.
Now, with the overblown police-state madness, it'll be even harder to save it.
I know.
But it's still fun.

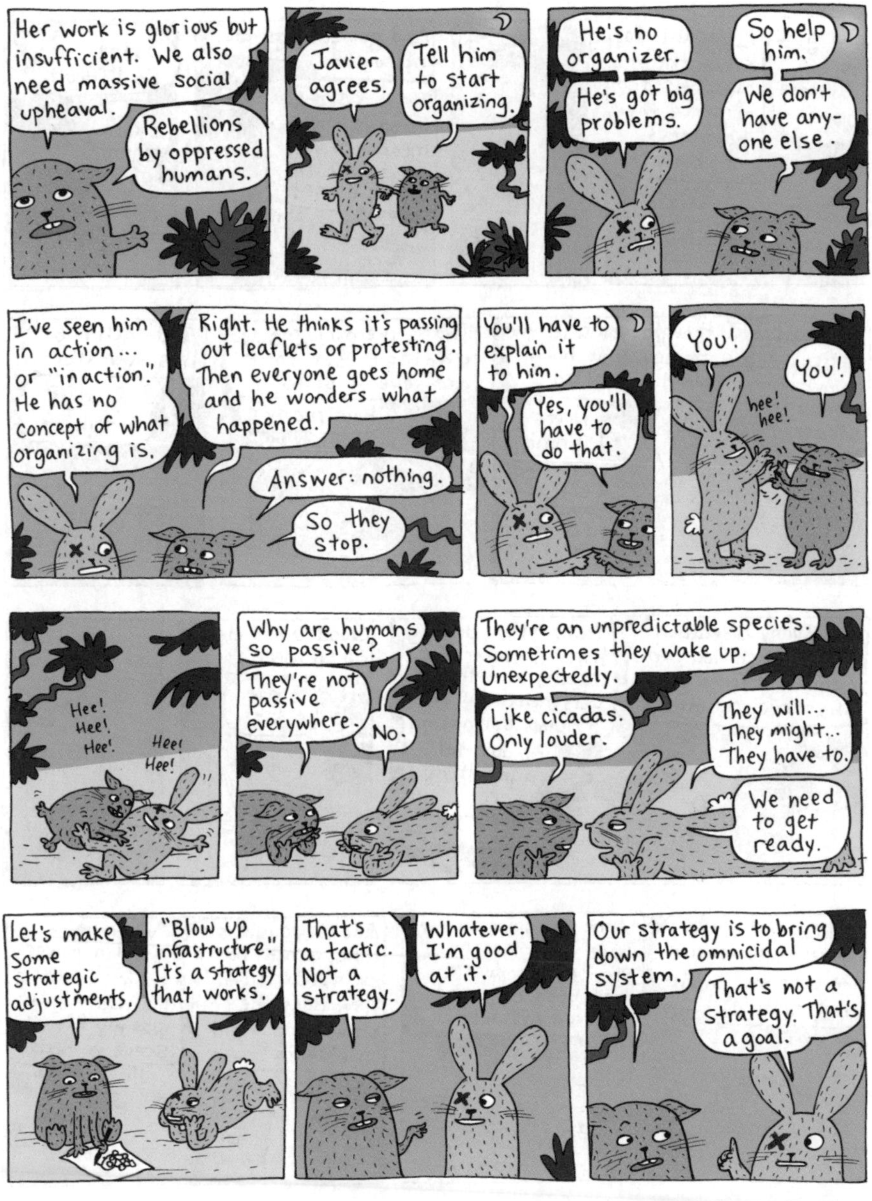

Her work is glorious but insufficient. We also need massive social upheaval.
Rebellions by oppressed humans.
Javier agrees.
Tell him to start organizing.
He's no organizer.
He's got big problems.
So help him.
We don't have any-one else.
I've seen him in action... or "inaction." He has no concept of what organizing is.
Right. He thinks it's passing out leaflets or protesting. Then everyone goes home and he wonders what happened.
Answer: nothing.
So they stop.
You'll have to explain it to him.
Yes, you'll have to do that.
You!
You!
hee! hee!
Hee! Hee! Hee!
Hee! Hee!
Why are humans so passive?
They're not passive everywhere.
No.
They're an unpredictable species. Sometimes they wake up. Unexpectedly.
Like cicadas. Only louder.
They will... They might... They have to.
We need to get ready.
Let's make some strategic adjustments.
"Blow up infrastructure." It's a strategy that works.
That's a tactic. Not a strategy.
Whatever. I'm good at it.
Our strategy is to bring down the omnicidal system.
That's not a strategy. That's a goal.

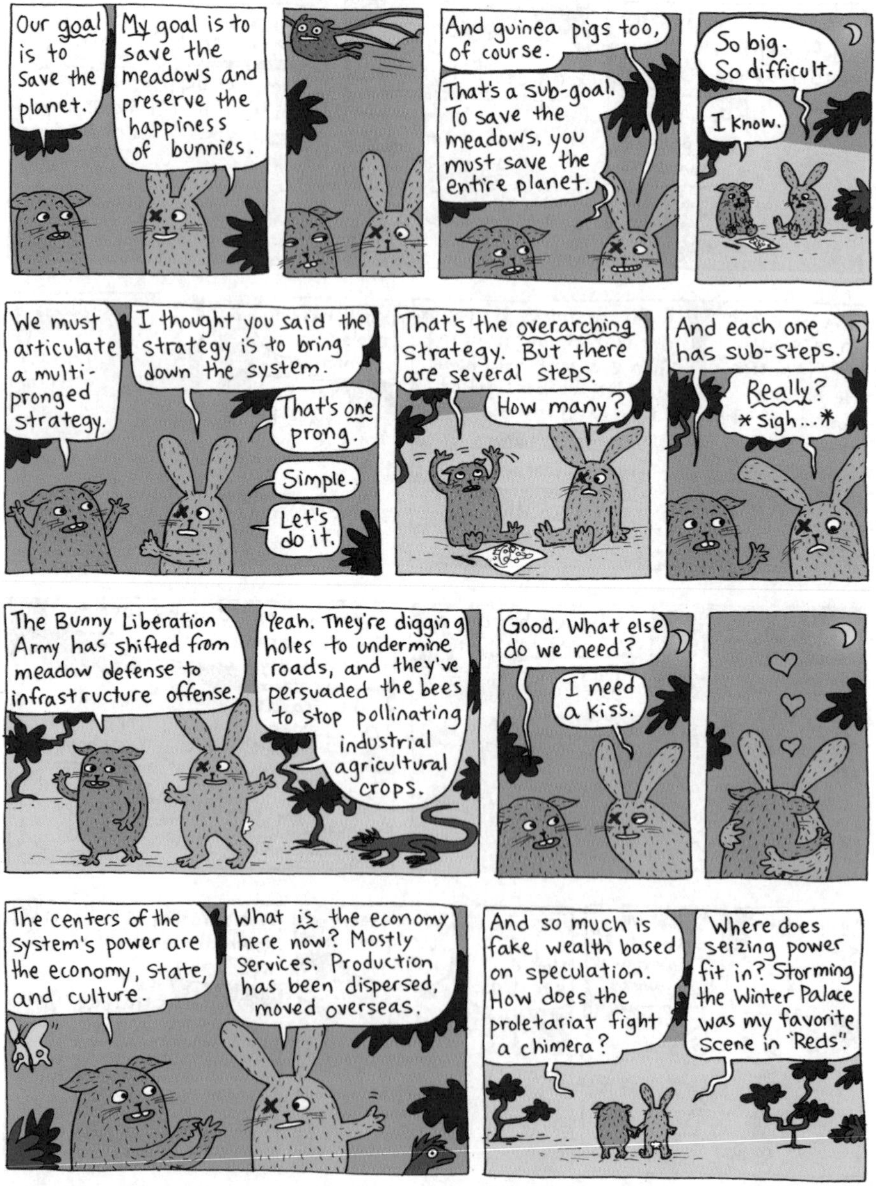
Our goal is to save the planet.
My goal is to save the meadows and preserve the happiness of bunnies.
And guinea pigs too, of course.
That's a sub-goal. To save the meadows, you must save the entire planet.
So big. So difficult.
I know.
We must articulate a multi-pronged strategy.
I thought you said the strategy is to bring down the system.
That's one prong.
Simple.
Let's do it.
That's the overarching strategy. But there are several steps.
How many?
And each one has sub-steps.
Really? *sigh...*
The Bunny Liberation Army has shifted from meadow defense to infrastructure offense.
Yeah. They're digging holes to undermine roads, and they've persuaded the bees to stop pollinating industrial agricultural crops.
Good. What else do we need?
I need a kiss.
The centers of the system's power are the economy, state, and culture.
What is the economy here now? Mostly services. Production has been dispersed, moved overseas.
And so much is fake wealth based on speculation. How does the proletariat fight a chimera?
Where does seizing power fit in? Storming the Winter Palace was my favorite scene in "Reds".

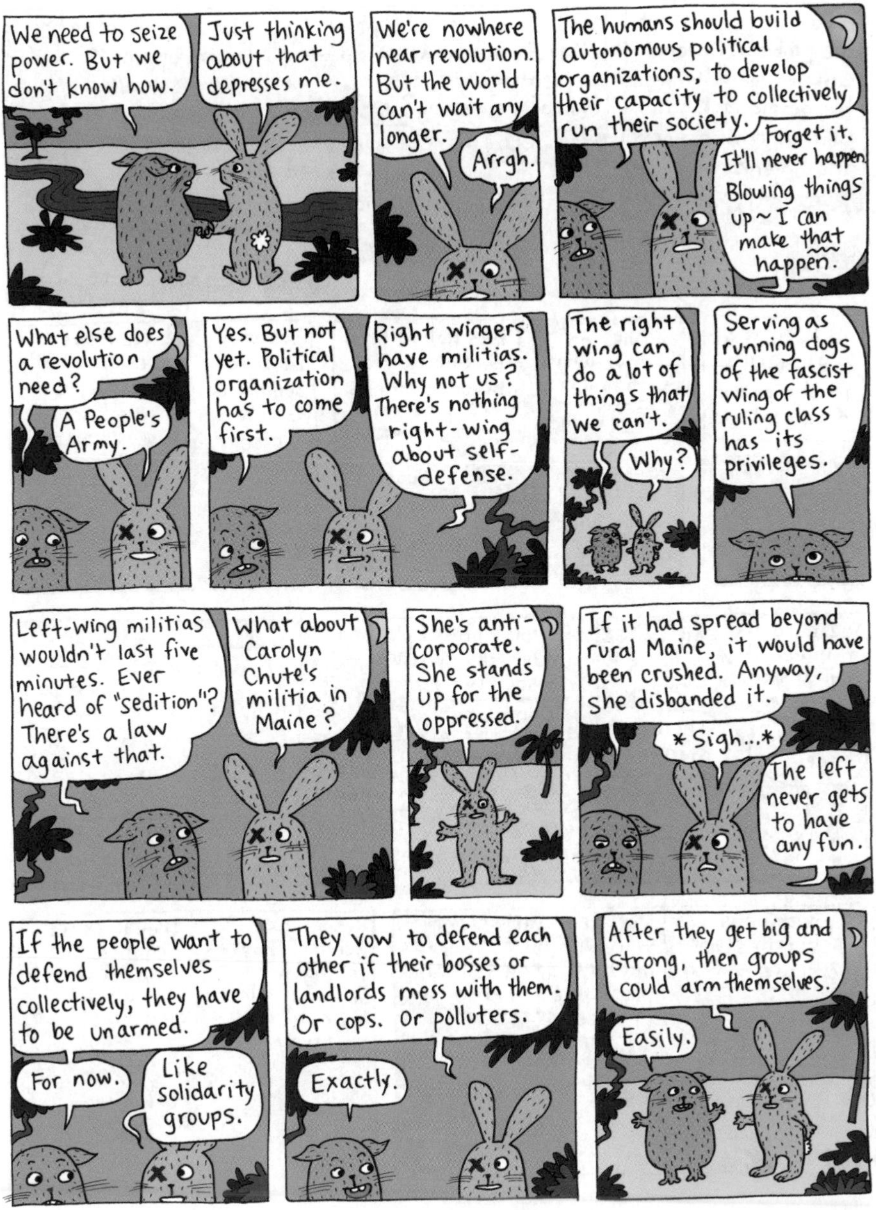
We need to seize power. But we don't know how.
Just thinking about that depresses me.
We're nowhere near revolution. But the world can't wait any longer.
Arrgh.
The humans should build autonomous political organizations, to develop their capacity to collectively run their society.
Forget it. It'll never happen.
Blowing things up ~ I can make that happen.
What else does a revolution need?
A People's Army.
Yes. But not yet. Political organization has to come first.
Right wingers have militias. Why not us? There's nothing right-wing about self-defense.
The right wing can do a lot of things that we can't.
Why?
Serving as running dogs of the fascist wing of the ruling class has its privileges.
Left-wing militias wouldn't last five minutes. Ever heard of "sedition"? There's a law against that.
What about Carolyn Chute's militia in Maine?
She's anti-corporate. She stands up for the oppressed.
If it had spread beyond rural Maine, it would have been crushed. Anyway, she disbanded it.
* Sigh... *
The left never gets to have any fun.
If the people want to defend themselves collectively, they have to be unarmed.
For now.
Like solidarity groups.
They vow to defend each other if their bosses or landlords mess with them. Or cops. Or polluters.
Exactly.
After they get big and strong, then groups could arm themselves.
Easily.

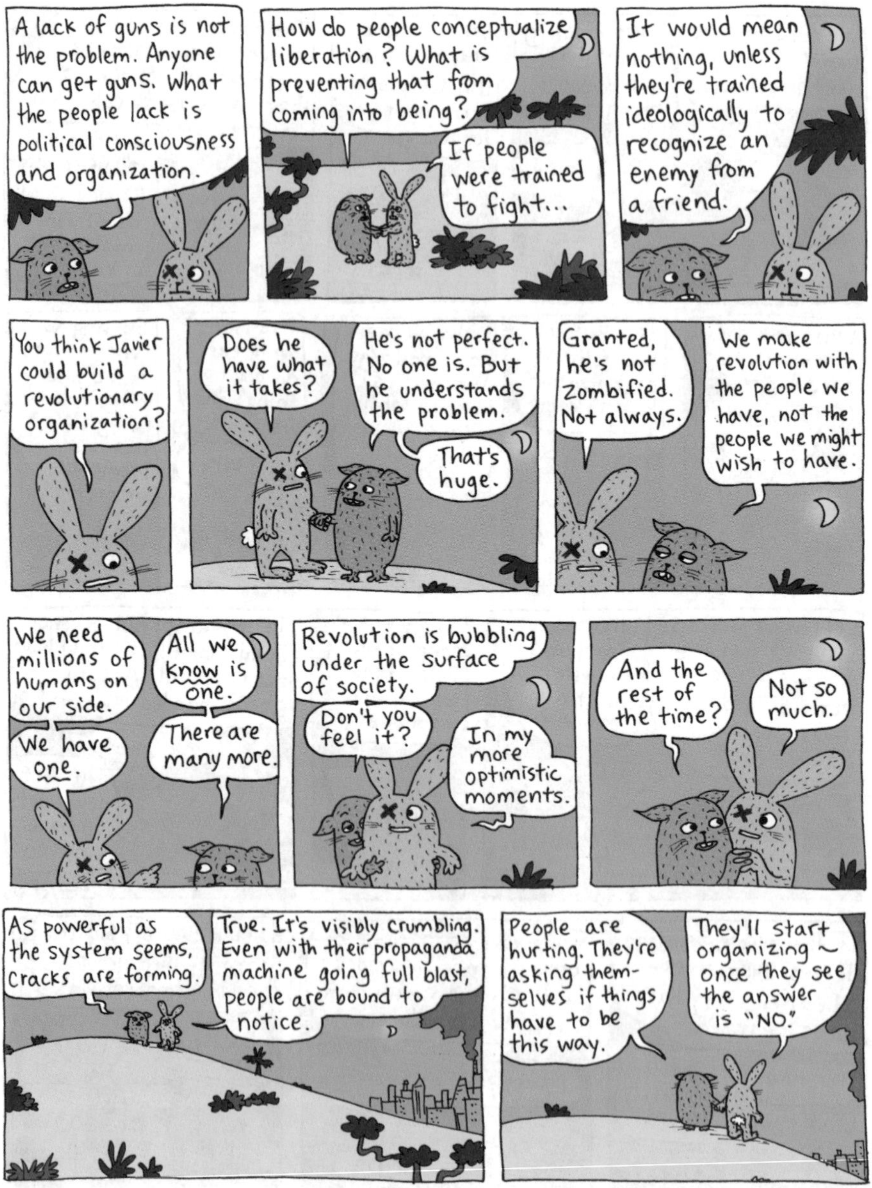
A lack of guns is not the problem. Anyone can get guns. What the people lack is political consciousness and organization.
How do people conceptualize liberation? What is preventing that from coming into being?
If people were trained to fight...
It would mean nothing, unless they're trained ideologically to recognize an enemy from a friend.
You think Javier could build a revolutionary organization?
Does he have what it takes?
He's not perfect. No one is. But he understands the problem.
That's huge.
Granted, he's not Zombified. Not always.
We make revolution with the people we have, not the people we might wish to have.
We need millions of humans on our side.
All we know is one.
We have one.
There are many more.
Revolution is bubbling under the surface of society.
Don't you feel it?
In my more optimistic moments.
And the rest of the time?
Not so much.
As powerful as the system seems, cracks are forming.
True. It's visibly crumbling. Even with their propaganda machine going full blast, people are bound to notice.
People are hurting. They're asking themselves if things have to be this way.
They'll start organizing ~ once they see the answer is "NO."

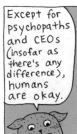

Except for psychopaths and CEOs (insofar as there's any difference), humans are okay.

Yeah. They're social animals with a big empathy chip. They help eachother in crises. It's cute.

But they're not allowed to do anything that's not system-approved.

Even the ones not in prison are trapped. They just don't see the bars.

We'll help make the bars visible.

And then show how much better it is outside.

If we build organizations now, then when the humans inevitably rise up, they can convert their raw rage into revolutionary energy.

It's going to be hard to build a movement from scratch.

Extremely.

We'll probably fail.

We have to try. Even if it means starting with one flawed person.

You're cute. You win.

I'll talk to Javier.

The exploitation of human labor and the extraction of natural material are two intertwined elements in capitalism's main process: creating surplus value.

You're sooooo cute when you're abstract.

This nation was founded on land theft, genocide and slavery. All to convert life into commodities for the accumulation of wealth by a few.

Now it's global.

The form has changed, but not the essence.

We must stop the system at two points of profit-creation: extraction and exploitation.

Please, let's get concrete. "Not one more inch of land. Not one more stolen life."

How's that?

I can't argue with it.

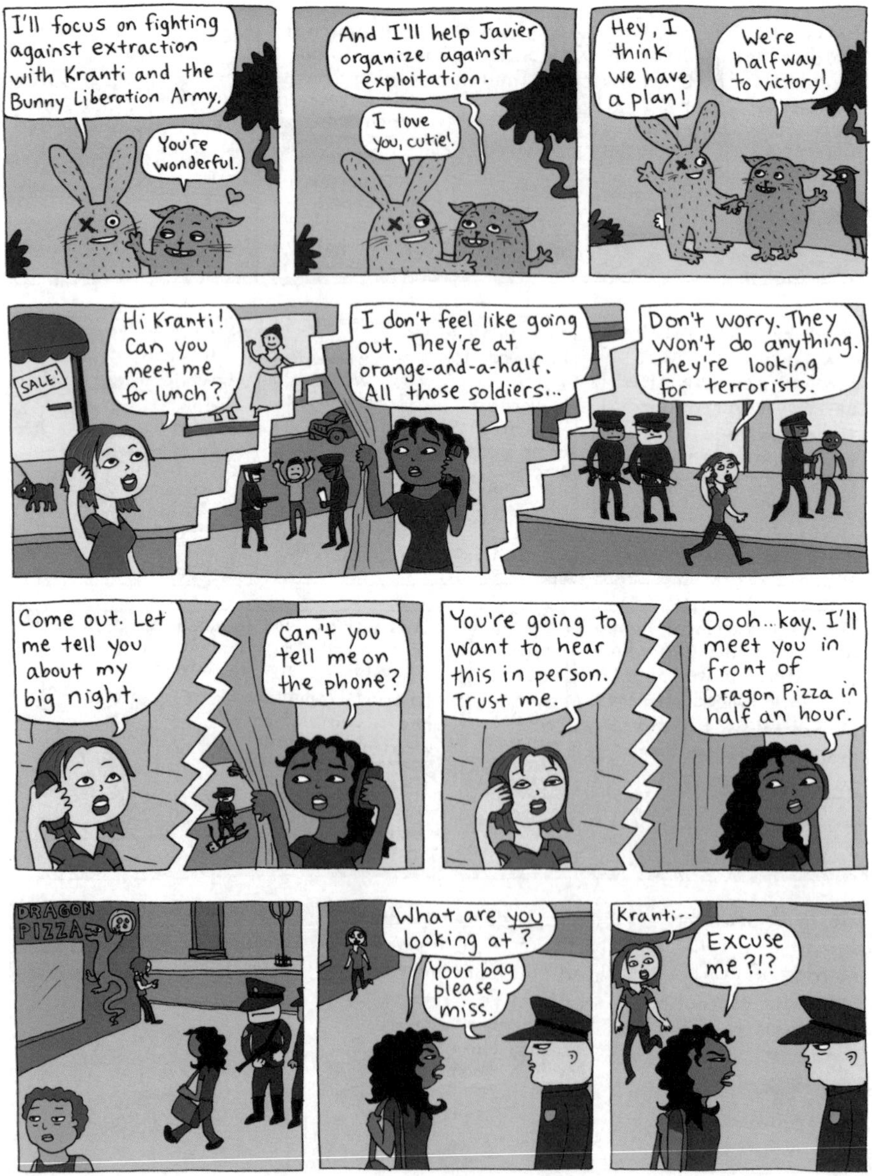
I'll focus on fighting against extraction with Kranti and the Bunny Liberation Army.
You're wonderful.
And I'll help Javier organize against exploitation.
I love you, cutie!
Hey, I think we have a plan!
We're halfway to victory!
SALE!
Hi Kranti! Can you meet me for lunch?
I don't feel like going out. They're at orange-and-a-half. All those soldiers...
Don't worry. They won't do anything. They're looking for terrorists.
Come out. Let me tell you about my big night.
Can't you tell me on the phone?
You're going to want to hear this in person. Trust me.
Oooh...kay. I'll meet you in front of Dragon Pizza in half an hour.
DRAGON PIZZA
What are you looking at?
Your bag please, miss.
Kranti--
Excuse me?!?

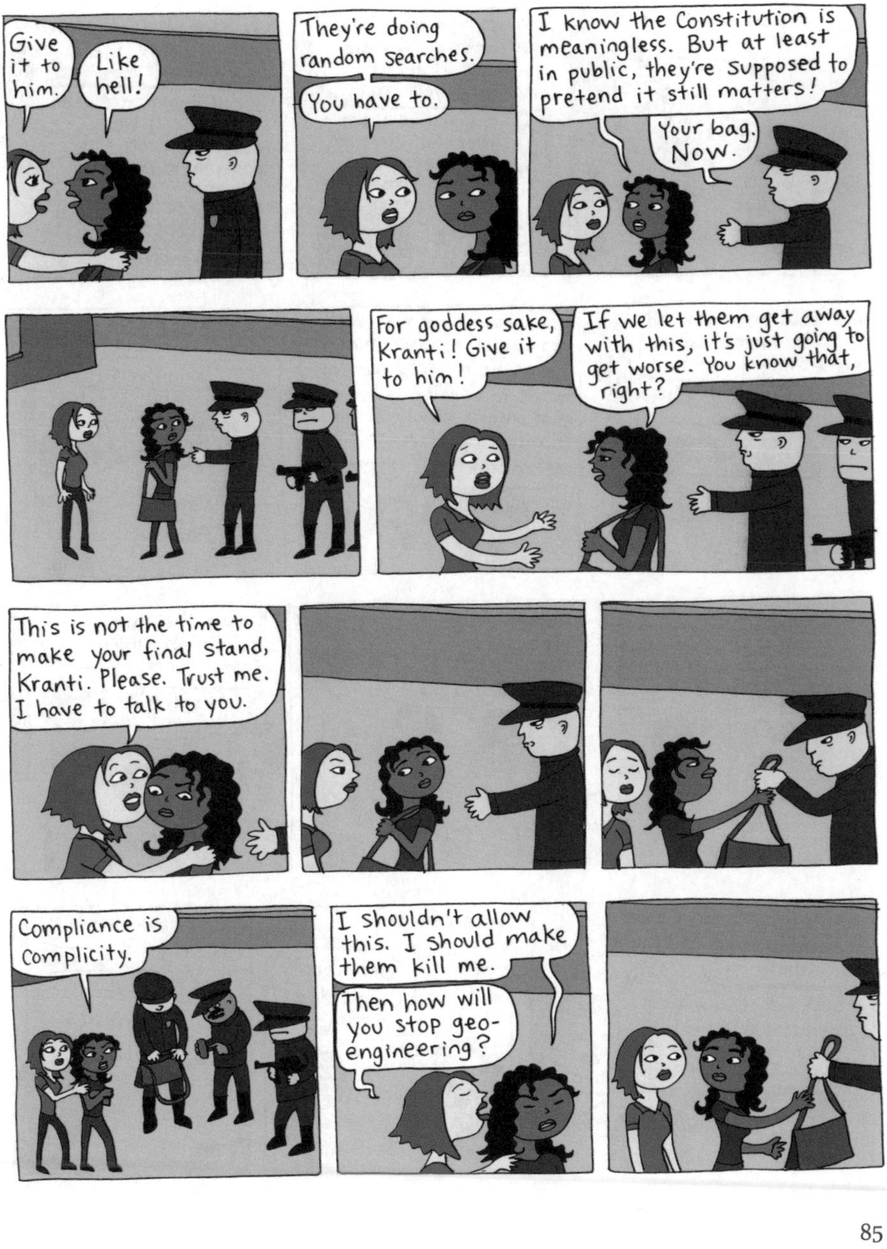
Give it to him.
Like hell!
They're doing random searches.
You have to.
I know the Constitution is meaningless. But at least in public, they're supposed to pretend it still matters!
Your bag. Now.
For goddess sake, Kranti! Give it to him!
If we let them get away with this, it's just going to get worse. You know that, right?
This is not the time to make your final stand, Kranti. Please. Trust me. I have to talk to you.
Compliance is complicity.
I shouldn't allow this. I should make them kill me.
Then how will you stop geo-engineering?

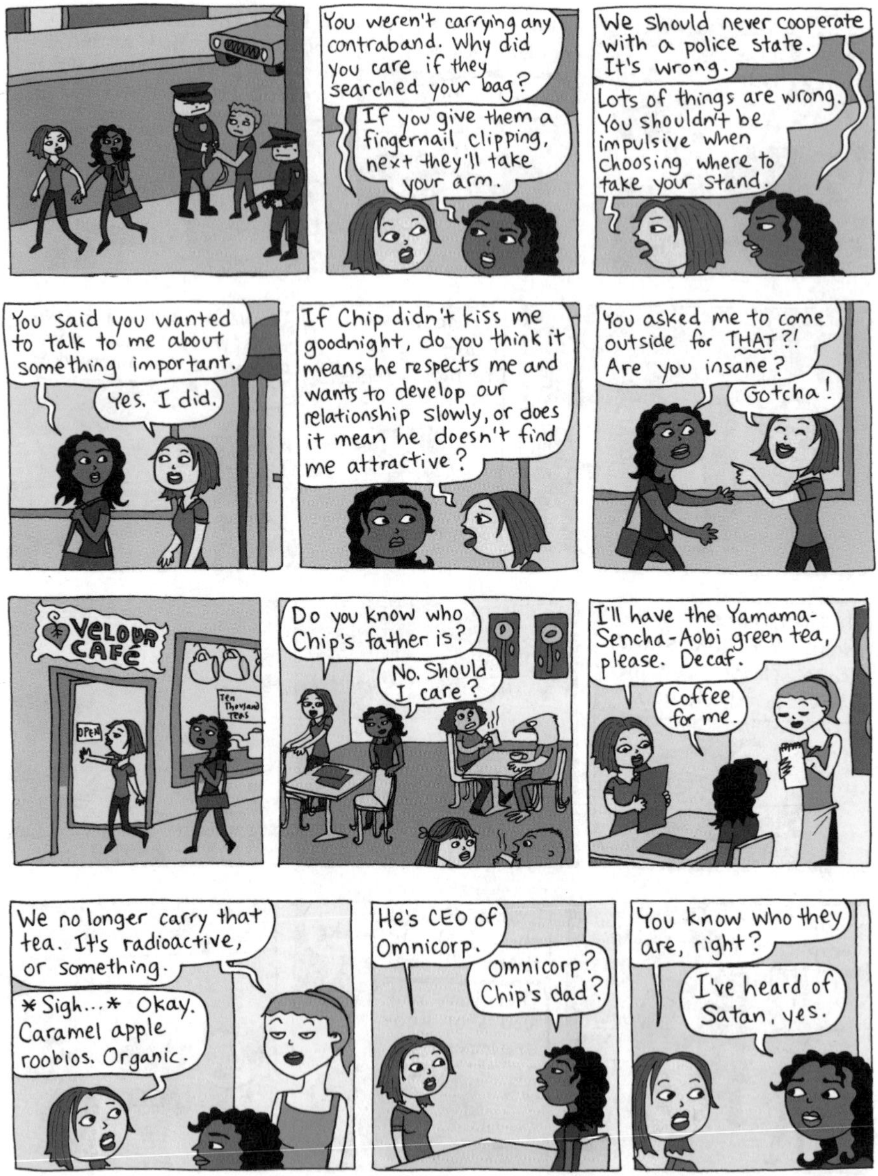
You weren't carrying any contraband. Why did you care if they searched your bag?
If you give them a fingernail clipping, next they'll take your arm.
We should never cooperate with a police state. It's wrong.
Lots of things are wrong. You shouldn't be impulsive when choosing where to take your stand.
You said you wanted to talk to me about something important.
Yes. I did.
If Chip didn't kiss me goodnight, do you think it means he respects me and wants to develop our relationship slowly, or does it mean he doesn't find me attractive?
You asked me to come outside for THAT?! Are you insane?
Gotcha!
VELOUR CAFÉ
OPEN
Ten Thousand Teas
Do you know who Chip's father is?
No. Should I care?
I'll have the Yamama-Sencha-Aobi green tea, please. Decaf.
Coffee for me.
We no longer carry that tea. It's radioactive, or something.
Sigh... Okay. Caramel apple roobios. Organic.
He's CEO of Omnicorp.
Omnicorp? Chip's dad?
You know who they are, right?
I've heard of Satan, yes.

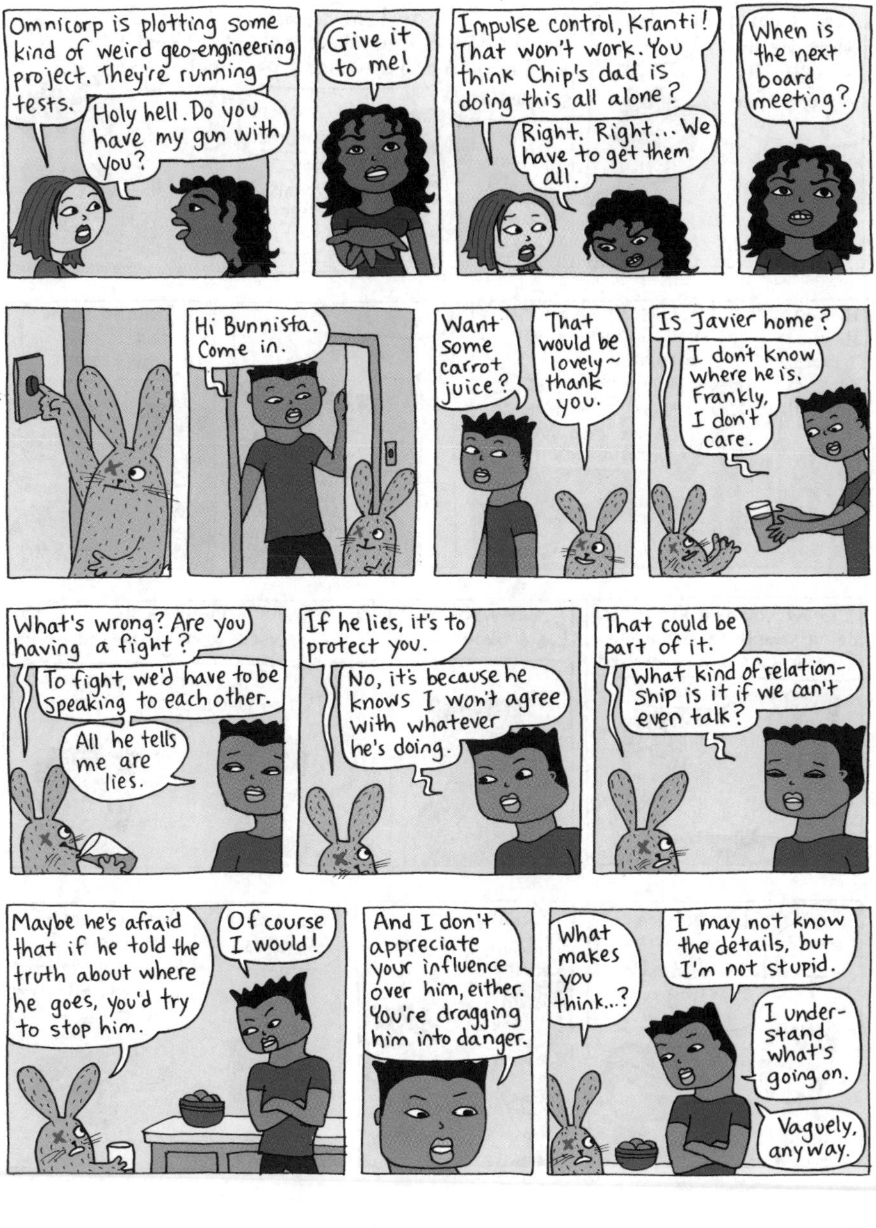
Omnicorp is plotting some kind of weird geo-engineering project. They're running tests.
Holy hell. Do you have my gun with you?
Give it to me!
Impulse control, Kranti! That won't work. You think Chip's dad is doing this all alone?
Right. Right... We have to get them all.
When is the next board meeting?
Hi Bunnista. Come in.
Want some carrot juice?
That would be lovely ~ thank you.
Is Javier home?
I don't know where he is. Frankly, I don't care.
What's wrong? Are you having a fight?
To fight, we'd have to be speaking to each other.
All he tells me are lies.
If he lies, it's to protect you.
No, it's because he knows I won't agree with whatever he's doing.
That could be part of it.
What kind of relationship is it if we can't even talk?
Maybe he's afraid that if he told the truth about where he goes, you'd try to stop him.
Of course I would!
And I don't appreciate your influence over him, either. You're dragging him into danger.
What makes you think...?
I may not know the details, but I'm not stupid.
I understand what's going on.
Vaguely, anyway.

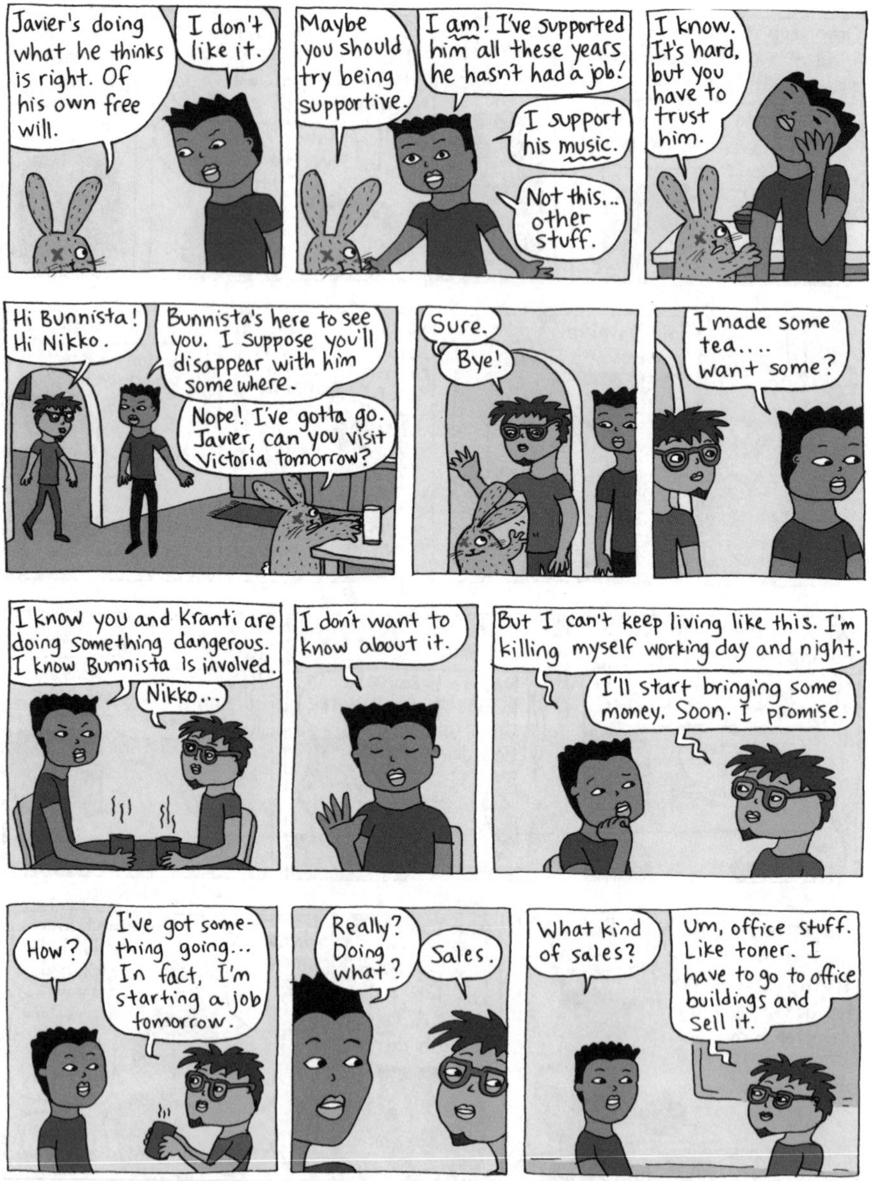
Javier's doing what he thinks is right. Of his own free will.
I don't like it.
Maybe you should try being supportive.
I am! I've supported him all these years he hasn't had a job!
I support his music.
Not this... other stuff.
I know. It's hard, but you have to trust him.
Hi Bunnista! Hi Nikko.
Bunnista's here to see you. I suppose you'll disappear with him somewhere.
Nope! I've gotta go. Javier, can you visit Victoria tomorrow?
Sure.
Bye!
I made some tea.... want some?
I know you and Kranti are doing something dangerous. I know Bunnista is involved.
Nikko...
I don't want to know about it.
But I can't keep living like this. I'm killing myself working day and night.
I'll start bringing some money. Soon. I promise.
How?
I've got some-thing going... In fact, I'm starting a job tomorrow.
Really? Doing what?
Sales.
What kind of sales?
Um, office stuff. Like toner. I have to go to office buildings and sell it.

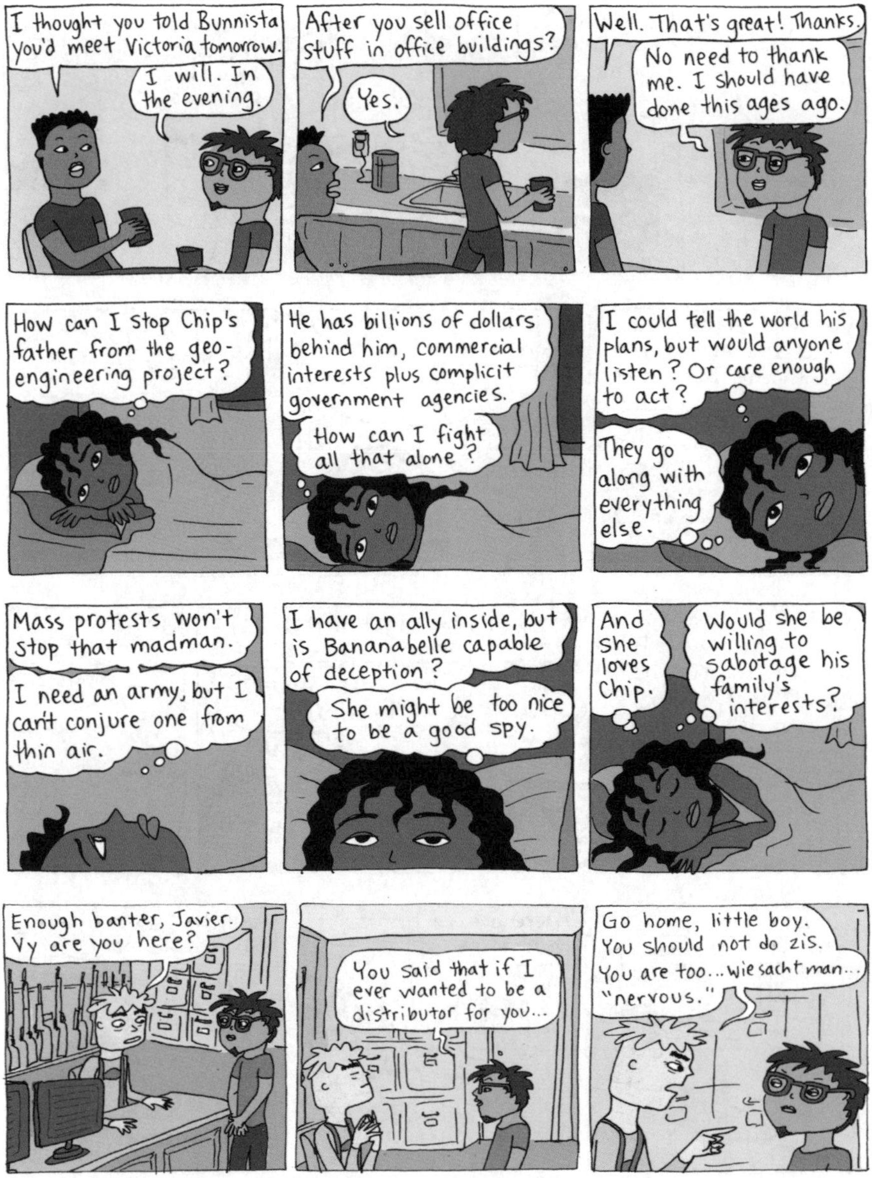
I thought you told Bunnista you'd meet Victoria tomorrow.
I will. In the evening.
After you sell office stuff in office buildings?
Yes.
Well. That's great! Thanks.
No need to thank me. I should have done this ages ago.
How can I stop Chip's father from the geo-engineering project?
He has billions of dollars behind him, commercial interests plus complicit government agencies.
How can I fight all that alone?
I could tell the world his plans, but would anyone listen? Or care enough to act?
They go along with everything else.
Mass protests won't stop that madman.
I need an army, but I can't conjure one from thin air.
I have an ally inside, but is Bananabelle capable of deception?
She might be too nice to be a good spy.
And she loves Chip.
Would she be willing to sabotage his family's interests?
Enough banter, Javier. Vy are you here?
You said that if I ever wanted to be a distributor for you...
Go home, little boy. You should not do zis. You are too... wie sacht man... "nervous."

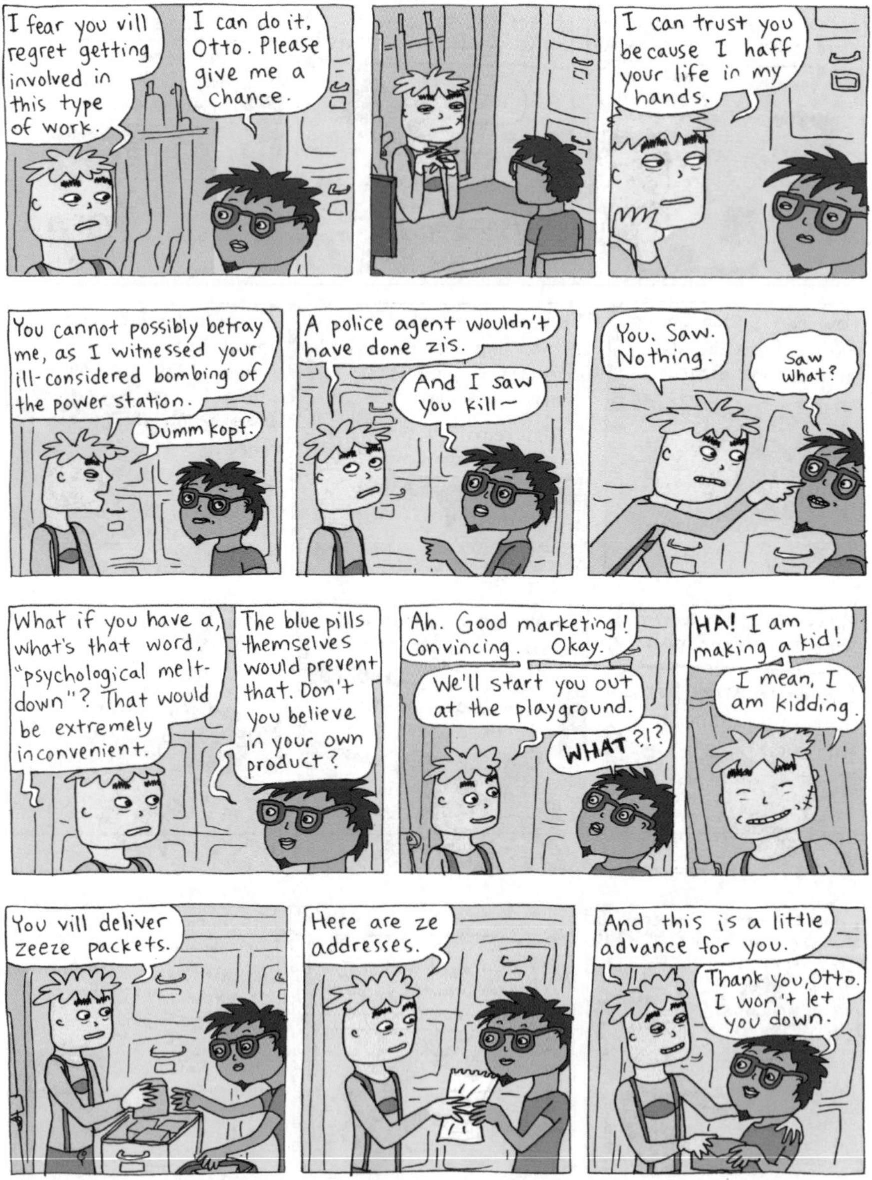
I fear you vill regret getting involved in this type of work.
I can do it, Otto. Please give me a chance.
I can trust you because I haff your life in my hands.
You cannot possibly betray me, as I witnessed your ill-considered bombing of the power station.
Dumm kopf.
A police agent wouldn't have done zis.
And I saw you kill~
You. Saw. Nothing.
Saw what?
What if you have a, what's that word, "psychological melt-down"? That would be extremely inconvenient.
The blue pills themselves would prevent that. Don't you believe in your own product?
Ah. Good marketing! Convincing. Okay.
We'll start you out at the playground.
WHAT?!?
HA! I am making a kid!
I mean, I am kidding.
You vill deliver zeeze packets.
Here are ze addresses.
And this is a little advance for you.
Thank you, Otto. I won't let you down.

...AND NOW IT'S TIME FOR A MONTAGE!
Finally.
Thank you, sonny!
A sight for sore eyes.
Can I get a better deal on this?
I just deliver.
GOING OUT OF BUSINESS SALE
THE LAST BOOKSTORE
open
You wanted to see me?
Greetings, human. I expected you earlier.
I brought you a gift.
"Deep Green Resistance"! I've been meaning to order this!
But how? You never have any money.
I got a job!
Doing what?
Not playing the accordion in a hotdog costume again, I hope.
Sadly, that job is no longer available.
I'm in Sales.
What kind of sales?
Um, office stuff. In office buildings.
Bo-ring!
But thanks for the book!

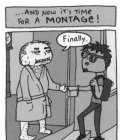

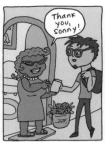

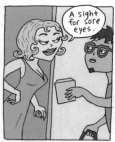

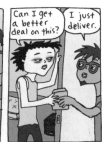

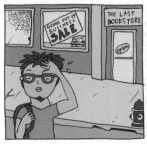

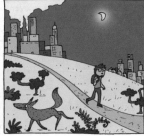

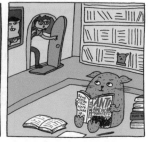

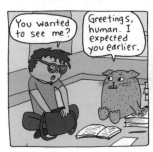

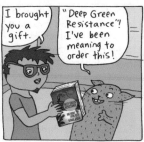

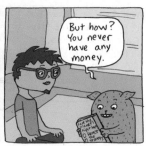

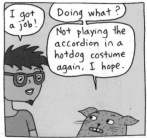

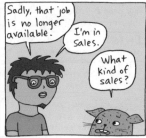

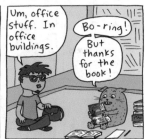

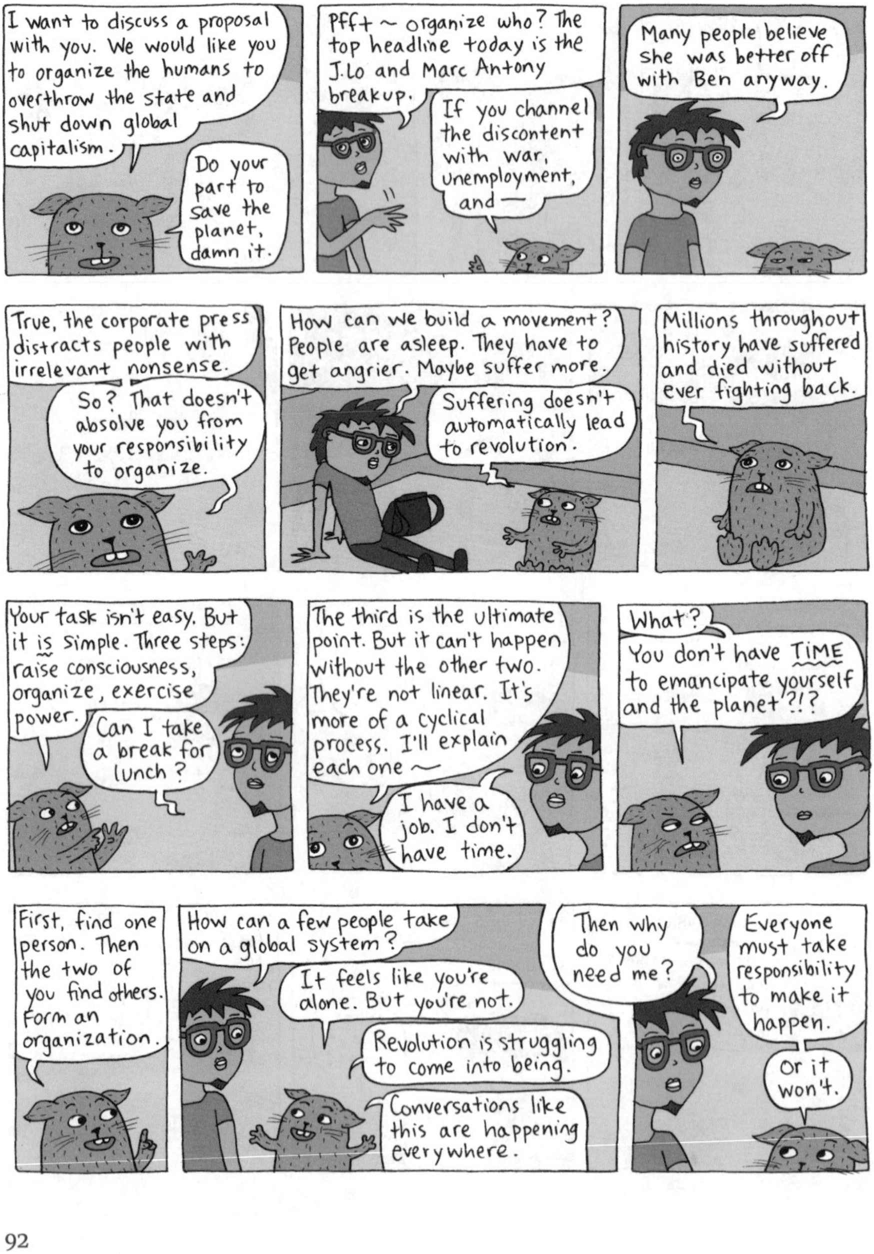
I want to discuss a proposal with you. We would like you to organize the humans to overthrow the state and shut down global capitalism.
Do your part to save the planet, damn it.
Pff+ ~ organize who? The top headline today is the J.Lo and Marc Antony breakup.
If you channel the discontent with war, unemployment, and —
Many people believe she was better off with Ben anyway.
True, the corporate press distracts people with irrelevant nonsense.
So? That doesn't absolve you from your responsibility to organize.
How can we build a movement? People are asleep. They have to get angrier. Maybe suffer more.
Suffering doesn't automatically lead to revolution.
Millions throughout history have suffered and died without ever fighting back.
Your task isn't easy. But it is simple. Three steps: raise consciousness, organize, exercise power.
Can I take a break for lunch?
The third is the ultimate point. But it can't happen without the other two. They're not linear. It's more of a cyclical process. I'll explain each one ~
I have a job. I don't have time.
What?
You don't have TIME to emancipate yourself and the planet?!?
First, find one person. Then the two of you find others. Form an organization.
How can a few people take on a global system?
It feels like you're alone. But you're not.
Revolution is struggling to come into being.
Conversations like this are happening everywhere.
Then why do you need me?
Everyone must take responsibility to make it happen.
Or it won't.

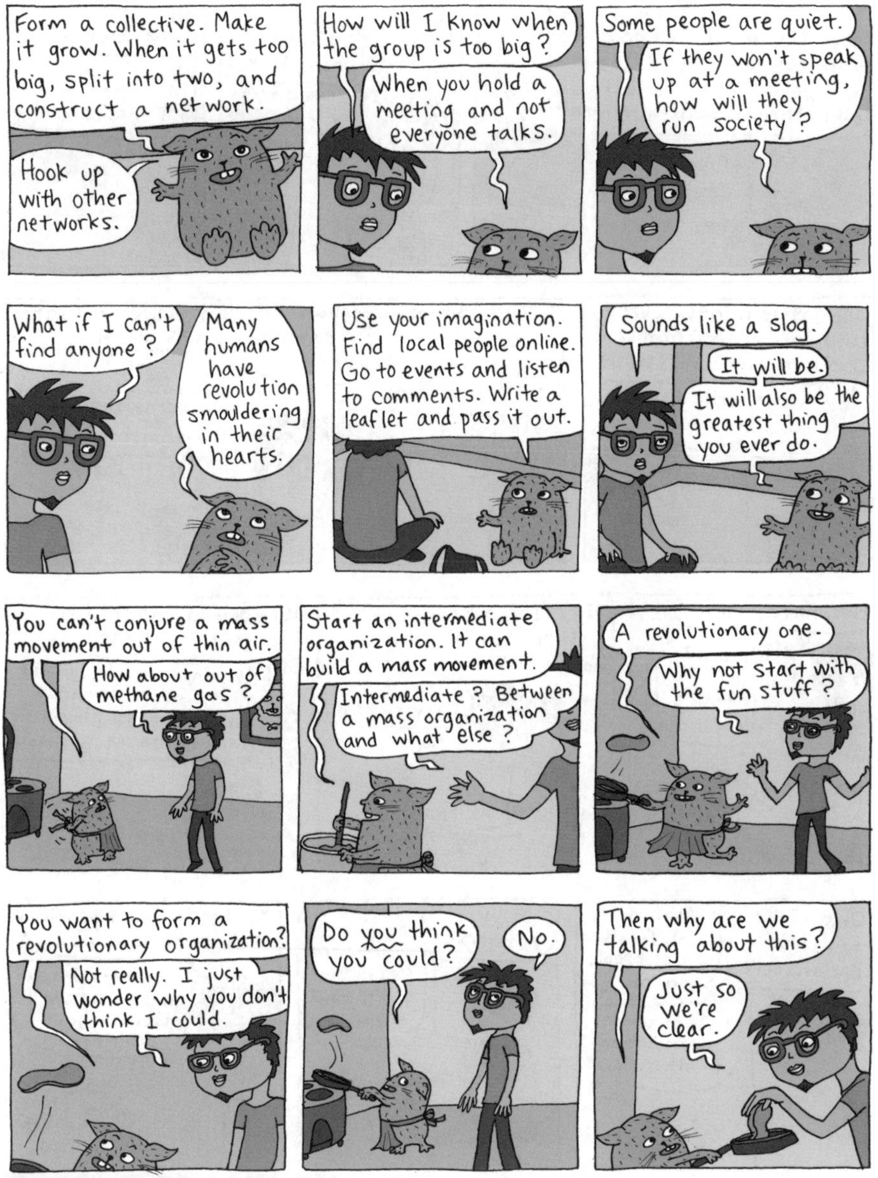
Form a collective. Make it grow. When it gets too big, split into two, and construct a network.
Hook up with other networks.
How will I know when the group is too big?
When you hold a meeting and not everyone talks.
Some people are quiet.
If they won't speak up at a meeting, how will they run society?
What if I can't find anyone?
Many humans have revolution smouldering in their hearts.
Use your imagination. Find local people online. Go to events and listen to comments. Write a leaflet and pass it out.
Sounds like a slog.
It will be.
It will also be the greatest thing you ever do.
You can't conjure a mass movement out of thin air.
How about out of methane gas?
Start an intermediate organization. It can build a mass movement.
Intermediate? Between a mass organization and what else?
A revolutionary one.
Why not start with the fun stuff?
You want to form a revolutionary organization?
Not really. I just wonder why you don't think I could.
Do you think you could?
No.
Then why are we talking about this?
Just so we're clear.

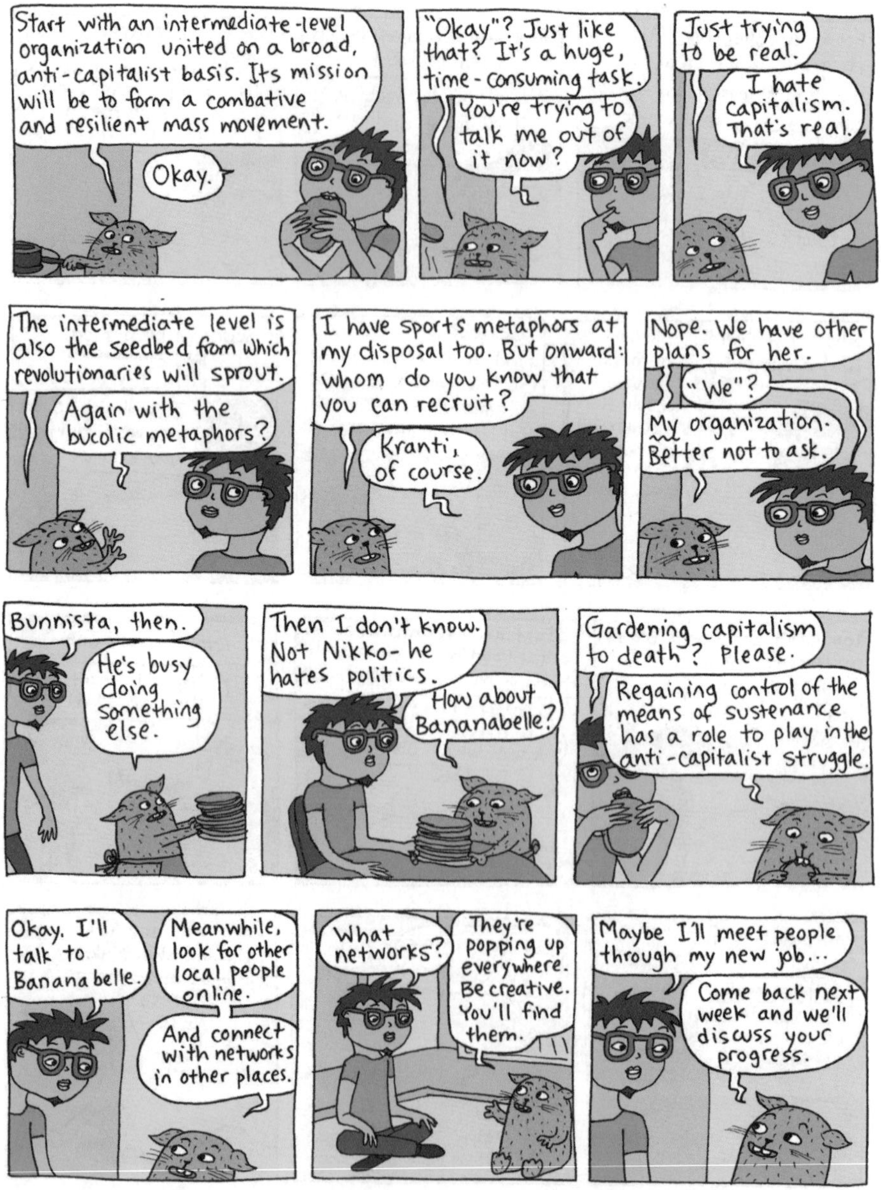

Start with an intermediate-level organization united on a broad, anti-capitalist basis. Its mission will be to form a combative and resilient mass movement.
Okay.
"Okay"? Just like that? It's a huge, time-consuming task.
You're trying to talk me out of it now?
Just trying to be real.
I hate capitalism. That's real.
The intermediate level is also the seedbed from which revolutionaries will sprout.
Again with the bucolic metaphors?
I have sports metaphors at my disposal too. But onward: whom do you know that you can recruit?
Kranti, of course.
Nope. We have other plans for her.
"We"?
My organization. Better not to ask.
Bunnista, then.
He's busy doing something else.
Then I don't know. Not Nikko- he hates politics.
How about Bananabelle?
Gardening capitalism to death? Please.
Regaining control of the means of sustenance has a role to play in the anti-capitalist struggle.
Okay. I'll talk to Bananabelle.
Meanwhile, look for other local people online.
And connect with networks in other places.
What networks?
They're popping up everywhere. Be creative. You'll find them.
Maybe I'll meet people through my new job...
Come back next week and we'll discuss your progress.

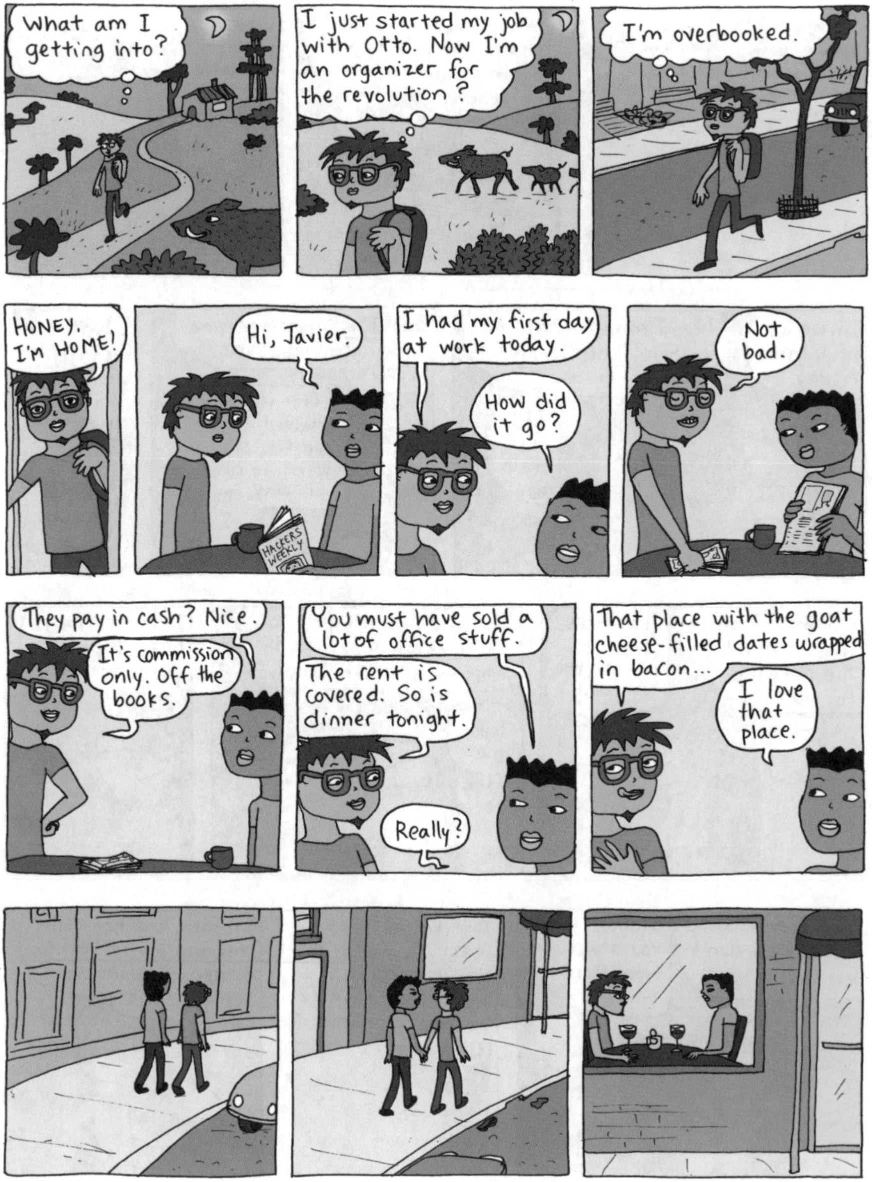
What am I getting into?
I just started my job with Otto. Now I'm an organizer for the revolution?
I'm overbooked.
HONEY, I'M HOME!
Hi, Javier.
HACKERS WEEKLY
I had my first day at work today.
How did it go?
Not bad.
They pay in cash? Nice.
It's commission only. Off the books.
You must have sold a lot of office stuff.
The rent is covered. So is dinner tonight.
Really?
That place with the goat cheese-filled dates wrapped in bacon...
I love that place.

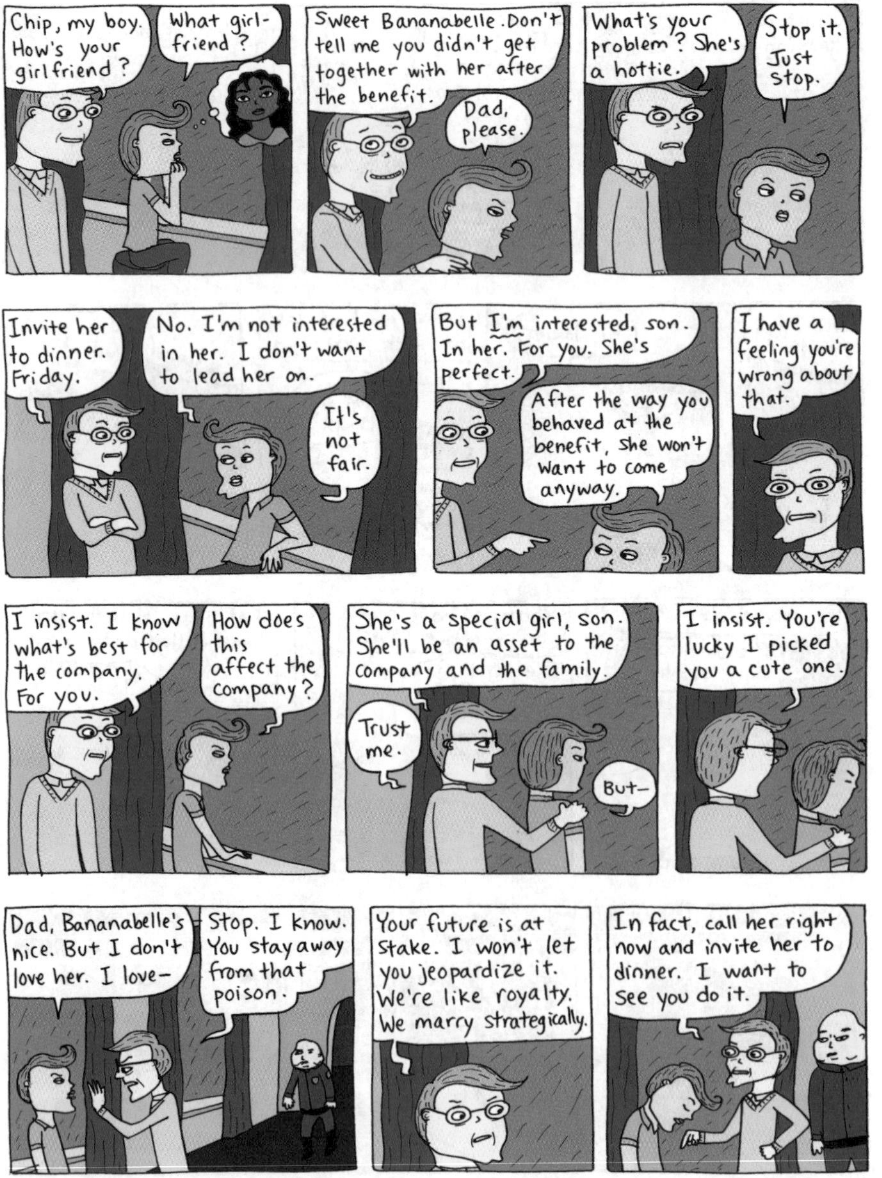

Chip, my boy. How's your girlfriend?
What girl-friend?
Sweet Bananabelle. Don't tell me you didn't get together with her after the benefit.
Dad, please.
What's your problem? She's a hottie.
Stop it. Just stop.
Invite her to dinner. Friday.
No. I'm not interested in her. I don't want to lead her on.
It's not fair.
But I'm interested, son. In her. For you. She's perfect.
After the way you behaved at the benefit, she won't want to come anyway.
I have a feeling you're wrong about that.
I insist. I know what's best for the company. For you.
How does this affect the company?
She's a special girl, son. She'll be an asset to the company and the family.
Trust me.
But—
I insist. You're lucky I picked you a cute one.
Dad, Bananabelle's nice. But I don't love her. I love—
Stop. I know. You stay away from that poison.
Your future is at stake. I won't let you jeopardize it. We're like royalty. We marry strategically.
In fact, call her right now and invite her to dinner. I want to see you do it.

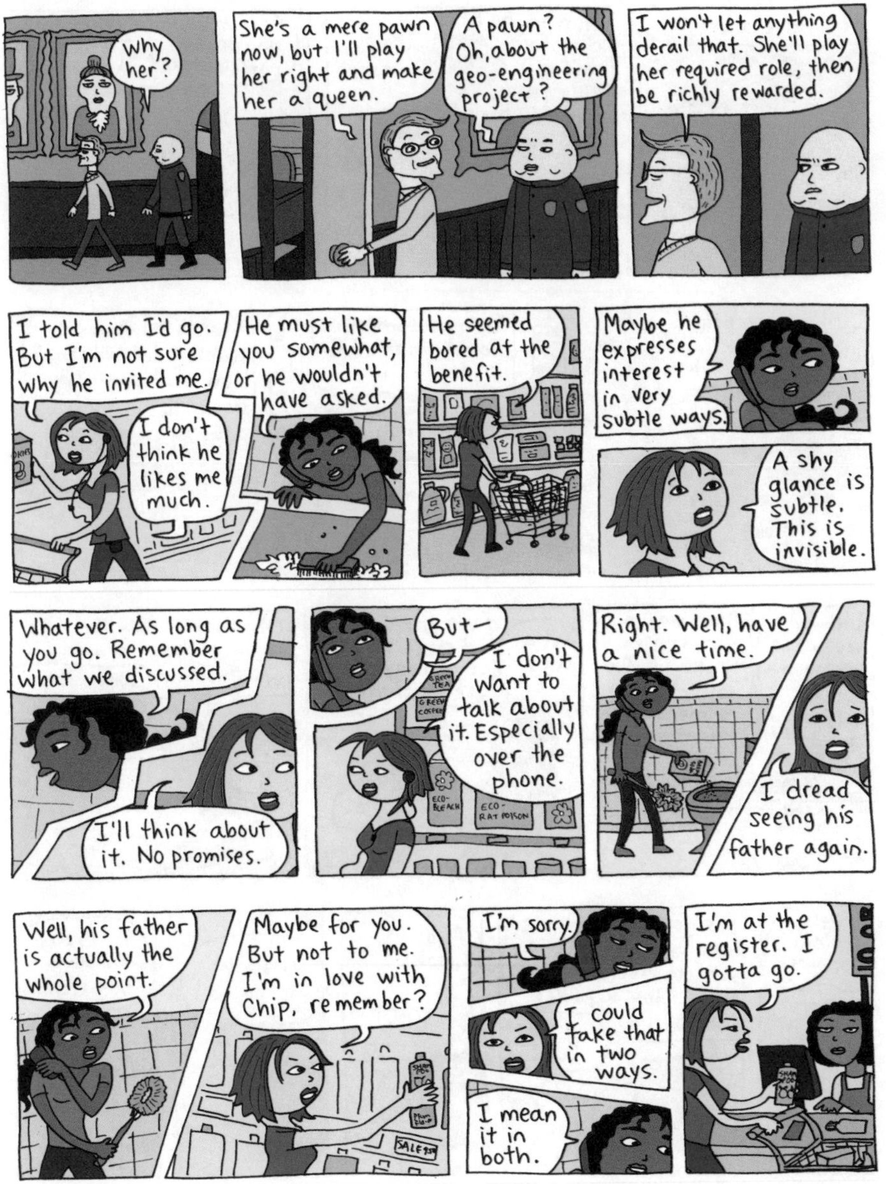

Why her?
She's a mere pawn now, but I'll play her right and make her a queen.
A pawn? Oh, about the geo-engineering project?
I won't let anything derail that. She'll play her required role, then be richly rewarded.
I told him I'd go. But I'm not sure why he invited me.
I don't think he likes me much.
He must like you somewhat, or he wouldn't have asked.
He seemed bored at the benefit.
Maybe he expresses interest in very subtle ways.
A shy glance is subtle. This is invisible.
Whatever. As long as you go. Remember what we discussed.
I'll think about it. No promises.
But—
I don't want to talk about it. Especially over the phone.
Right. Well, have a nice time.
I dread seeing his father again.
Well, his father is actually the whole point.
Maybe for you. But not to me. I'm in love with Chip, remember?
I'm sorry.
I could take that in two ways.
I mean it in both.
I'm at the register. I gotta go.

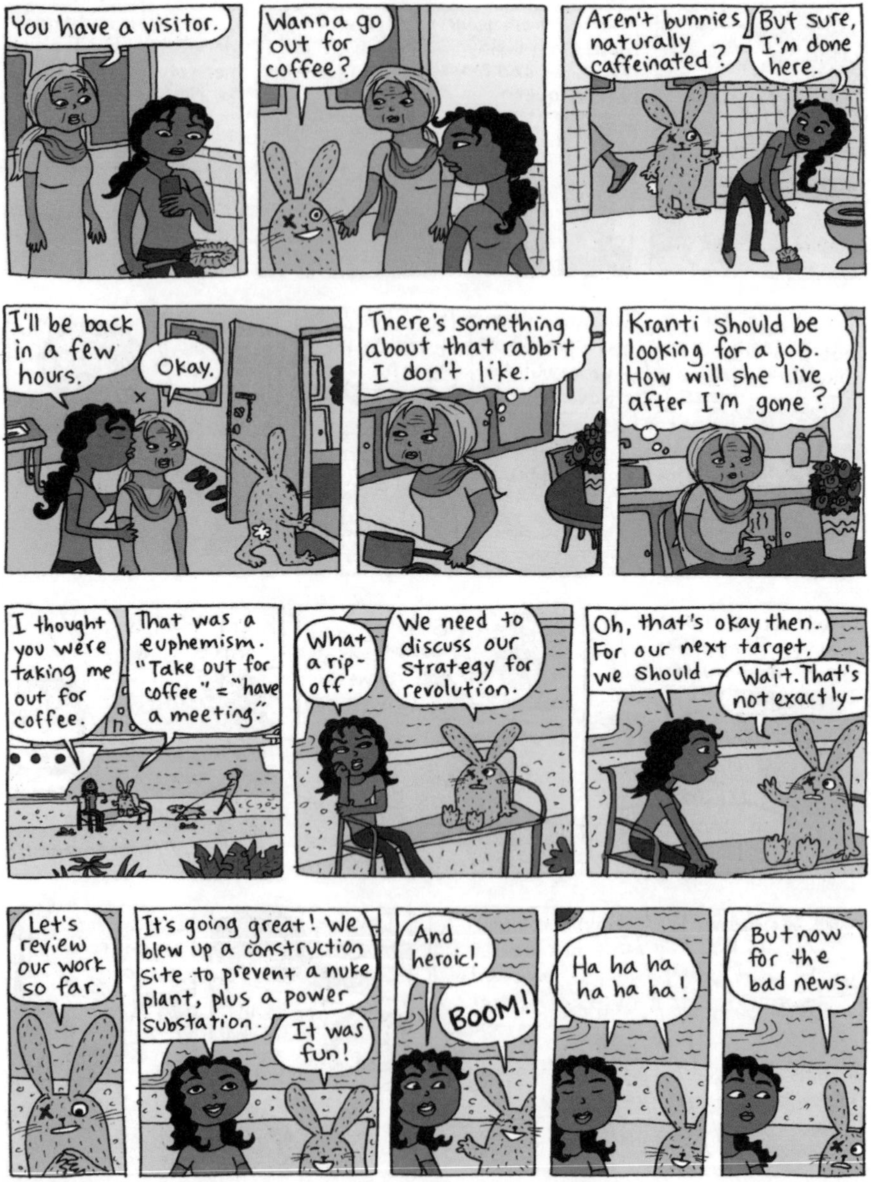
You have a visitor.
Wanna go out for coffee?
Aren't bunnies naturally caffeinated?
But sure, I'm done here.
I'll be back in a few hours.
Okay.
There's something about that rabbit I don't like.
Kranti should be looking for a job. How will she live after I'm gone?
I thought you were taking me out for coffee.
That was a euphemism. "Take out for coffee" = "have a meeting."
What a rip-off.
We need to discuss our strategy for revolution.
Oh, that's okay then. For our next target, we should—
Wait. That's not exactly—
Let's review our work so far.
It's going great! We blew up a construction site to prevent a nuke plant, plus a power substation.
It was fun!
And heroic!
BOOM!
Ha ha ha ha ha ha!
But now for the bad news.

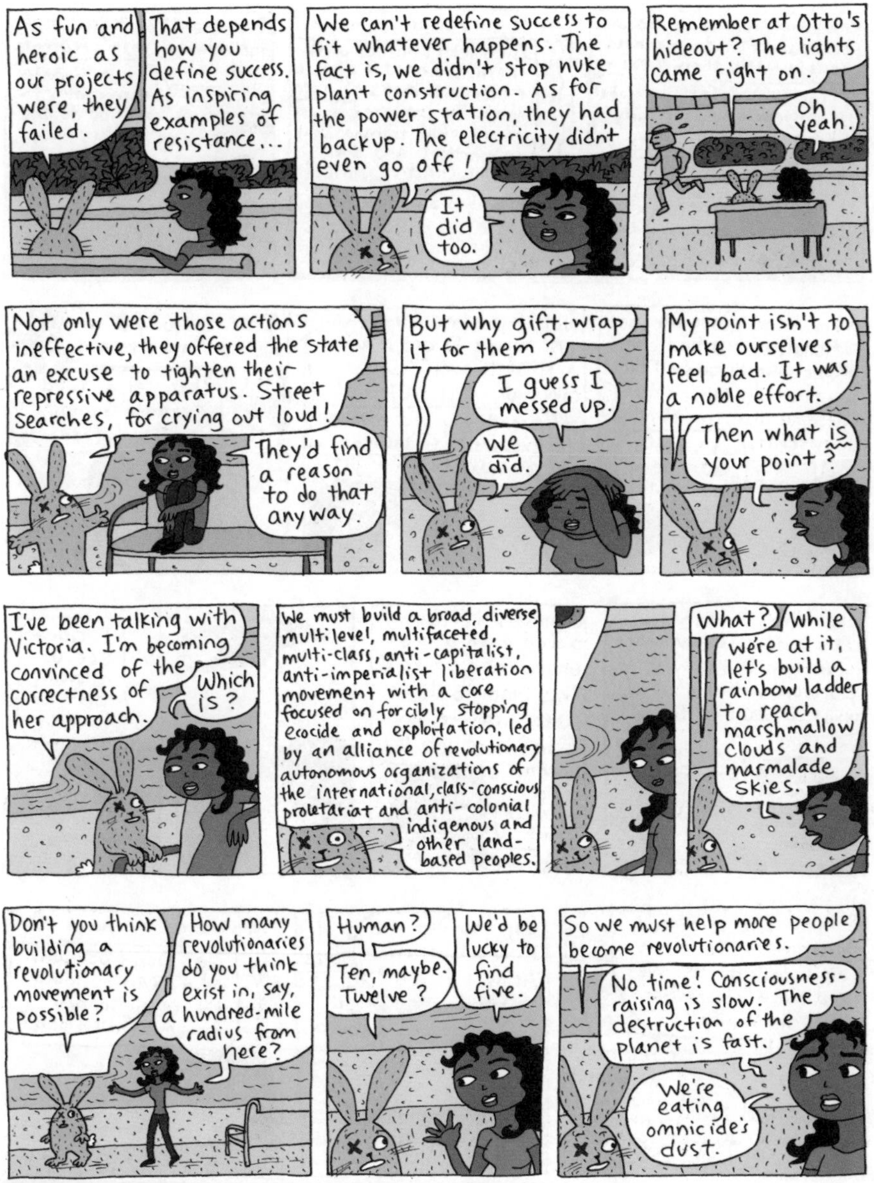

As fun and heroic as our projects were, they failed.
That depends how you define success. As inspiring examples of resistance...
We can't redefine success to fit whatever happens. The fact is, we didn't stop nuke plant construction. As for the power station, they had backup. The electricity didn't even go off!
It did too.
Remember at Otto's hideout? The lights came right on.
Oh yeah.
Not only were those actions ineffective, they offered the state an excuse to tighten their repressive apparatus. Street searches, for crying out loud!
They'd find a reason to do that anyway.
But why gift-wrap it for them?
I guess I messed up.
We did.
My point isn't to make ourselves feel bad. It was a noble effort.
Then what is your point?
I've been talking with Victoria. I'm becoming convinced of the correctness of her approach.
Which is?
We must build a broad, diverse, multilevel, multifaceted, multi-class, anti-capitalist, anti-imperialist liberation movement with a core focused on forcibly stopping ecocide and exploitation, led by an alliance of revolutionary autonomous organizations of the international, class-conscious proletariat and anti-colonial indigenous and other land-based peoples.
What?
While we're at it, let's build a rainbow ladder to reach marshmallow clouds and marmalade skies.
Don't you think building a revolutionary movement is possible?
How many revolutionaries do you think exist in, say, a hundred-mile radius from here?
Human?
Ten, maybe. Twelve?
We'd be lucky to find five.
So we must help more people become revolutionaries.
No time! Consciousness-raising is slow. The destruction of the planet is fast.
We're eating omnicide's dust.

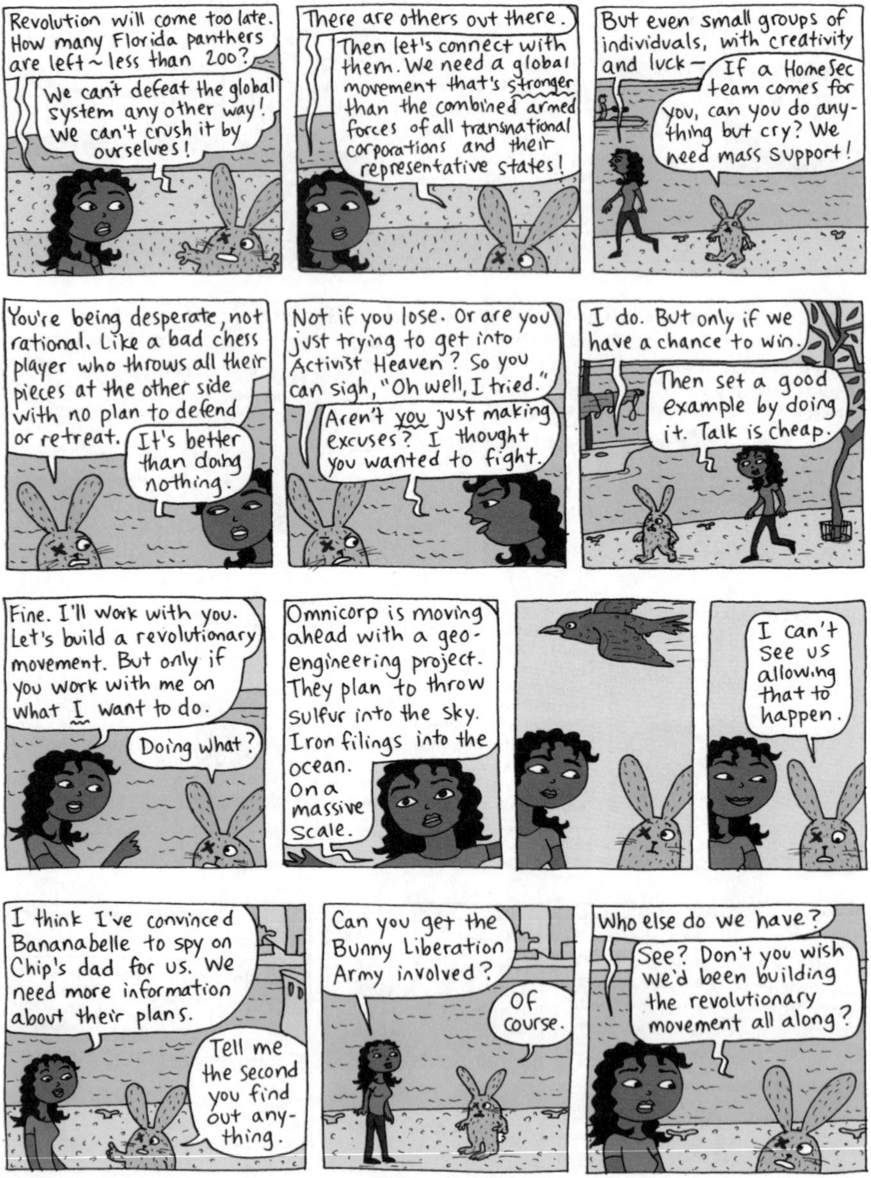
Revolution will come too late. How many Florida panthers are left ~ less than 200?
We can't defeat the global system any other way! We can't crush it by ourselves!
There are others out there.
Then let's connect with them. We need a global movement that's stronger than the combined armed forces of all transnational corporations and their representative states!
But even small groups of individuals, with creativity and luck —
If a HomeSec team comes for you, can you do anything but cry? We need mass support!
You're being desperate, not rational. Like a bad chess player who throws all their pieces at the other side with no plan to defend or retreat.
It's better than doing nothing.
Not if you lose. Or are you just trying to get into Activist Heaven? So you can sigh, "Oh well, I tried."
Aren't you just making excuses? I thought you wanted to fight.
I do. But only if we have a chance to win.
Then set a good example by doing it. Talk is cheap.
Fine. I'll work with you. Let's build a revolutionary movement. But only if you work with me on what I want to do.
Doing what?
Omnicorp is moving ahead with a geo-engineering project. They plan to throw sulfur into the sky. Iron filings into the ocean. On a massive scale.
I can't see us allowing that to happen.
I think I've convinced Bananabelle to spy on Chip's dad for us. We need more information about their plans.
Tell me the second you find out anything.
Can you get the Bunny Liberation Army involved?
Of course.
Who else do we have?
See? Don't you wish we'd been building the revolutionary movement all along?

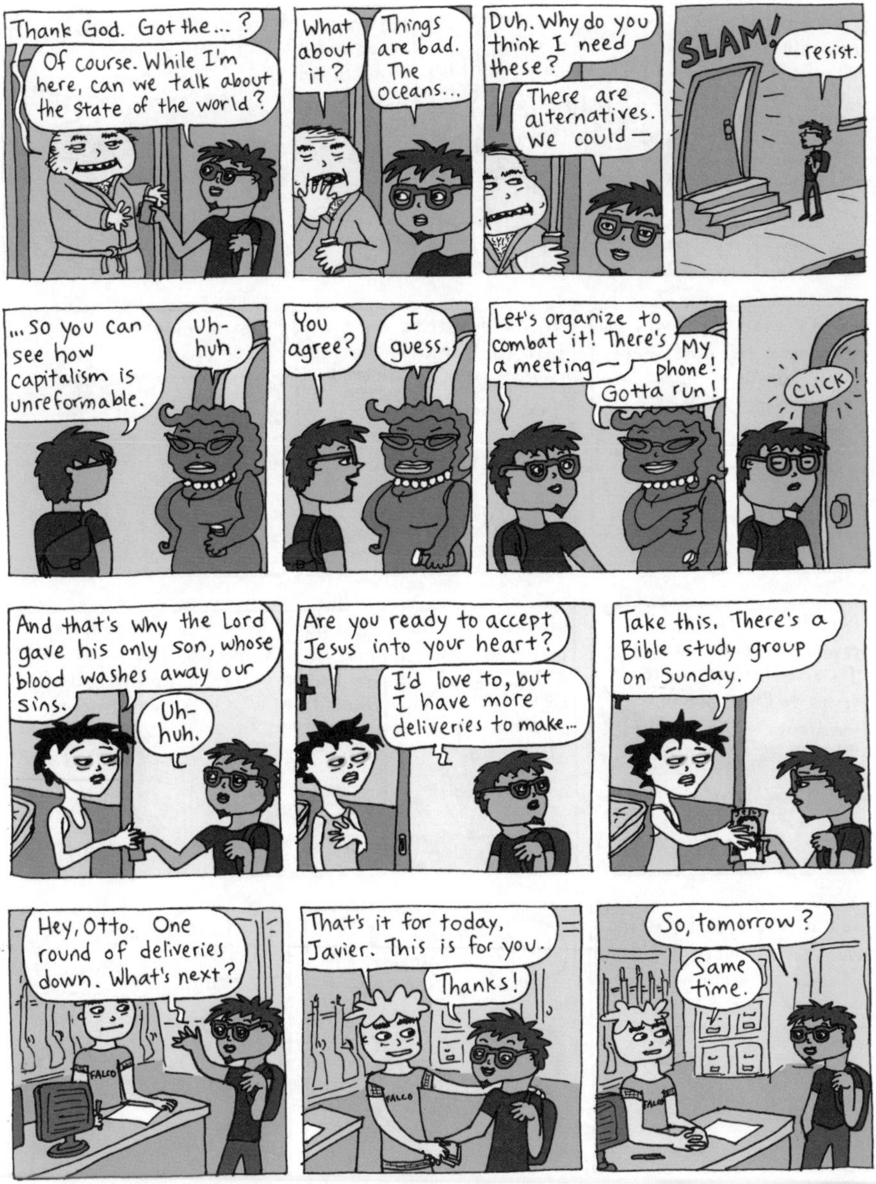
Thank God. Got the...?
Of course. While I'm here, can we talk about the state of the world?
What about it?
Things are bad. The oceans...
Duh. Why do you think I need these?
There are alternatives. We could—
SLAM!
—resist.
...so you can see how capitalism is unreformable.
Uh-huh.
You agree?
I guess.
Let's organize to combat it! There's a meeting—
My phone! Gotta run!
CLICK!
And that's why the Lord gave his only son, whose blood washes away our sins.
Uh-huh.
Are you ready to accept Jesus into your heart?
I'd love to, but I have more deliveries to make...
Take this. There's a Bible study group on Sunday.
Hey, Otto. One round of deliveries down. What's next?
FALCO
That's it for today, Javier. This is for you.
Thanks!
FALCO
So, tomorrow?
Same time.
FALCO

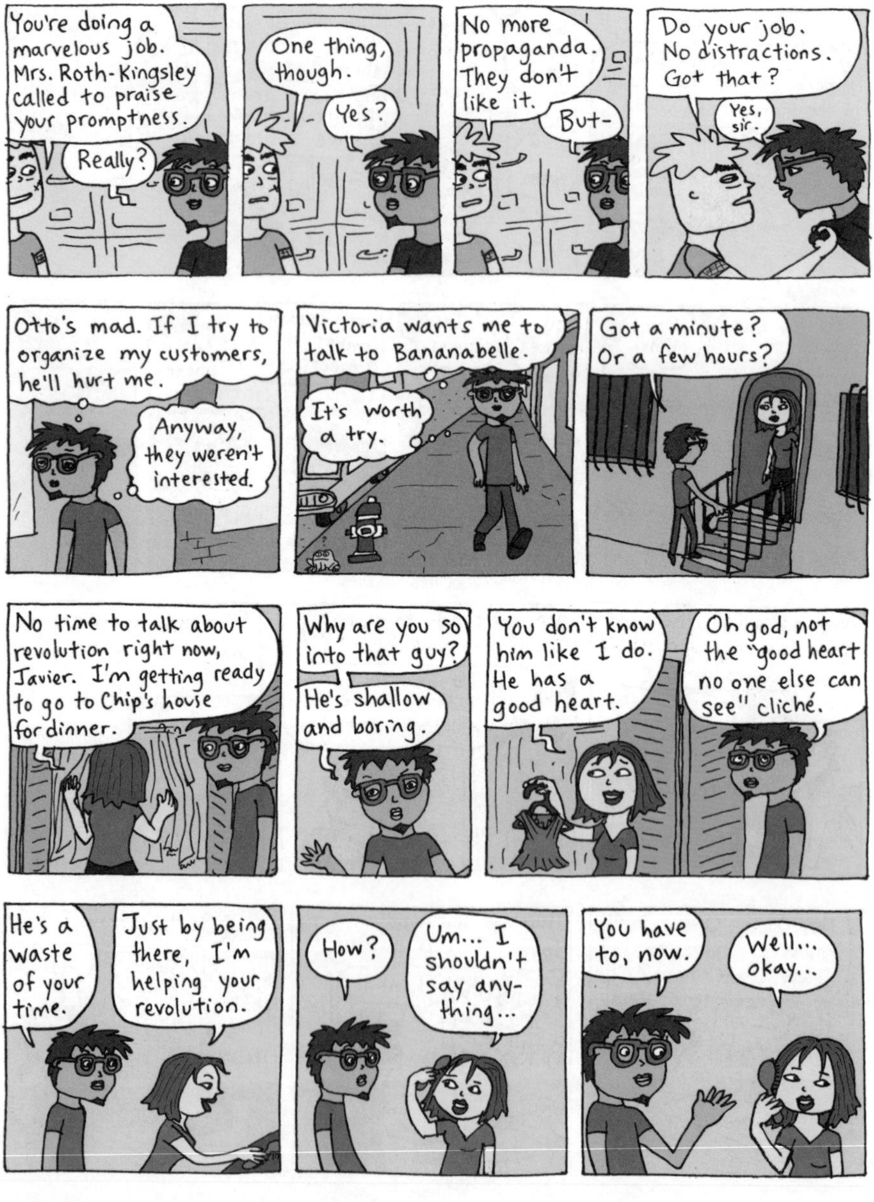
You're doing a marvelous job. Mrs. Roth-Kingsley called to praise your promptness.
Really?
One thing, though.
Yes?
No more propaganda. They don't like it.
But-
Do your job. No distractions. Got that?
Yes, sir.
Otto's mad. If I try to organize my customers, he'll hurt me.
Anyway, they weren't interested.
Victoria wants me to talk to Bananabelle.
It's worth a try.
Got a minute? Or a few hours?
No time to talk about revolution right now, Javier. I'm getting ready to go to Chip's house for dinner.
Why are you so into that guy?
He's shallow and boring.
You don't know him like I do. He has a good heart.
Oh god, not the "good heart no one else can see" cliché.
He's a waste of your time.
Just by being there, I'm helping your revolution.
How?
Um... I shouldn't say anything...
You have to, now.
Well... okay...

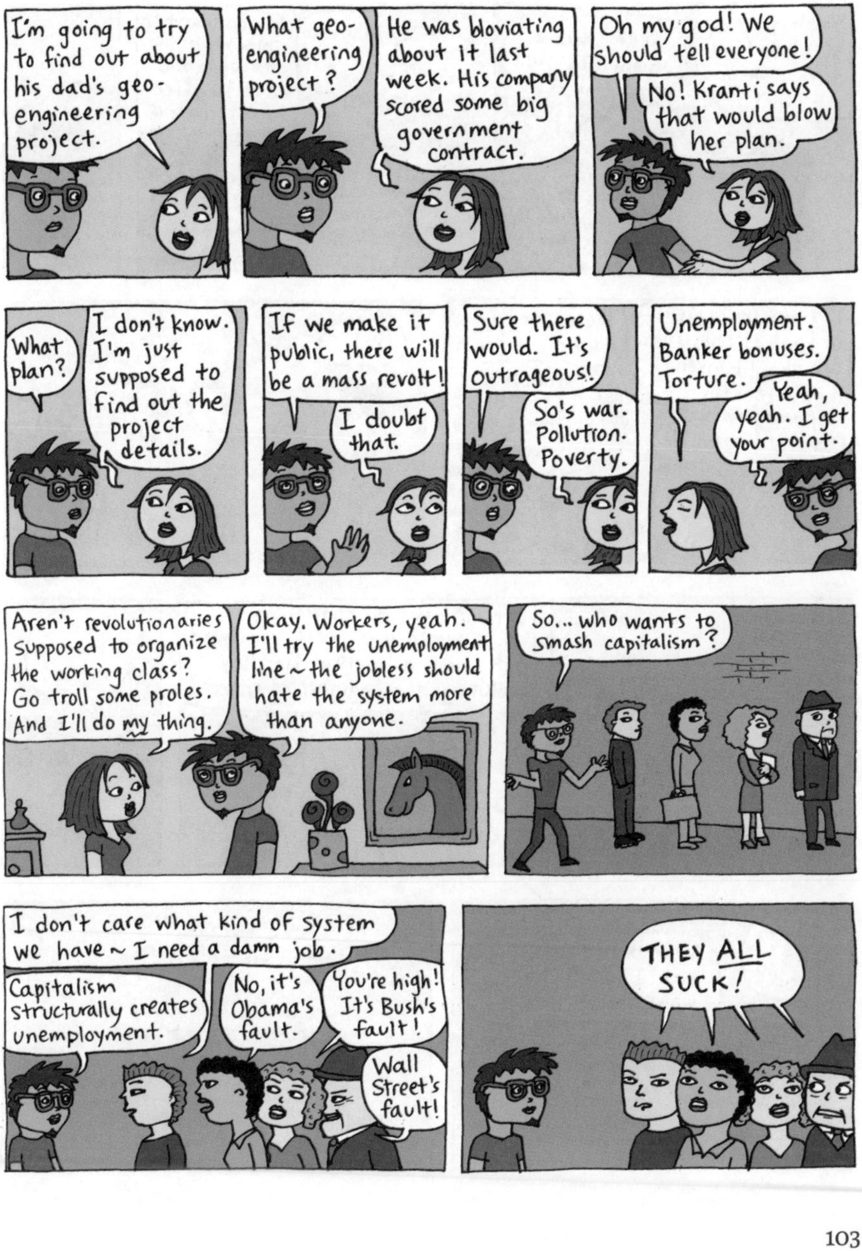
I'm going to try to find out about his dad's geo-engineering project.
What geo-engineering project?
He was bloviating about it last week. His company scored some big government contract.
Oh my god! We should tell everyone!
No! Kranti says that would blow her plan.
What plan?
I don't know. I'm just supposed to find out the project details.
If we make it public, there will be a mass revolt!
I doubt that.
Sure there would. It's outrageous!
So's war. Pollution. Poverty.
Unemployment. Banker bonuses. Torture.
Yeah, yeah. I get your point.
Aren't revolutionaries supposed to organize the working class? Go troll some proles. And I'll do my thing.
Okay. Workers, yeah. I'll try the unemployment line ~ the jobless should hate the system more than anyone.
So... who wants to smash capitalism?
I don't care what kind of system we have ~ I need a damn job.
Capitalism structurally creates unemployment.
No, it's Obama's fault.
You're high! It's Bush's fault!
Wall Street's fault!
THEY ALL SUCK!

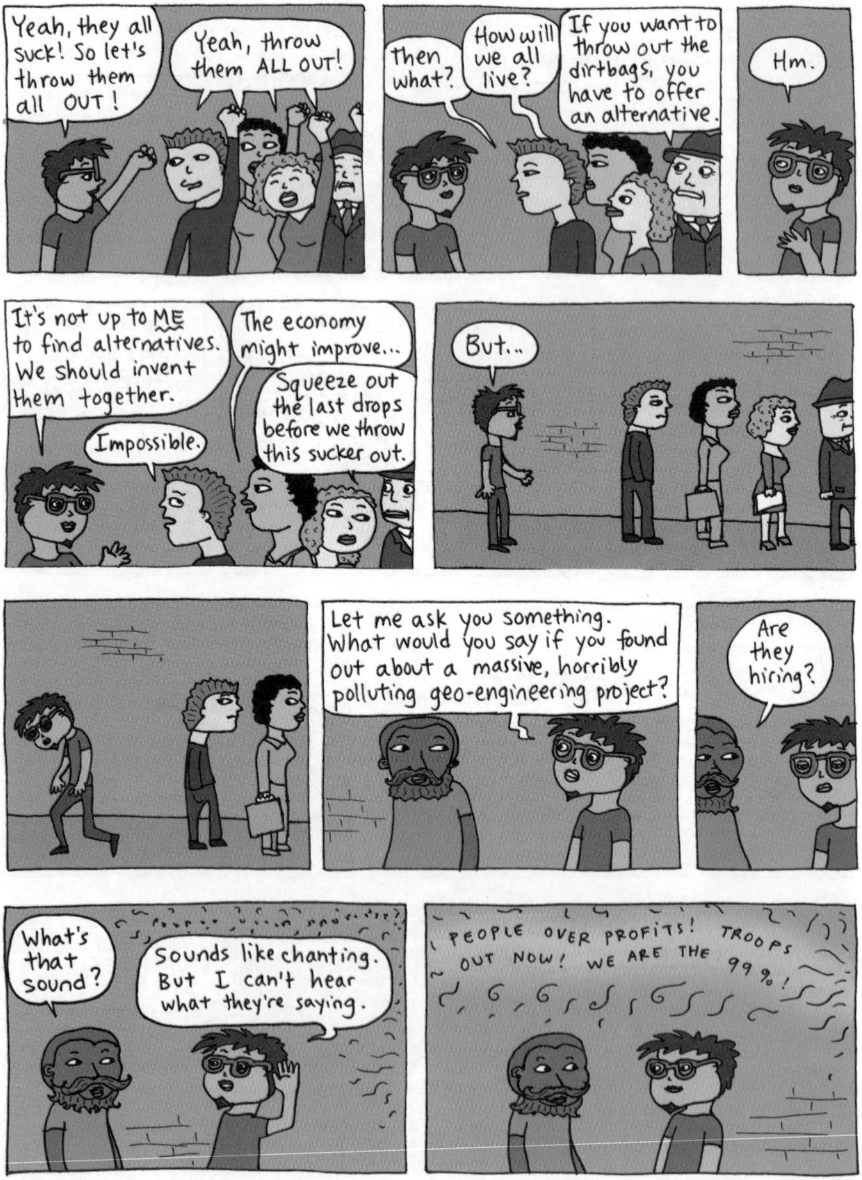

Yeah, they all suck! So let's throw them all OUT!
Yeah, throw them ALL OUT!
Then what?
How will we all live?
If you want to throw out the dirtbags, you have to offer an alternative.
Hm.
It's not up to ME to find alternatives. We should invent them together.
The economy might improve...
Squeeze out the last drops before we throw this sucker out.
Impossible.
But...
Let me ask you something. What would you say if you found out about a massive, horribly polluting geo-engineering project?
Are they hiring?
What's that sound?
Sounds like chanting. But I can't hear what they're saying.
PEOPLE OVER PROFITS! TROOPS OUT NOW! WE ARE THE 99%!

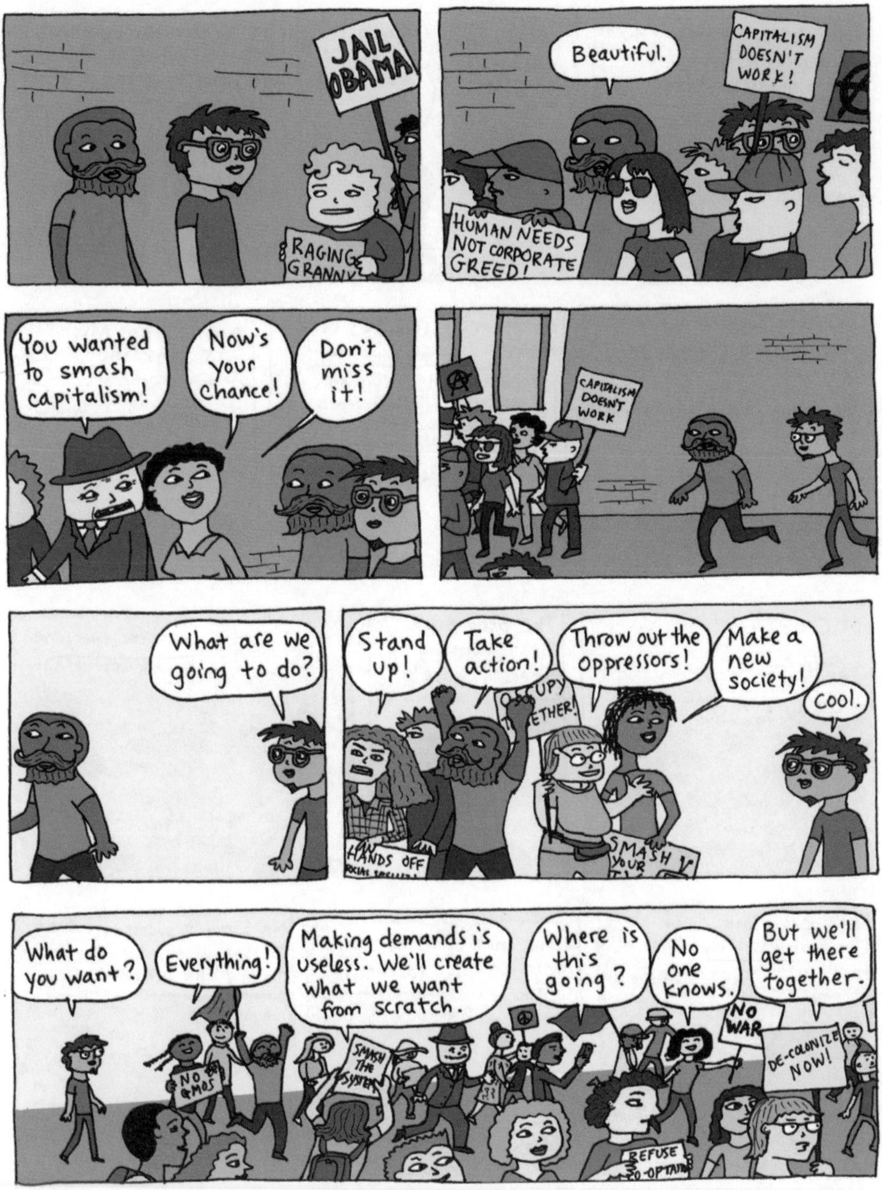
JAIL OBAMA
RAGING GRANNY
Beautiful.
CAPITALISM DOESN'T WORK!
HUMAN NEEDS NOT CORPORATE GREED!
You wanted to smash capitalism!
Now's your chance!
Don't miss it!
CAPITALISM DOESN'T WORK
What are we going to do?
Stand up!
Take action!
Throw out the oppressors!
Make a new society!
Cool.
HANDS OFF
SMASH YOUR
What do you want?
Everything!
Making demands is useless. We'll create what we want from scratch.
Where is this going?
No one knows.
But we'll get there together.
NO GMOS
SMASH THE SYSTEM
NO WAR
DE-COLONIZE NOW!
REFUSE

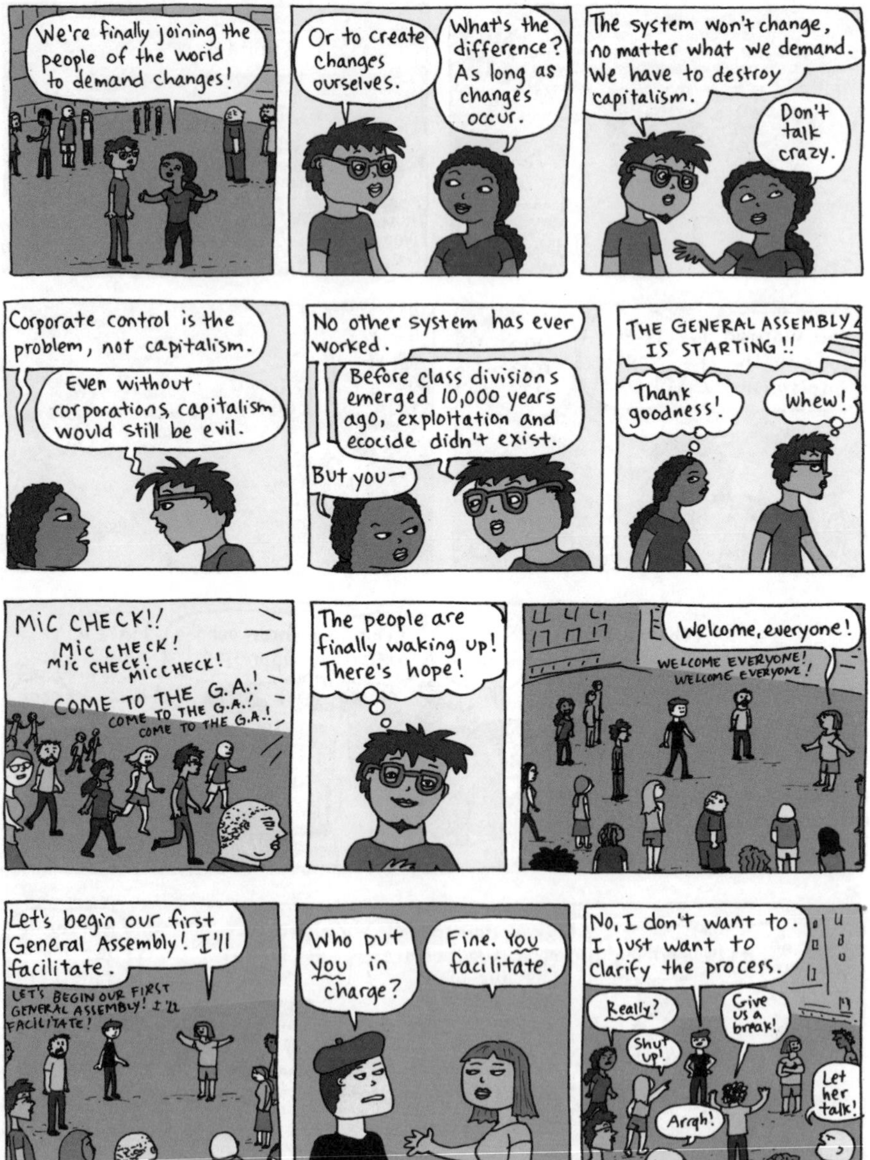

We're finally joining the people of the world to demand changes!
Or to create changes ourselves.
What's the difference? As long as changes occur.
The system won't change, no matter what we demand. We have to destroy capitalism.
Don't talk crazy.
Corporate control is the problem, not capitalism.
Even without corporations, capitalism would still be evil.
No other system has ever worked.
Before class divisions emerged 10,000 years ago, exploitation and ecocide didn't exist.
But you—
THE GENERAL ASSEMBLY IS STARTING!!
Thank goodness!
Whew!
MIC CHECK!!
MIC CHECK!
MIC CHECK!
MIC CHECK!
COME TO THE G.A.!
COME TO THE G.A.!
COME TO THE G.A.!
The people are finally waking up! There's hope!
Welcome, everyone!
WELCOME EVERYONE!
WELCOME EVERYONE!
Let's begin our first General Assembly! I'll facilitate.
LET'S BEGIN OUR FIRST GENERAL ASSEMBLY! I'LL FACILITATE!
Who put you in charge?
Fine. You facilitate.
No, I don't want to. I just want to clarify the process.
Really?
Shut up!
Give us a break!
Arrgh!
Let her talk!

Does anyone else want to facilitate?

May I begin?

Stay cool, girl! Can't let them know I'm a resistance mole.

Mustn't blow everything!

Um, hi. I'm Bananabelle? I'm expected for dinner.

Good evening, dear.

Hi. Care for a drink?

Uh, do you have juice?

See, son? It's not necessary to get blotto for every social occasion.

Unless the occasion involves Dear Old Dad.

I brought you fruit from our community garden.

What are those?

Carambola.... Star fruit. You've never had one? Try it! They're good!

Maybe later.

You're very thoughtful, my dear.

Take these to the kitchen, Griselda.

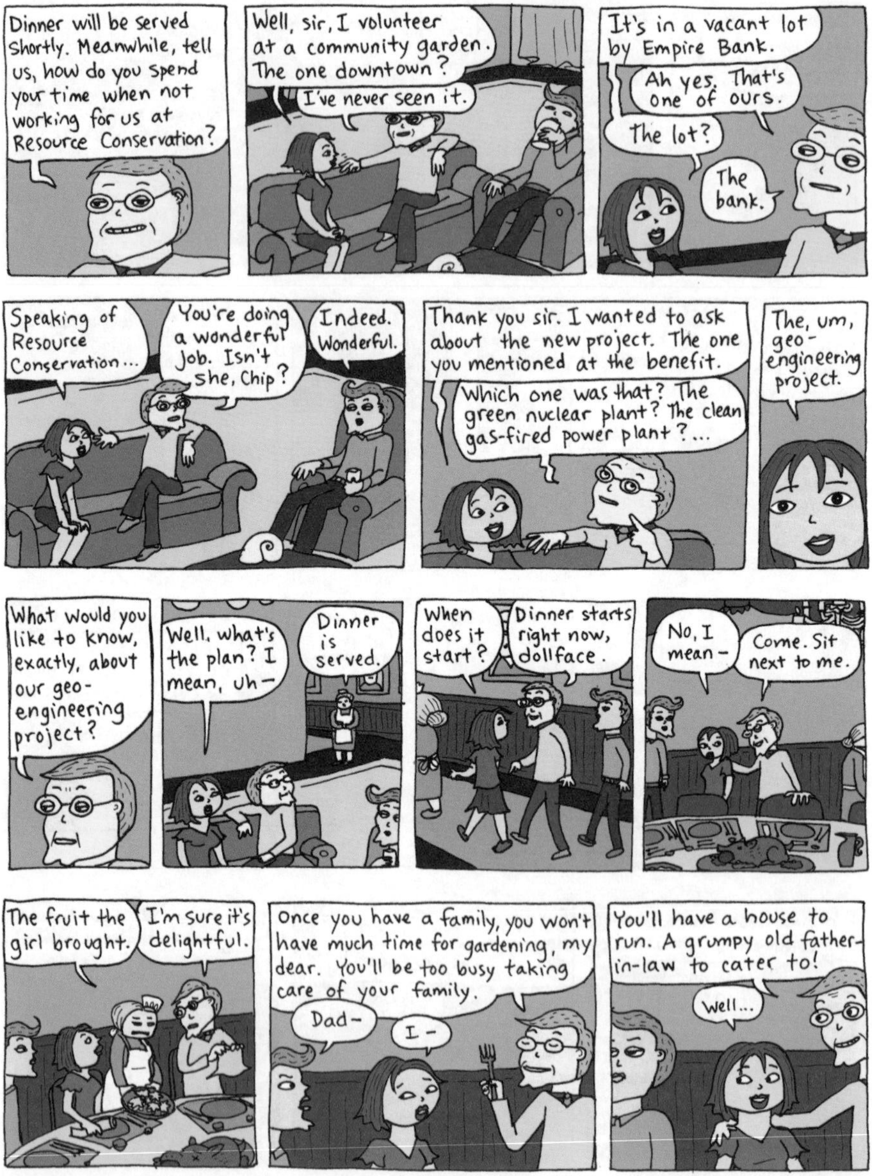
Dinner will be served shortly. Meanwhile, tell us, how do you spend your time when not working for us at Resource Conservation?
Well, sir, I volunteer at a community garden. The one downtown?
I've never seen it.
It's in a vacant lot by Empire Bank.
Ah yes. That's one of ours.
The lot?
The bank.
Speaking of Resource Conservation...
You're doing a wonderful job. Isn't she, Chip?
Indeed. Wonderful.
Thank you sir. I wanted to ask about the new project. The one you mentioned at the benefit.
Which one was that? The green nuclear plant? The clean gas-fired power plant?...
The, um, geo-engineering project.
What would you like to know, exactly, about our geo-engineering project?
Well, what's the plan? I mean, uh—
Dinner is served.
When does it start?
Dinner starts right now, dollface.
No, I mean—
Come. Sit next to me.
The fruit the girl brought.
I'm sure it's delightful.
Once you have a family, you won't have much time for gardening, my dear. You'll be too busy taking care of your family.
Dad—
I—
You'll have a house to run. A grumpy old father-in-law to cater to!
Well...

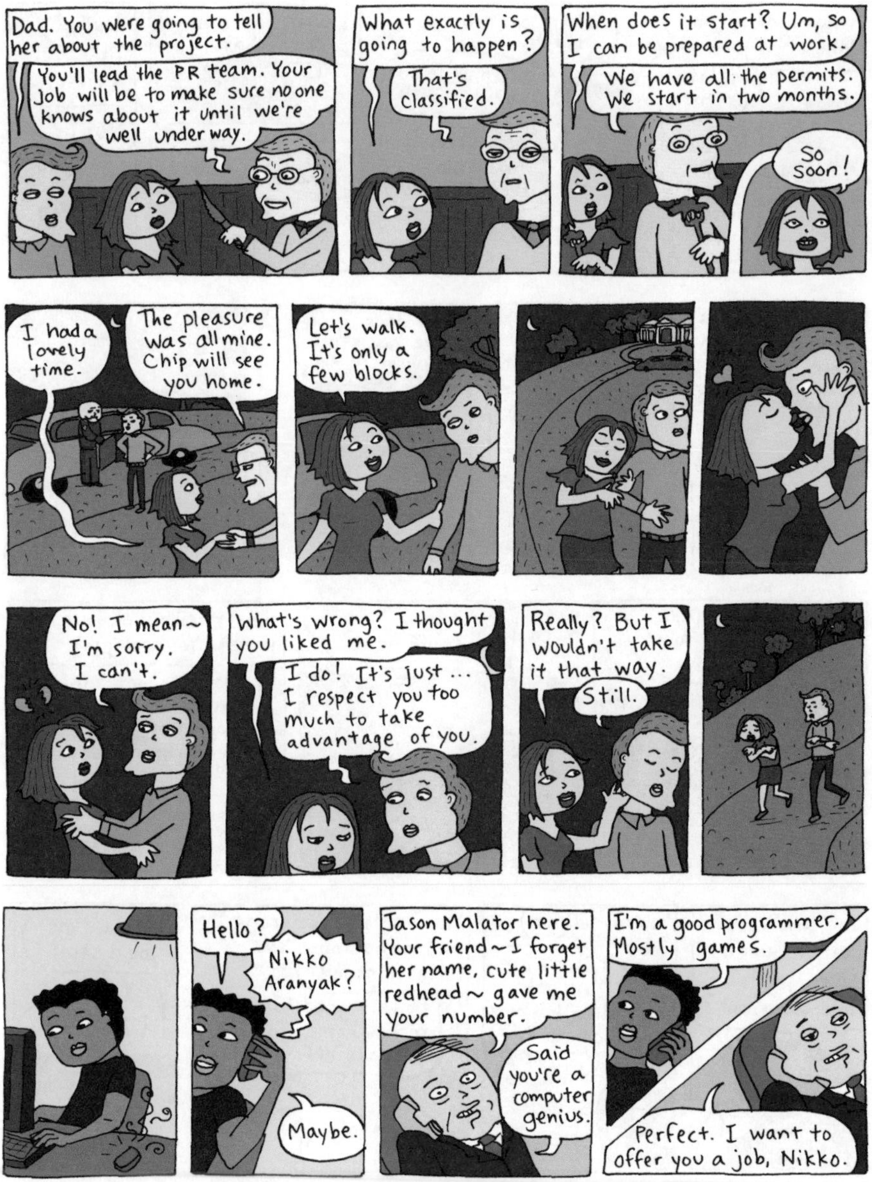
Dad. You were going to tell her about the project.
You'll lead the PR team. Your Job will be to make sure no one knows about it until we're well under way.
What exactly is going to happen?
That's classified.
When does it start? Um, so I can be prepared at work.
We have all the permits. We start in two months.
So soon!
I had a lovely time.
The pleasure was all mine. Chip will see you home.
Let's walk. It's only a few blocks.
No! I mean~ I'm sorry. I can't.
What's wrong? I thought you liked me.
I do! It's just ... I respect you too much to take advantage of you.
Really? But I wouldn't take it that way.
Still.
Hello?
Nikko Aranyak?
Maybe.
Jason Malator here. Your friend~I forget her name, cute little redhead~gave me your number.
Said you're a computer genius.
I'm a good programmer. Mostly games.
Perfect. I want to offer you a job, Nikko.

What kind of job? Where?

Malator Defense. We supply the world's major security forces. Including the U.S. of A.

You're an arms dealer.

We provide our clients with every means necessary to maintain their security.

I won't have any part of that.

Even for $500 grand a year?

To start.

Really?

Gosh...

No!

No.

I can't believe I just turned down $500 grand.

But I can't work for an evil company like that.

Why does Javier leave his stuff everywhere?

CLUNK!

Hi Nikko. Want some tea?

We need to talk.

You're going through my stuff now?

No! It fell out of your jacket. You're a junkie?

No! I'm not taking these. Well, only sometimes.

When I really need one.

You know that "office supply sales job" I told you about?

You're selling them?

There are no jobs. I didn't know what to do.

You can't. It's wrong, and dangerous. You have to stop!

It felt good to bring money home. To take pressure off you.

Promise me you'll stop.

Okay. I promise.

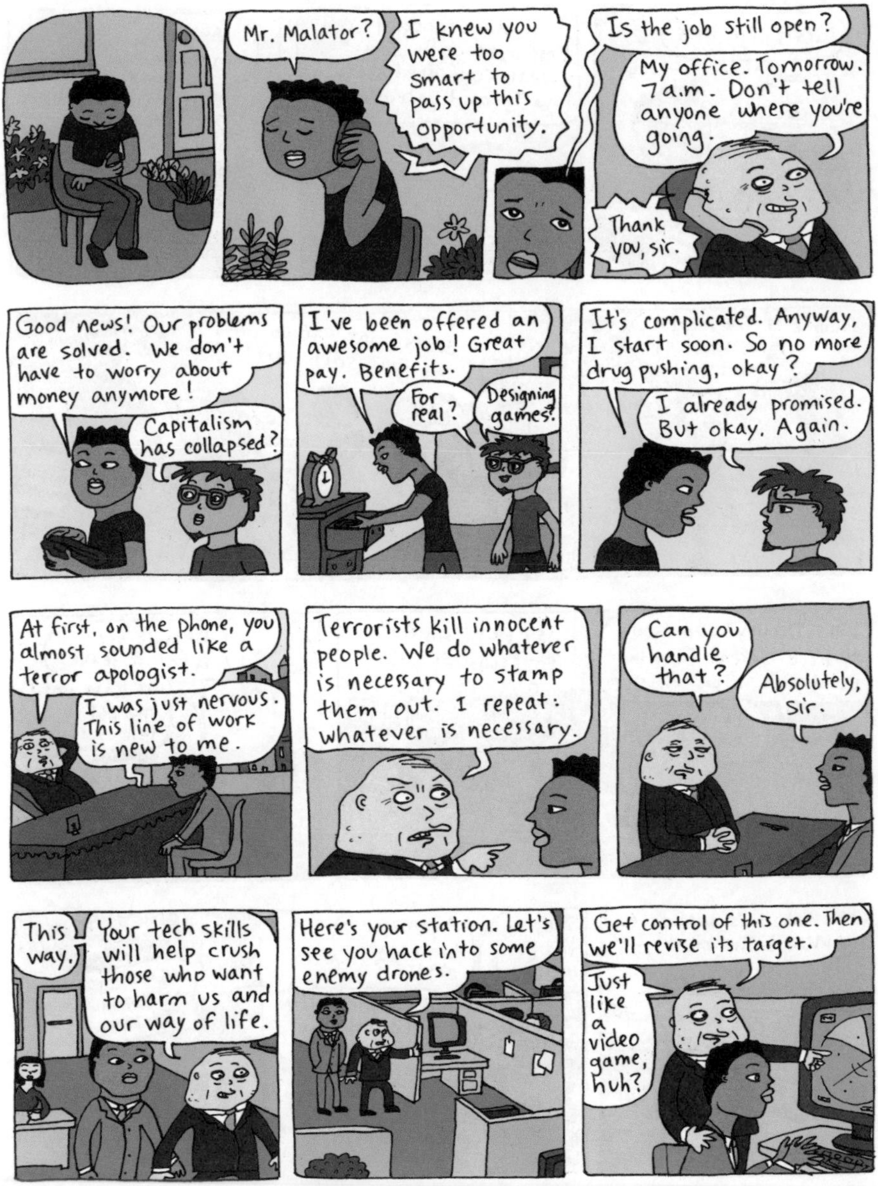

Mr. Malator?
I knew you were too smart to pass up this opportunity.
Is the job still open?
My office. Tomorrow. 7 a.m. Don't tell anyone where you're going.
Thank you, sir.
Good news! Our problems are solved. We don't have to worry about money anymore!
Capitalism has collapsed?
I've been offered an awesome job! Great pay. Benefits.
For real?
Designing games?
It's complicated. Anyway, I start soon. So no more drug pushing, okay?
I already promised. But okay. Again.
At first, on the phone, you almost sounded like a terror apologist.
I was just nervous. This line of work is new to me.
Terrorists kill innocent people. We do whatever is necessary to stamp them out. I repeat: whatever is necessary.
Can you handle that?
Absolutely, Sir.
This way.
Your tech skills will help crush those who want to harm us and our way of life.
Here's your station. Let's see you hack into some enemy drones.
Get control of this one. Then we'll revise its target.
Just like a video game, huh?

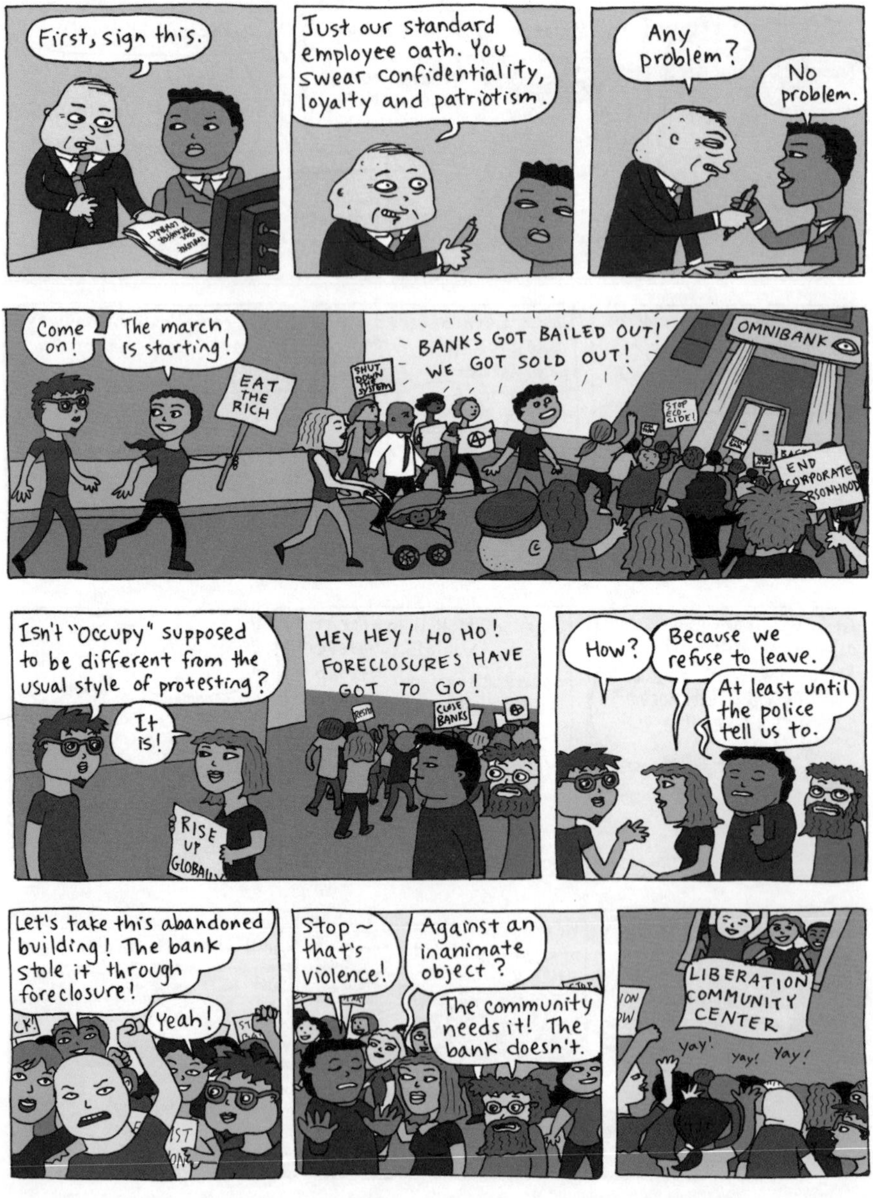

First, sign this.
Just our standard employee oath. You swear confidentiality, loyalty and patriotism.
Any problem?
No problem.
Come on!
The march is starting!
EAT THE RICH
SHUT DOWN THE SYSTEM
BANKS GOT BAILED OUT! WE GOT SOLD OUT!
OMNIBANK
STOP ECO-CIDE!
END CORPORATE PERSONHOOD
Isn't "Occupy" supposed to be different from the usual style of protesting?
It is!
RISE UP GLOBALLY
HEY HEY! HO HO! FORECLOSURES HAVE GOT TO GO!
CLOSE BANKS
How?
Because we refuse to leave.
At least until the police tell us to.
Let's take this abandoned building! The bank stole it through foreclosure!
Yeah!
Stop ~ that's violence!
Against an inanimate object?
The community needs it! The bank doesn't.
LIBERATION COMMUNITY CENTER
yay! yay! Yay!

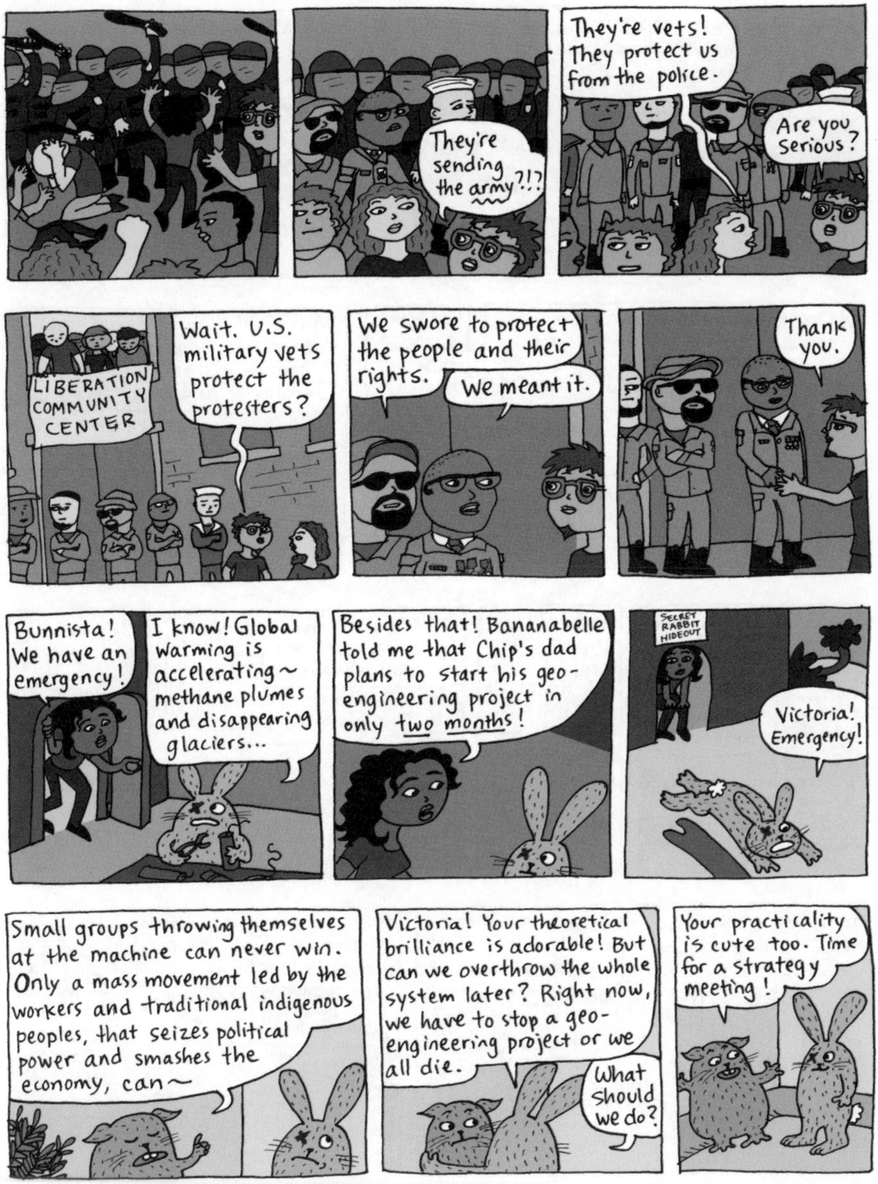
They're sending the army?!?
They're vets! They protect us from the police.
Are you serious?
LIBERATION COMMUNITY CENTER
Wait. U.S. military vets protect the protesters?
We swore to protect the people and their rights.
We meant it.
Thank you.
Bunnista! We have an emergency!
I know! Global warming is accelerating~ methane plumes and disappearing glaciers...
Besides that! Bananabelle told me that Chip's dad plans to start his geo-engineering project in only two months!
SECRET RABBIT HIDEOUT
Victoria! Emergency!
Small groups throwing themselves at the machine can never win. Only a mass movement led by the workers and traditional indigenous peoples, that seizes political power and smashes the economy, can~
Victoria! Your theoretical brilliance is adorable! But can we overthrow the whole system later? Right now, we have to stop a geo-engineering project or we all die.
What should we do?
Your practicality is cute too. Time for a strategy meeting!

Javier, have you organized the Occupy protesters into a powerful fighting force for revolution yet?

Um, not exactly.

Why not?

It's not that simple! Ideologically, they're all over the place.

They use consensus. Their process is slow...

We don't have time for slow.

We must organize a massive People's Army!

What if we can't convince enough people in time? What if they insist on campaigning and writing petitions? Then Omnicorp will know we're onto them. They'll harden their targets.

We have to do this ourselves!

That's not relying properly on the masses, who are the true makers of history. It's adventurist and voluntarist...

We don't have time to be politically correct!

We could get Otto to help us.

I knew that loose end would loop back into the plot somehow!

He has organization, weapons, and safe houses. He can't snitch. We saw him kill a cop, remember?

I hate Otto. Bunnista, why can't you just steal weapons like you always do?

Surveillance is pervasive. This would be easier.

He's a bad guy.

We don't have time to be pure.

Your work obviously requires a disciplined organization.

I haff excellent people. I haff built a powerful machine.

But our work isn't drugs~ it's revolution. Still, we need a disciplined organization too.

May we borrow yours?

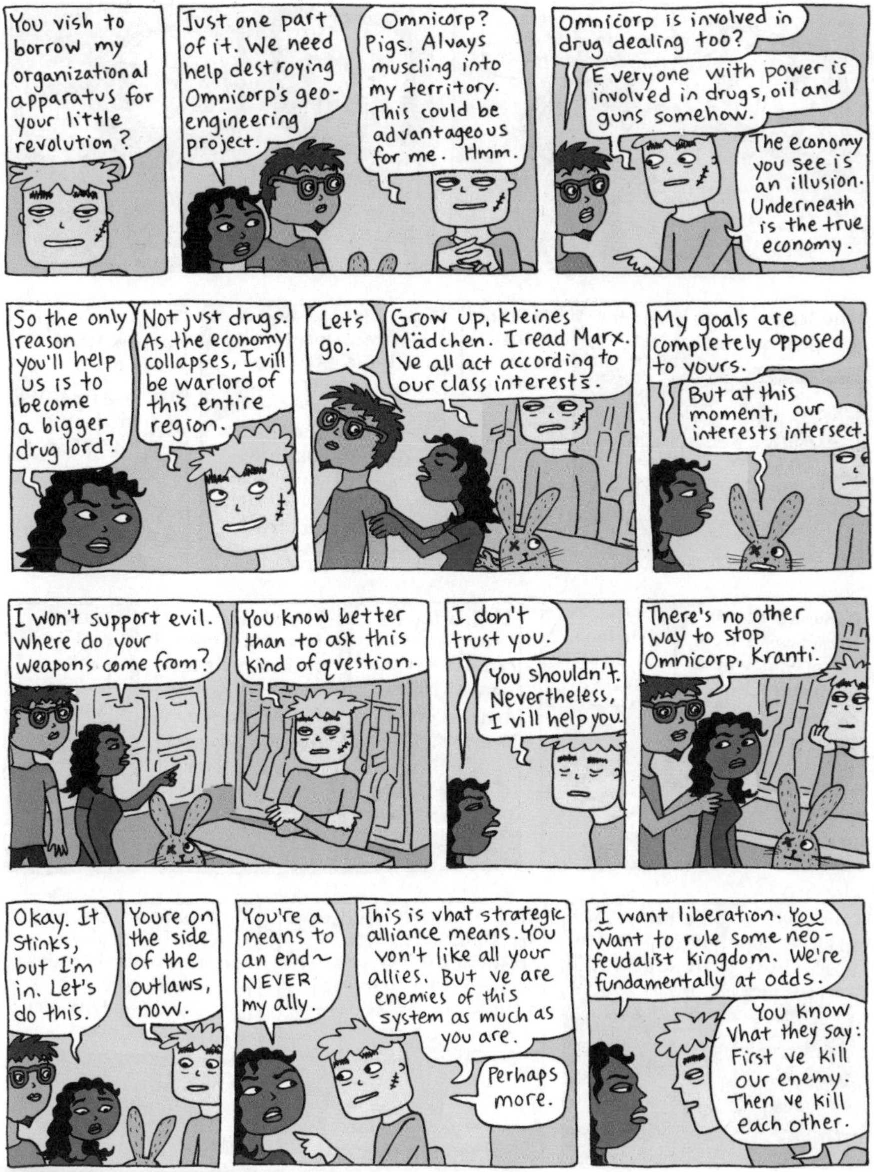
You vish to borrow my organizational apparatus for your little revolution?
Just one part of it. We need help destroying Omnicorp's geo-engineering project.
Omnicorp? Pigs. Alvays muscling into my territory. This could be advantageous for me. Hmm.
Omnicorp is involved in drug dealing too?
Everyone with power is involved in drugs, oil and guns somehow.
The economy you see is an illusion. Underneath is the true economy.
So the only reason you'll help us is to become a bigger drug lord?
Not just drugs. As the economy collapses, I vill be warlord of this entire region.
Let's go.
Grow up, kleines Mädchen. I read Marx. Ve all act according to our class interests.
My goals are completely opposed to yours.
But at this moment, our interests intersect.
I won't support evil. Where do your weapons come from?
You know better than to ask this kind of qvestion.
I don't trust you.
You shouldn't. Nevertheless, I vill help you.
There's no other way to stop Omnicorp, Kranti.
Okay. It stinks, but I'm in. Let's do this.
Youre on the side of the outlaws, now.
You're a means to an end~ NEVER my ally.
This is vhat strategic alliance means. You von't like all your allies. But ve are enemies of this system as much as you are.
Perhaps more.
I want liberation. You want to rule some neo-feudalist kingdom. We're fundamentally at odds.
You know vhat they say: First ve kill our enemy. Then ve kill each other.

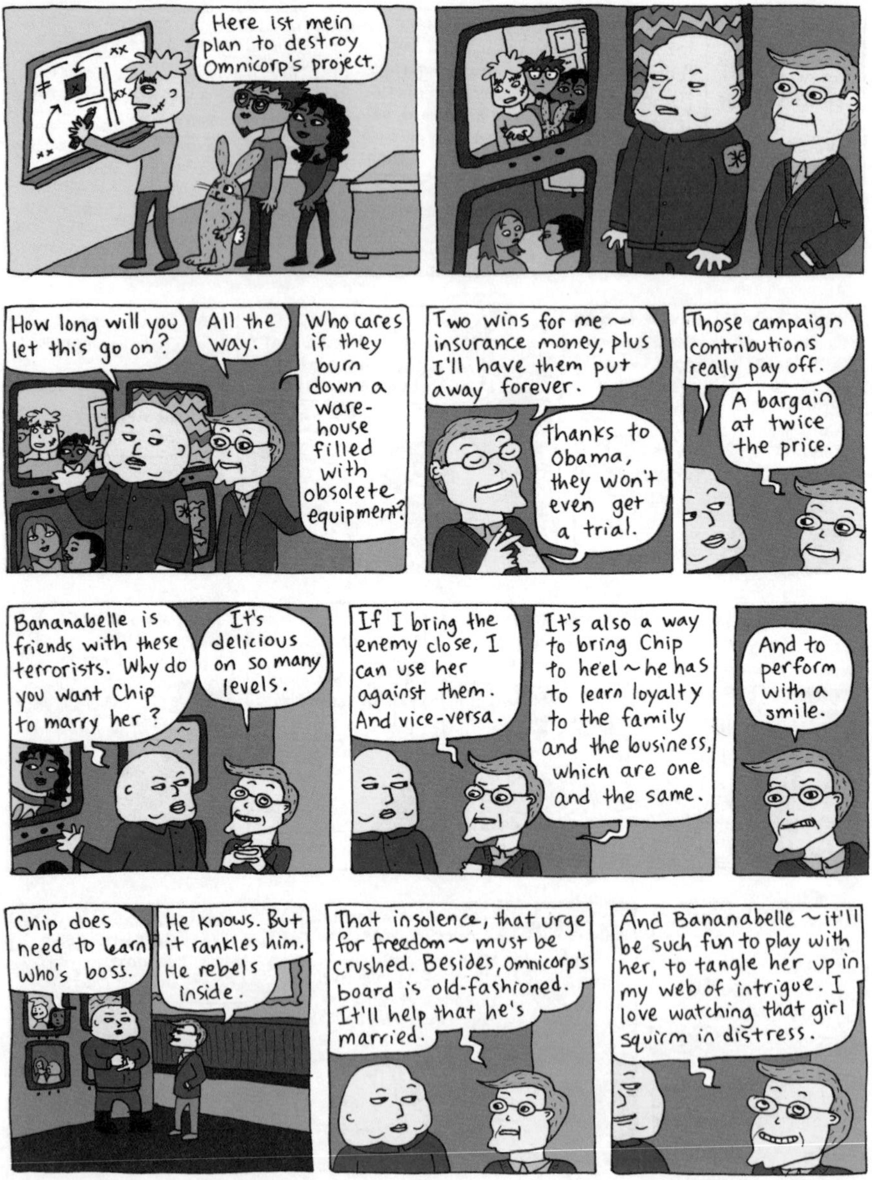

Here ist mein plan to destroy Omnicorp's project.
How long will you let this go on?
All the way.
Who cares if they burn down a ware-house filled with obsolete equipment?
Two wins for me ~ insurance money, plus I'll have them put away forever.
thanks to Obama, they won't even get a trial.
Those campaign contributions really pay off.
A bargain at twice the price.
Bananabelle is friends with these terrorists. Why do you want Chip to marry her?
It's delicious on so many levels.
If I bring the enemy close, I can use her against them. And vice-versa.
It's also a way to bring Chip to heel ~ he has to learn loyalty to the family and the business, which are one and the same.
And to perform with a smile.
Chip does need to learn who's boss.
He knows. But it rankles him. He rebels inside.
That insolence, that urge for freedom ~ must be crushed. Besides, Omnicorp's board is old-fashioned. It'll help that he's married.
And Bananabelle ~ it'll be such fun to play with her, to tangle her up in my web of intrigue. I love watching that girl squirm in distress.

She sure is pretty.

Indeed.

By the way, arrange for Empire Bank to purchase that lot next to our downtown branch.

The one with her community garden on it.

Dad, are you busy? I need some money. It's for—

Chip, I'm glad you stopped by.

Sit.

Twenty thou should do. Until the weekend—

Son, it's been weeks since Bananabelle was here.

So?

I want your engagement finalized. Tonight.

But Dad—

No more dithering.

Don't you see what's going on in the world?

Climate change. Food and energy disruptions. Global political uprisings. Soon we'll have martial law. Labor camps. Civil war. Maybe nuclear.

We must strategically position ourselves if we're going to wind up on top of the wreckage.

Don't be so alarmist.

It'll be uglier than you can imagine. The coming world order is neo-feudalism. It's unstoppable. It'll be Mad Max meets the Wild West.

Omnicorp is our institutional fortress. If you're elected to the board, with my other allies we'll get a majority. Then you and I will seize control.

I've got it all figured out.

I've got secret deals in the works to make Omnicorp the global market leader in information, food, energy, private militaries, and detention services.

We'll dominate it all. You and me, kid. But nothing can be left to chance.

Your hubris is terrifying.

Otherwise we end up with our heads on pikes. You want that?

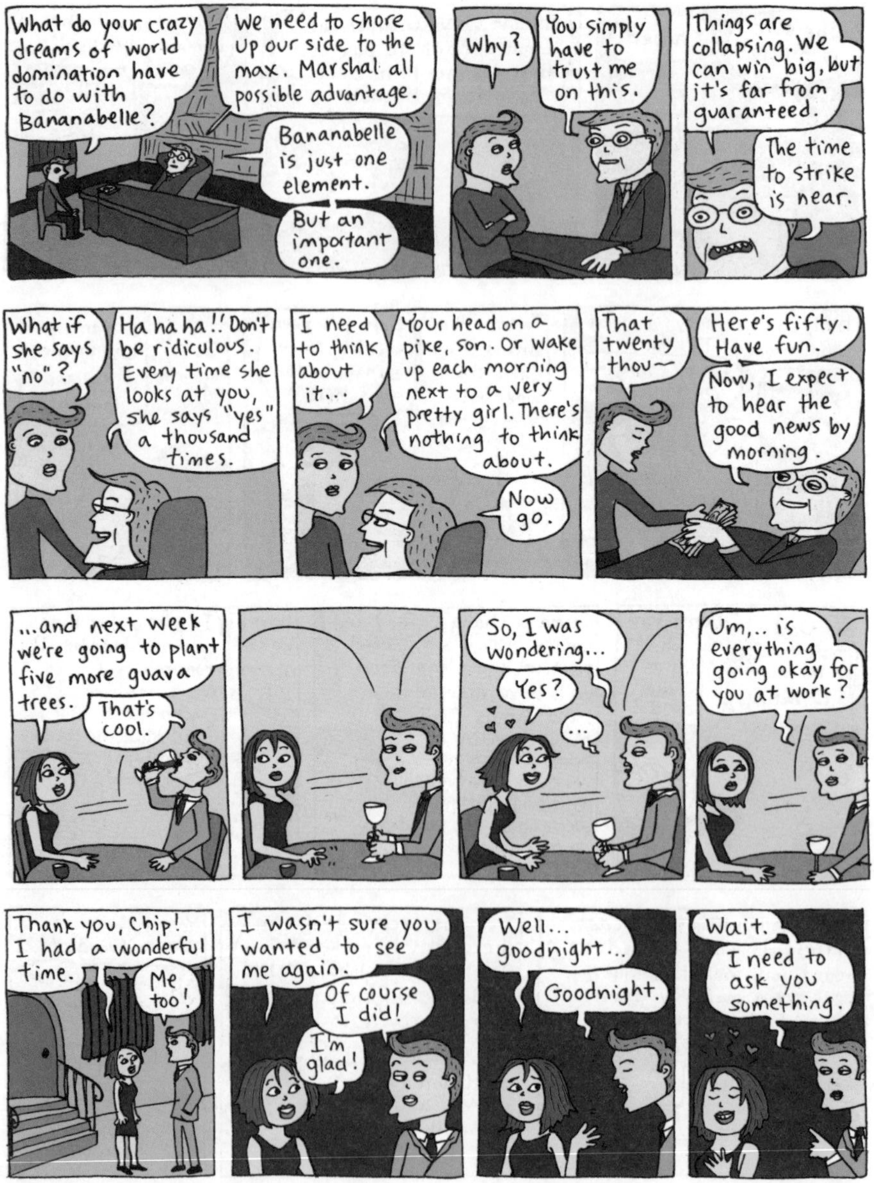
What do your crazy dreams of world domination have to do with Bananabelle?
We need to shore up our side to the max. Marshal all possible advantage.
Bananabelle is just one element.
But an important one.
Why?
You simply have to trust me on this.
Things are collapsing. We can win big, but it's far from guaranteed.
The time to strike is near.
What if she says "no"?
Ha ha ha!! Don't be ridiculous. Every time she looks at you, she says "yes" a thousand times.
I need to think about it...
Your head on a pike, son. Or wake up each morning next to a very pretty girl. There's nothing to think about.
Now go.
That twenty thou~
Here's fifty. Have fun.
Now, I expect to hear the good news by morning.
...and next week we're going to plant five more guava trees.
That's cool.
So, I was wondering...
Yes?
...
Um,... is everything going okay for you at work?
Thank you, Chip! I had a wonderful time.
Me too!
I wasn't sure you wanted to see me again.
Of course I did!
I'm glad!
Well... goodnight...
Goodnight.
Wait.
I need to ask you something.

KRANTI!! KRANTI!!

What's wrong?!

I'm getting MARRIED!?

To whom? And, why?

Chip, of course! It wasn't exactly the proposal I'd dreamed of. But we'll be so happy!!

I appreciate your sacrifice for the cause...

But going this far? Too heroic, maybe?

But I love him!

What about his awful family? Their evil company?

Love has no rules.

And denial has no bounds.

You're really going to marry into that family? They're the enemy!

His father is. But that's not Chip's fault. He's different.

How do you know? Based on what evidence?

I can just tell.

He's not like his father. He has problems, sure ~ but my love will save him. He'll become sweet. And less drunk.

Bill. Junk. Junk. Bill. Bill.

Pay stub?

"Malator Defense Holding Co., Ltd."?

Um, sweetie?

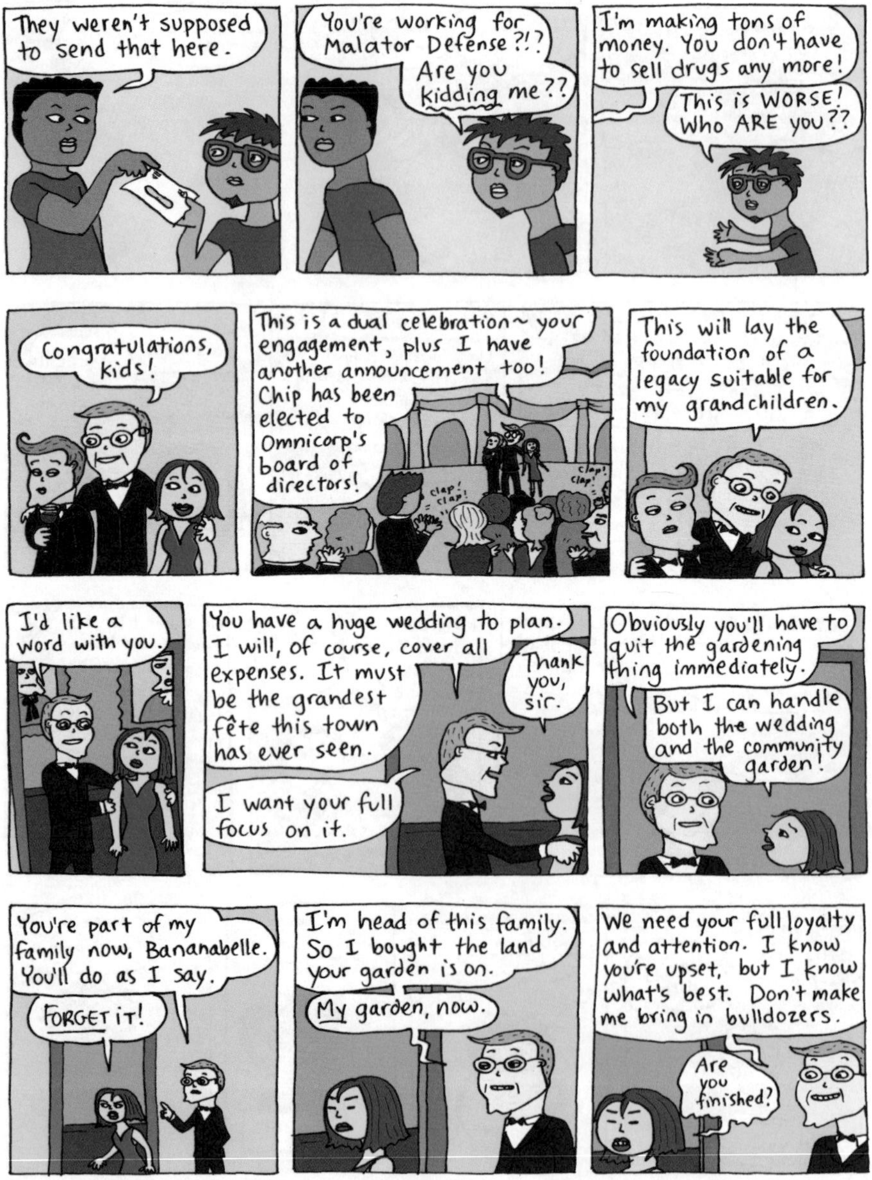
They weren't supposed to send that here.
You're working for Malator Defense?!?
Are you kidding me??
I'm making tons of money. You don't have to sell drugs any more!
This is WORSE! Who ARE you??
Congratulations, kids!
This is a dual celebration~ your engagement, plus I have another announcement too! Chip has been elected to Omnicorp's board of directors!
clap! clap!
clap! clap!
This will lay the foundation of a legacy suitable for my grandchildren.
I'd like a word with you.
You have a huge wedding to plan. I will, of course, cover all expenses. It must be the grandest fête this town has ever seen.
Thank you, sir.
I want your full focus on it.
Obviously you'll have to quit the gardening thing immediately.
But I can handle both the wedding and the community garden!
You're part of my family now, Bananabelle. You'll do as I say.
FORGET IT!
I'm head of this family. So I bought the land your garden is on.
My garden, now.
We need your full loyalty and attention. I know you're upset, but I know what's best. Don't make me bring in bulldozers.
Are you finished?

What should I do??

Chip's dad is EVIL!!

What a trap! If you don't comply with his whims, in come the bulldozers. If you do, at least the garden can still exist without you.

I WON'T let him push me around like this!

What choice do you have? He has all the power.

You don't care about me. You just want me to spy on them.

I do care. I love you.

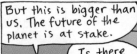

But this is bigger than us. The future of the planet is at stake.

Is there any sacrifice, including our lives, that isn't worth making?

Of course not. But only if we succeed.

We have to succeed.

I hate to tell the other gardeners, but I have to quit.

You do.

I feel awful. I want to tell them the real reason.

You can't! Even if they think you're a bad person. This is part of your sacrifice.

I could tell John. I trust him.

Trust no one. He might say the wrong thing to the wrong person, even by accident.

... so Carolyn can take my place for the Thursday seed exchange...

Why are you quitting?

Well, I'm getting married soon, and, um...there's a lot of planning and stuff to do...

You're abandoning our work to become a slave of the patriarchy? How could you?

I expected better from you, Bananabelle.

I never thought you would sell yourself out.

There's something else. Last week, this land was sold. To Omnicorp.
Are you serious? How do you know?
She's marrying the company golden boy. I saw it on the society page of the corporate rag.
Our land belongs to THEM? Why did you let that happen?
John, I didn't know until it was done.
There's something fishy going on.
PREPARING FOR ATTACK: ANOTHER MONTAGE
TNT
TNT
I've booked Chez Luxe for the reception. And I've arranged for a private showing of Chloe Bridal's top gowns from Paris. 2p.m. Tuesday.
That's very generous of you, Charles.
Call me "Daddy," my sweet girl.
Oh my god. Really, Dad?
I've always wanted a daughter. Now my family is complete.
I'll be right back. I need to, um, powder my nose.
PASSWORD: CØnQUEST

Smitty will drive you home. See you tomorrow, Bananabelle.

Thank you for a lovely time.

Don't forget our meeting with the invitations designer. Promptly at 10.

Yes, sir.

yawn!

♪

She went for the password.

I knew she would. Little vixen.

OMNICORP BULLETS HIGH QUALITY

The password for Charles' computer.

You're a hero.

I don't feel like one.

X

Kiss

The password to Omnicorp's computer.

Nicely done, comrade.

123

Oh Bananabelle, you're a perfect princess!
I think this is the one, don't you?
Whatever you say.
That's my girl.
Are you alone?
Yeah.
This is the password for Omnicorp's CEO. We need you to hack into—
NO.
The geo-engineering project starts in only—
I said "No." I don't want to be involved.
You're not putting me in this position.
A lot is at stake. Including your loved ones, if you don't care about any-one else.
Don't guilt trip me for your decisions. You never consulted me.
SLAM!
Nikko refused to help.
I'm not surprised. He's never agreed with what we're doing.
We should have talked with him more.
Javier told us he wasn't open to it.
We can't convince everyone.
That's the problem.
zzzz

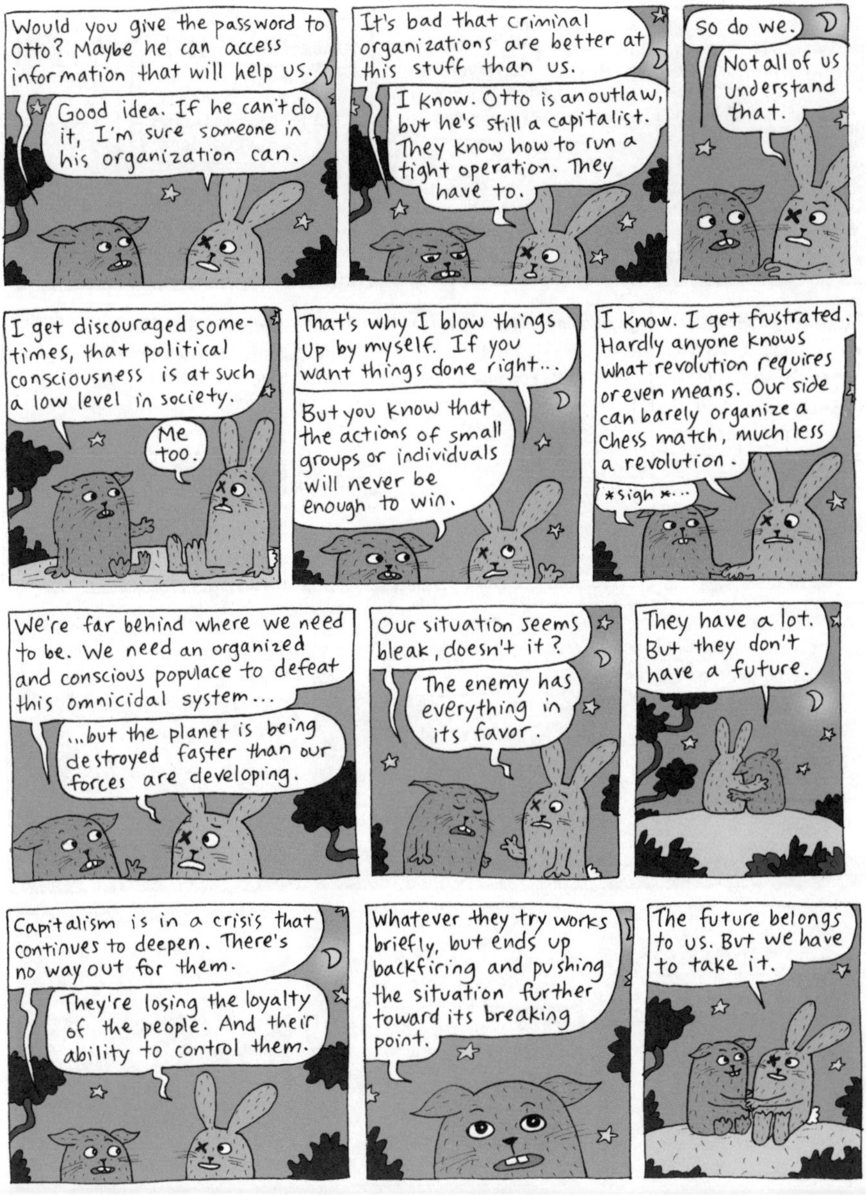
Would you give the password to Otto? Maybe he can access information that will help us.
Good idea. If he can't do it, I'm sure someone in his organization can.
It's bad that criminal organizations are better at this stuff than us.
I know. Otto is an outlaw, but he's still a capitalist. They know how to run a tight operation. They have to.
So do we.
Not all of us understand that.
I get discouraged sometimes, that political consciousness is at such a low level in society.
Me too.
That's why I blow things up by myself. If you want things done right...
But you know that the actions of small groups or individuals will never be enough to win.
I know. I get frustrated. Hardly anyone knows what revolution requires or even means. Our side can barely organize a chess match, much less a revolution.
sigh...
We're far behind where we need to be. We need an organized and conscious populace to defeat this omnicidal system...
...but the planet is being destroyed faster than our forces are developing.
Our situation seems bleak, doesn't it?
The enemy has everything in its favor.
They have a lot. But they don't have a future.
Capitalism is in a crisis that continues to deepen. There's no way out for them.
They're losing the loyalty of the people. And their ability to control them.
Whatever they try works briefly, but ends up backfiring and pushing the situation further toward its breaking point.
The future belongs to us. But we have to take it.

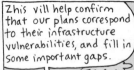

Here. This is the password for the CEO of Omnicorp.

Gold!

Zhis vill help confirm that our plans correspond to their infrastructure vulnerabilities, and fill in some important gaps.

Can you get in undetected?

I haff someone who can handle it. Not easy, but consider it done.

I knew you'd come through.

Sabina, take zhis password. I need everything about Omnicorp's geo-engineering project.

Location of materials, schedule of operations, security, personnel, chain of command — the usual.

Got it.

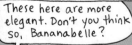

Work with Martin. He vill help summarize your reports.

This style comes with either embossed wedding bells or a pair of doves.

These here are more elegant. Don't you think so, Bananabelle?

Uh-huh.

It's settled, then. Sasha, come into my office so I can write your check.

Chip, do you really want to get married?

Of course I do.

But... you don't seem happy. I don't even know if you love me.

Of course I do...

But—

Tea is served.

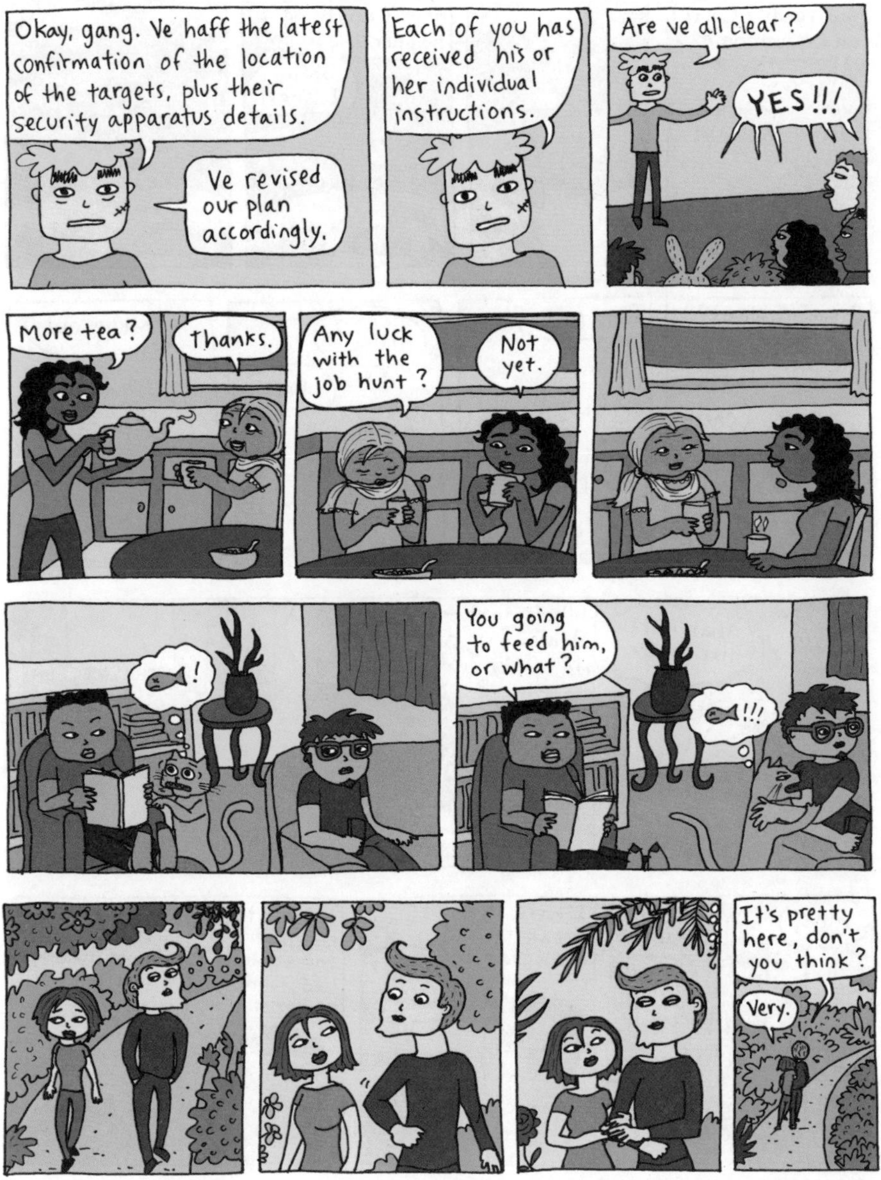
Okay, gang. Ve haff the latest confirmation of the location of the targets, plus their security apparatus details.
Ve revised our plan accordingly.
Each of you has received his or her individual instructions.
Are ve all clear?
YES!!!
More tea?
Thanks.
Any luck with the job hunt?
Not yet.
!
You going to feed him, or what?
!!!
It's pretty here, don't you think?
Very.

You ready? Clear on everything?

Yes.

Hey, if anything happens...

Shh. I know.

Communications?

Check!

Transport?

Check!

Arms?

Check.

Move out.

Hey...

That looks like Javier.

Who's that ~ a drug dealer? Or a customer? Or maybe Javier's cheating on me...?

Ma?

Oh. Hi, Kranti.

I have to break up with Javier.

What? Why?

I can't trust him any more. He lied to me.

I always wonder what he's up to. It's not healthy. I just saw him with some guy and I...

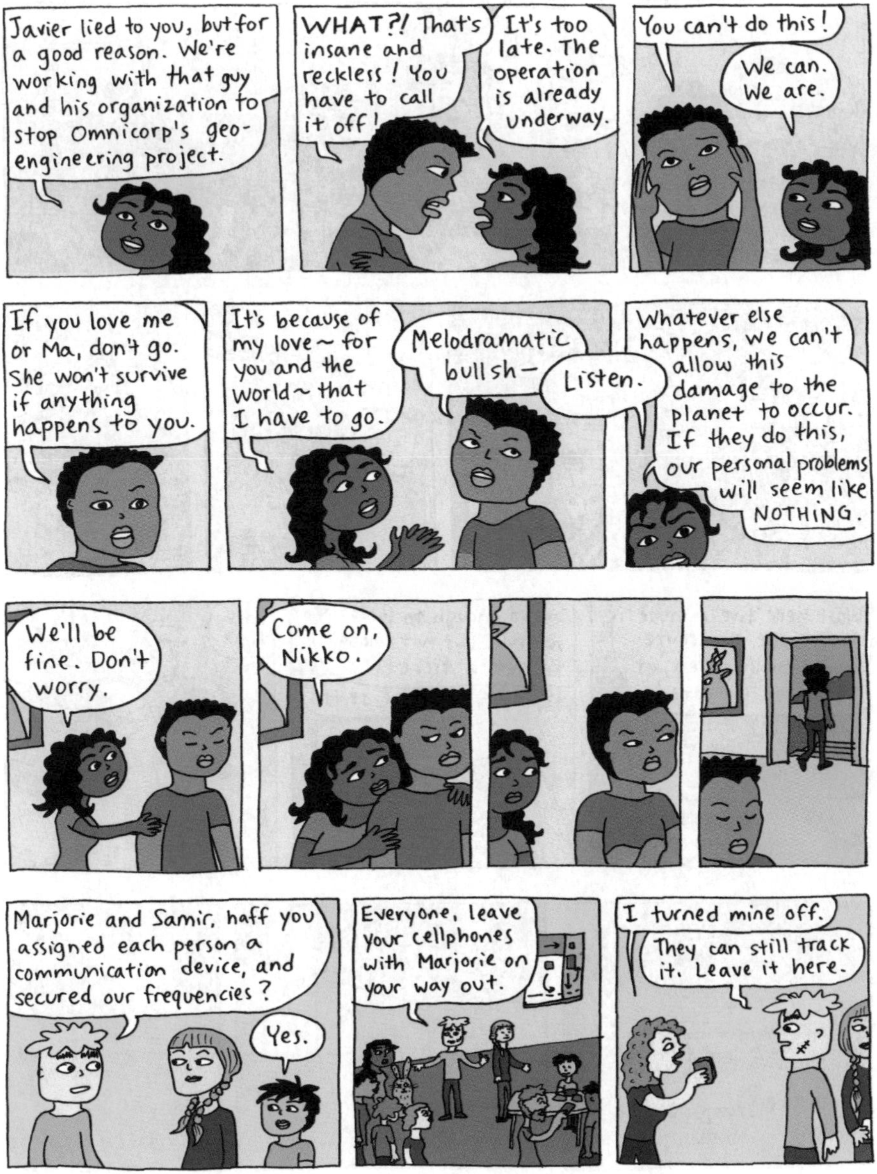
Javier lied to you, but for a good reason. We're working with that guy and his organization to stop Omnicorp's geo-engineering project.
WHAT?! That's insane and reckless! You have to call it off!
It's too late. The operation is already underway.
You can't do this!
We can. We are.
If you love me or Ma, don't go. She won't survive if anything happens to you.
It's because of my love~ for you and the world~ that I have to go.
Melodramatic bullsh—
Listen.
Whatever else happens, we can't allow this damage to the planet to occur. If they do this, our personal problems will seem like NOTHING.
We'll be fine. Don't worry.
Come on, Nikko.
Marjorie and Samir, haff you assigned each person a communication device, and secured our frequencies?
Yes.
Everyone, leave your cellphones with Marjorie on your way out.
I turned mine off.
They can still track it. Leave it here.

No-Fat!
No-Sugar!
No-Dairy!
No-ice!
PURE
ICE CREAM
Wait here five minutes. Then take the route you've been given, at the speed indicated.
Speed enough to look normal, but not enough to get a ticket.
Got it.
Viel Glück, Liebchen.
It's time.
Let's go.
Hair Clippers Unlimited

SLAM!
Rowr!
All Omnicorp's plans, laid out like a banquet.
Supplies, schematics, locations...
Something's wrong.
This is way too easy.
I need to get behind this layer...
There's got to be something else here.
Tap Tap Tap
Bingo.

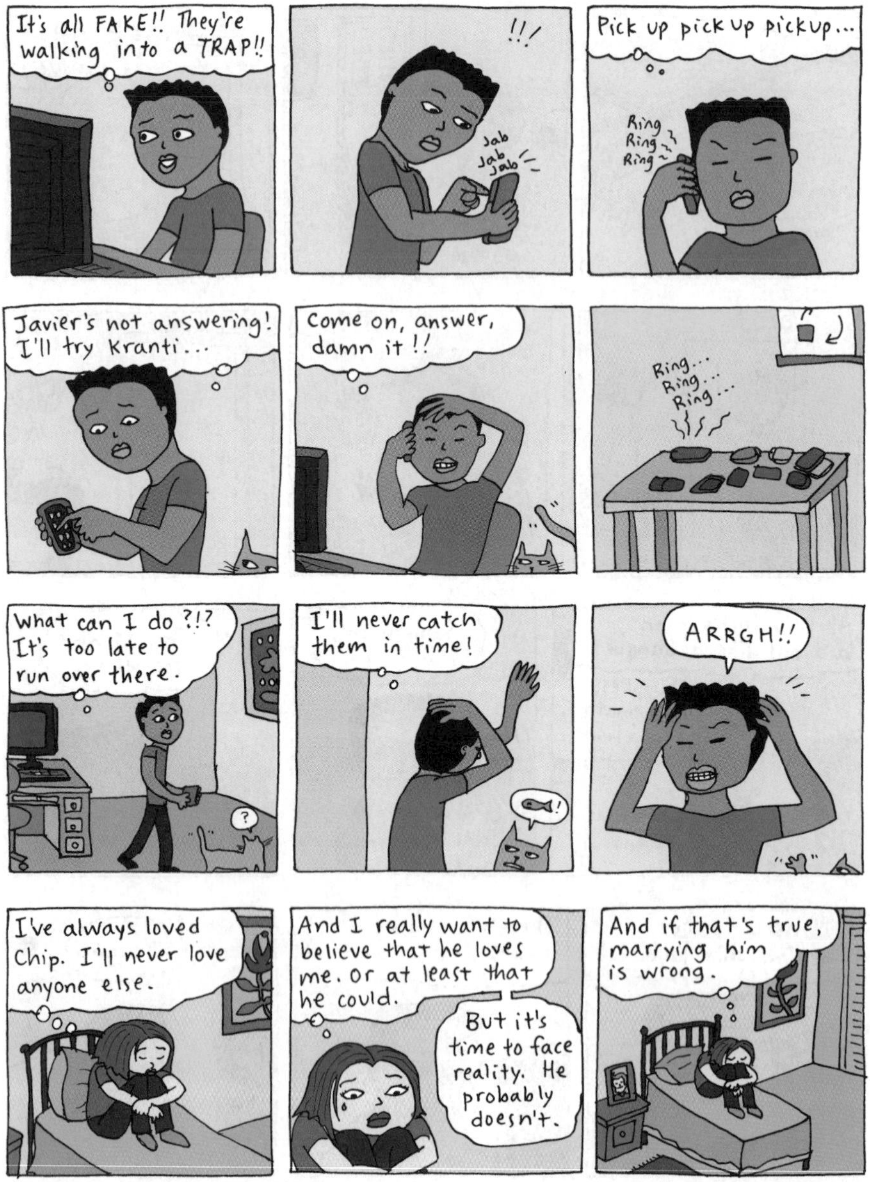
It's all FAKE!! They're walking into a TRAP!!
!!!
Jab Jab Jab
Pick up pick up pickup...
Ring Ring Ring
Javier's not answering! I'll try Kranti...
Come on, answer, damn it!!
Ring... Ring... Ring...
What can I do?!? It's too late to run over there.
?
I'll never catch them in time!
!
ARRGH!!
I've always loved Chip. I'll never love anyone else.
And I really want to believe that he loves me. Or at least that he could.
But it's time to face reality. He probably doesn't.
And if that's true, marrying him is wrong.

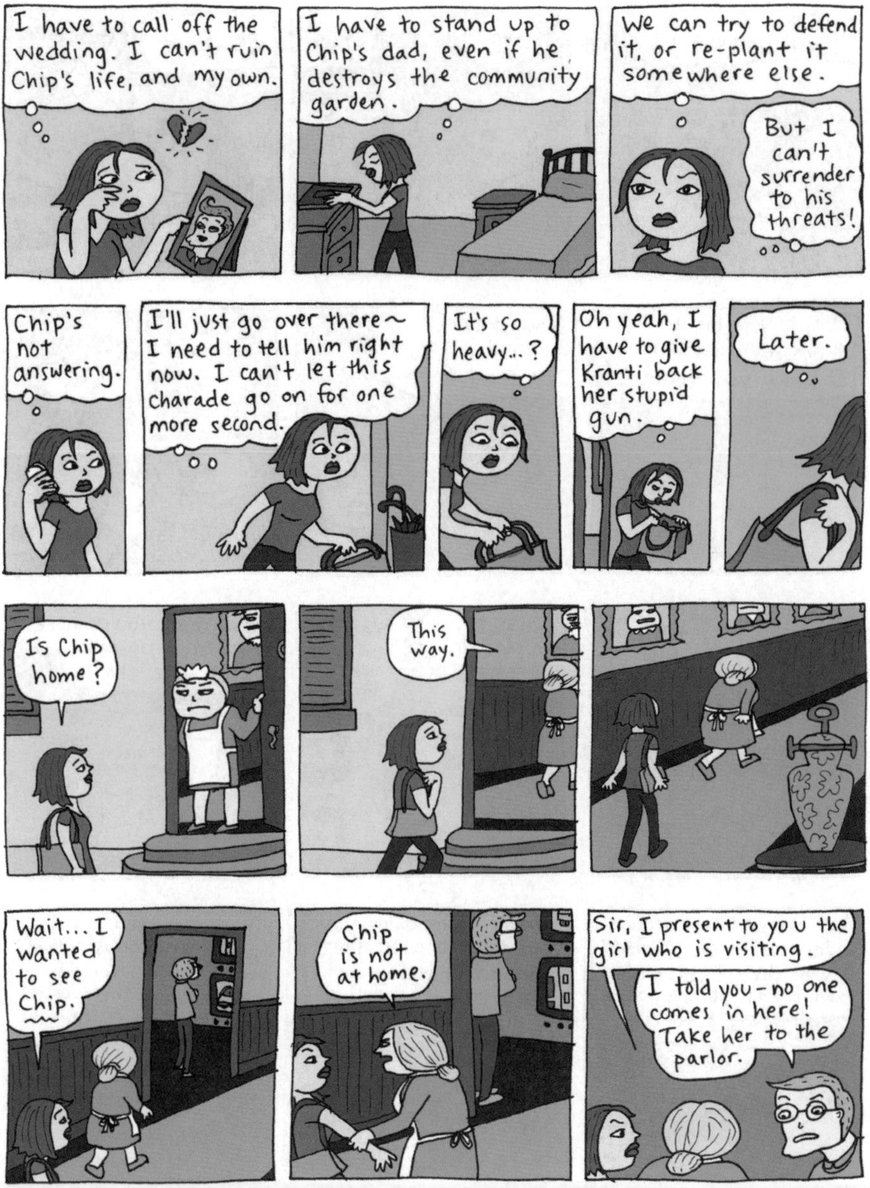
I have to call off the wedding. I can't ruin Chip's life, and my own.
I have to stand up to Chip's dad, even if he destroys the community garden.
We can try to defend it, or re-plant it somewhere else.
But I can't surrender to his threats!
Chip's not answering.
I'll just go over there~ I need to tell him right now. I can't let this charade go on for one more second.
It's so heavy...?
Oh yeah, I have to give Kranti back her stupid gun.
Later.
Is Chip home?
This way.
Wait... I wanted to see Chip.
Chip is not at home.
Sir, I present to you the girl who is visiting.
I told you - no one comes in here! Take her to the parlor.

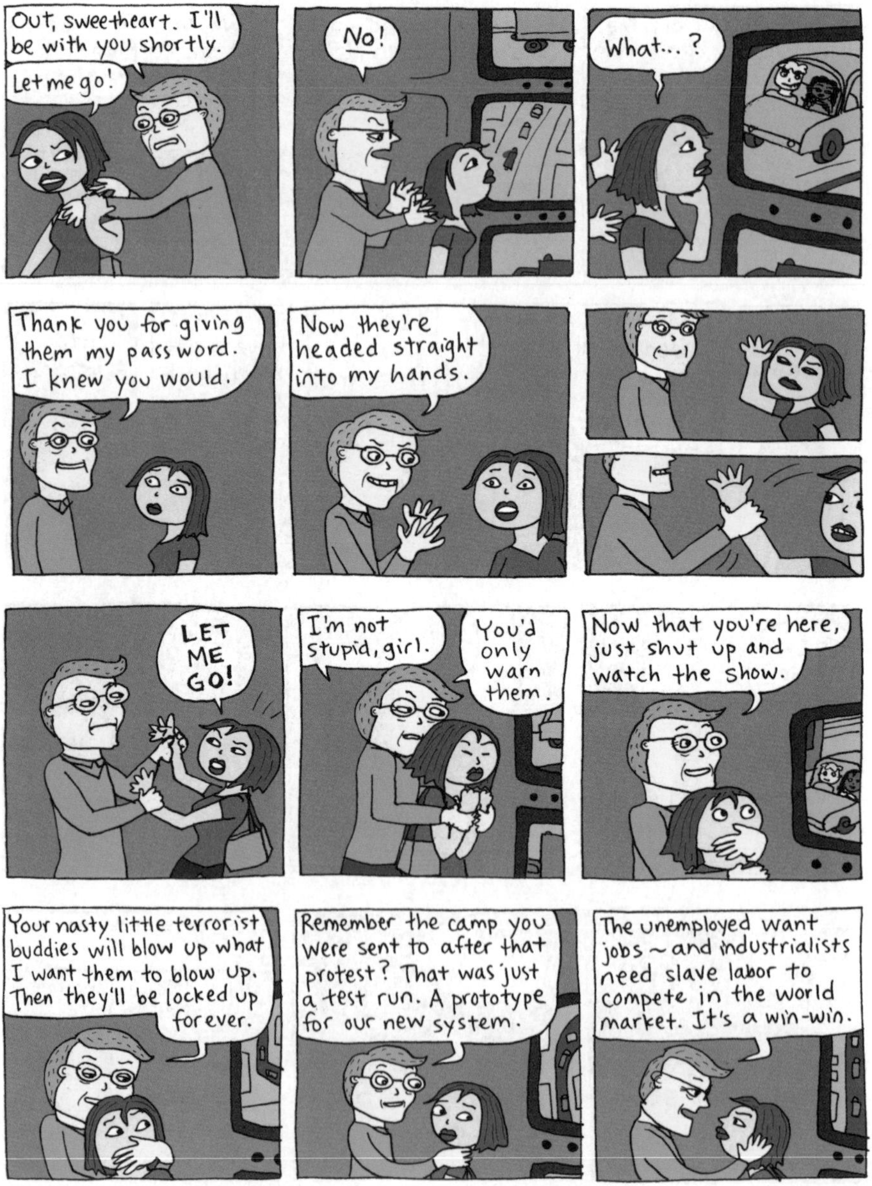
Out, sweetheart. I'll be with you shortly.
Let me go!
No!
What...?
Thank you for giving them my password. I knew you would.
Now they're headed straight into my hands.
LET ME GO!
I'm not stupid, girl.
You'd only warn them.
Now that you're here, just shut up and watch the show.
Your nasty little terrorist buddies will blow up what I want them to blow up. Then they'll be locked up forever.
Remember the camp you were sent to after that protest? That was just a test run. A prototype for our new system.
The unemployed want jobs ~ and industrialists need slave labor to compete in the world market. It's a win-win.

Why have a controlling interest in a security company if you can't use it on your own family? Hehheh.

Listen. You have to care, deep down inside, about doing the right thing.

I am doing the right thing. I'm preserving civilization. The geo-engineering project your friends are trying to destroy is a net good.

Don't you under-stand? Everything is at risk!

Exactly! That's what I'm saying!

We could stop global warming if we choose to live differently.

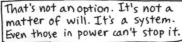
That's not an option. It's not a matter of will. It's a system. Even those in power can't stop it.

But we don't know what effects geo-engineering will have on the oceans.

Yes we do. It'll kill them. It'll cause massive algae blooms. It'll suck the oxygen out of the seas and kill every fish and mammal. Terrible. But it's a price we must pay. The good part is, it'll also sequester carbon.

You don't have a right to play God!

Watch me.

You're causing a disaster! You're risking all life on this planet! Don't you care that millions ~ maybe billions~ of people will DIE?

Can't anything change your mind?

No. Not even you, sweet pea. Not only am I right, I'm going to make a fortune.

I've always believed that every person has some good inside them.

That with compassion and understanding, that good part can be reached. That everyone can be reasoned with.

I was wrong.

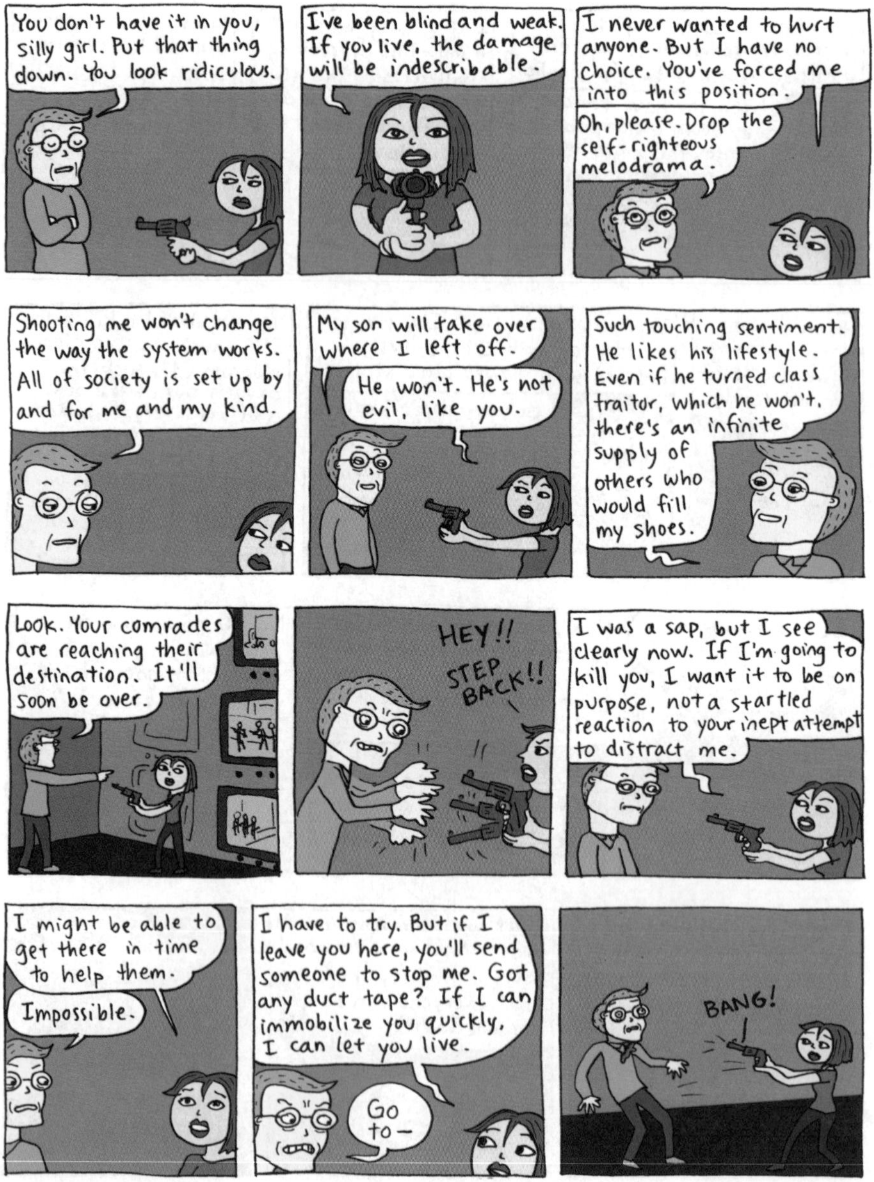

You don't have it in you, silly girl. Put that thing down. You look ridiculous.
I've been blind and weak. If you live, the damage will be indescribable.
I never wanted to hurt anyone. But I have no choice. You've forced me into this position.
Oh, please. Drop the self-righteous melodrama.
Shooting me won't change the way the system works. All of society is set up by and for me and my kind.
My son will take over where I left off.
He won't. He's not evil, like you.
Such touching sentiment. He likes his lifestyle. Even if he turned class traitor, which he won't, there's an infinite supply of others who would fill my shoes.
Look. Your comrades are reaching their destination. It'll soon be over.
HEY!!
STEP BACK!!
I was a sap, but I see clearly now. If I'm going to kill you, I want it to be on purpose, not a startled reaction to your inept attempt to distract me.
I might be able to get there in time to help them.
Impossible.
I have to try. But if I leave you here, you'll send someone to stop me. Got any duct tape? If I can immobilize you quickly, I can let you live.
Go to—
BANG!

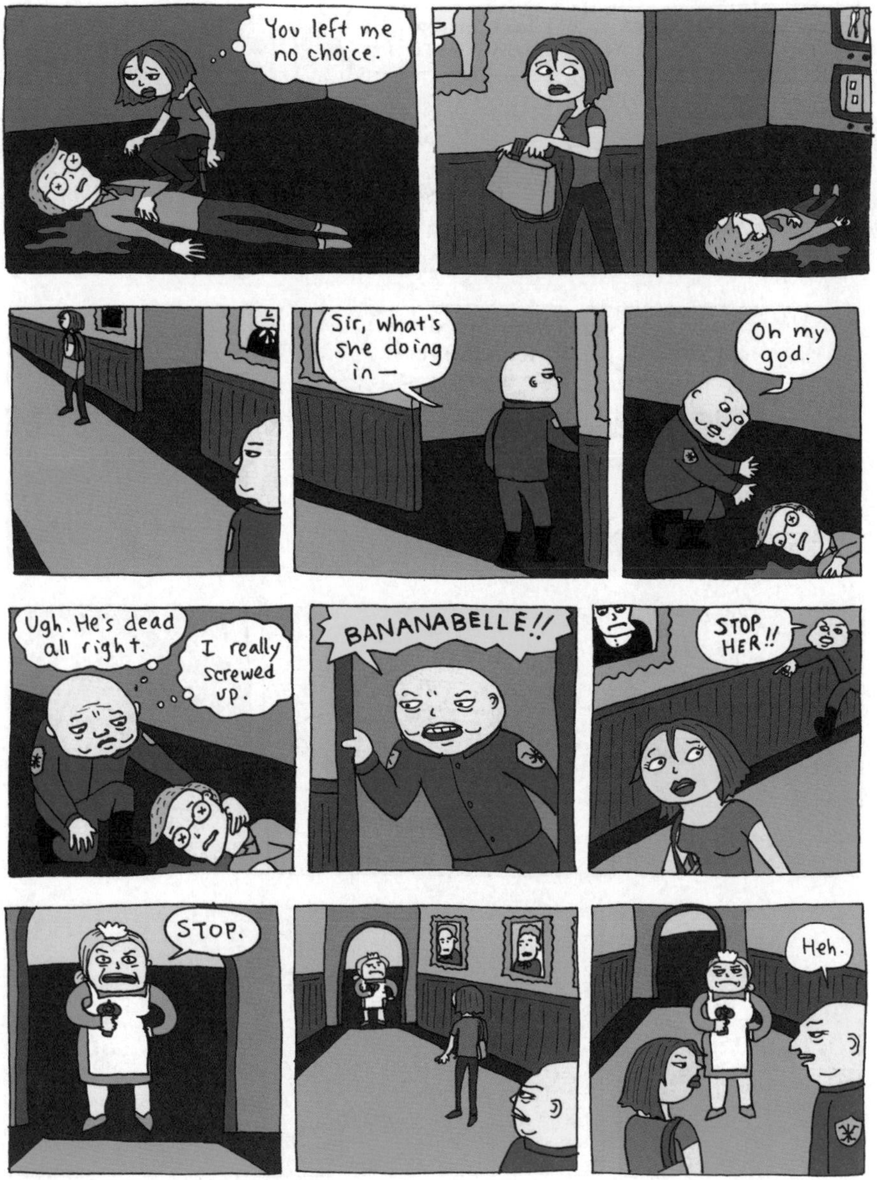
You left me no choice.
Sir, what's she doing in—
Oh my god.
Ugh. He's dead all right.
I really screwed up.
BANANABELLE!!
STOP HER!!
STOP.
Heh.

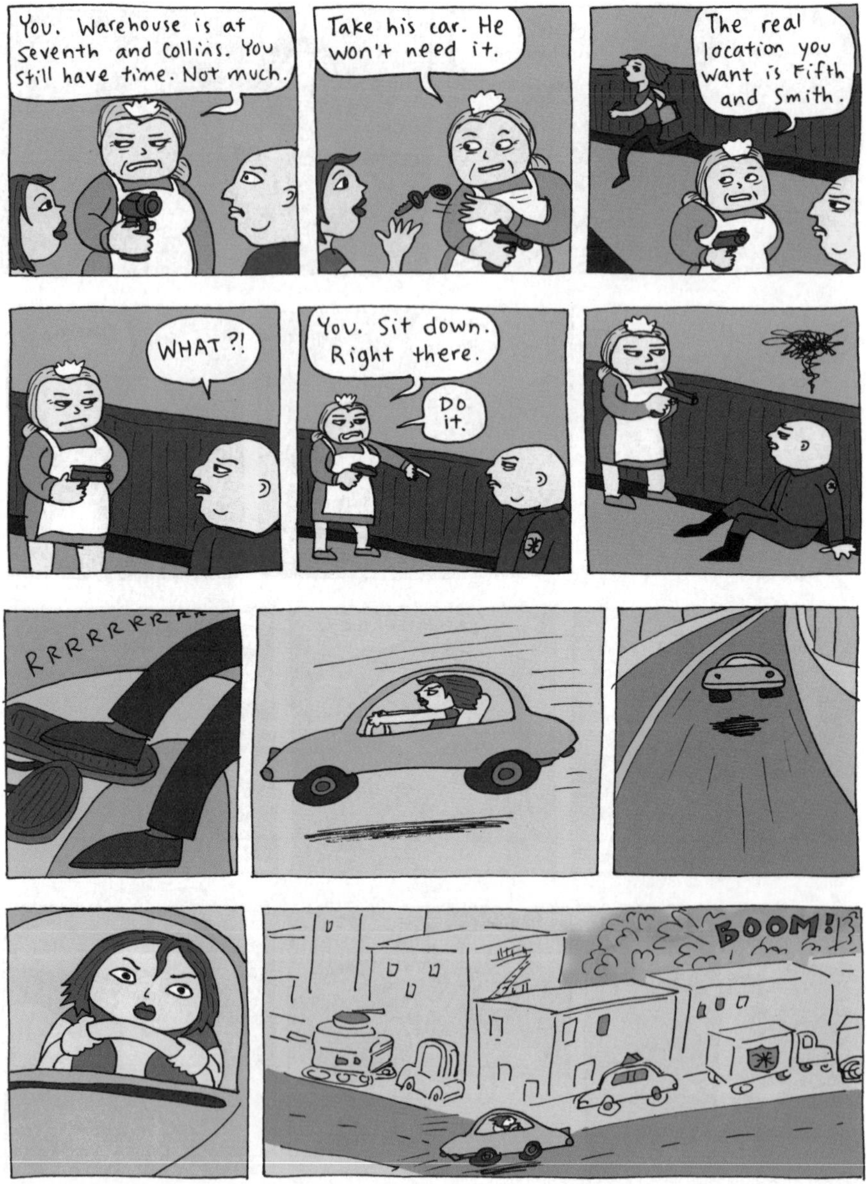
You. Warehouse is at Seventh and Collins. You still have time. Not much.
Take his car. He won't need it.
The real location you want is Fifth and Smith.
WHAT?!
You. Sit down. Right there.
Do it.
RRRRRRRRR
BOOM!

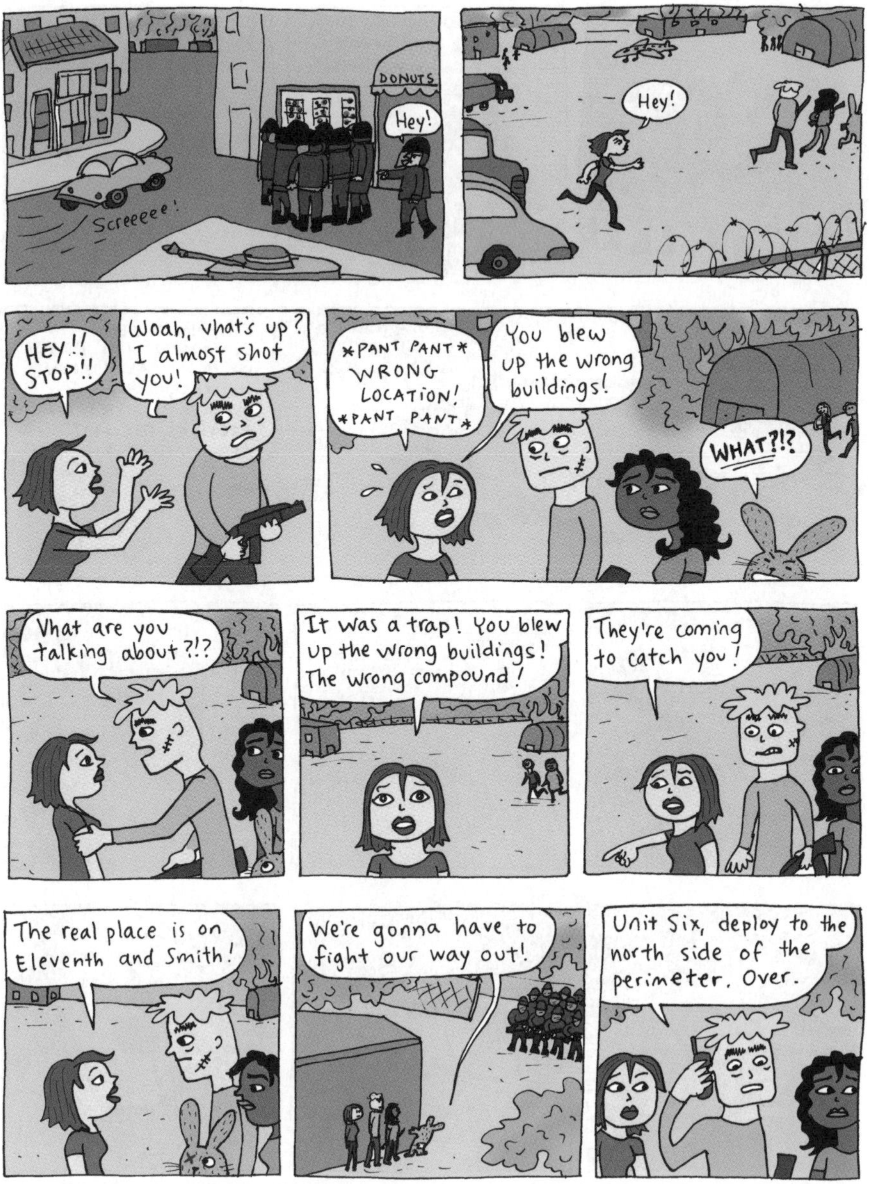
DONUTS
Hey!
Screeeee!
Hey!
HEY!! STOP!!
Woah, vhat's up? I almost shot you!
PANT PANT WRONG LOCATION! *PANT PANT*
You blew up the wrong buildings!
WHAT?!?
Vhat are you talking about?!?
It was a trap! You blew up the wrong buildings! The wrong compound!
They're coming to catch you!
The real place is on Eleventh and Smith!
We're gonna have to fight our way out!
Unit Six, deploy to the north side of the perimeter. Over.

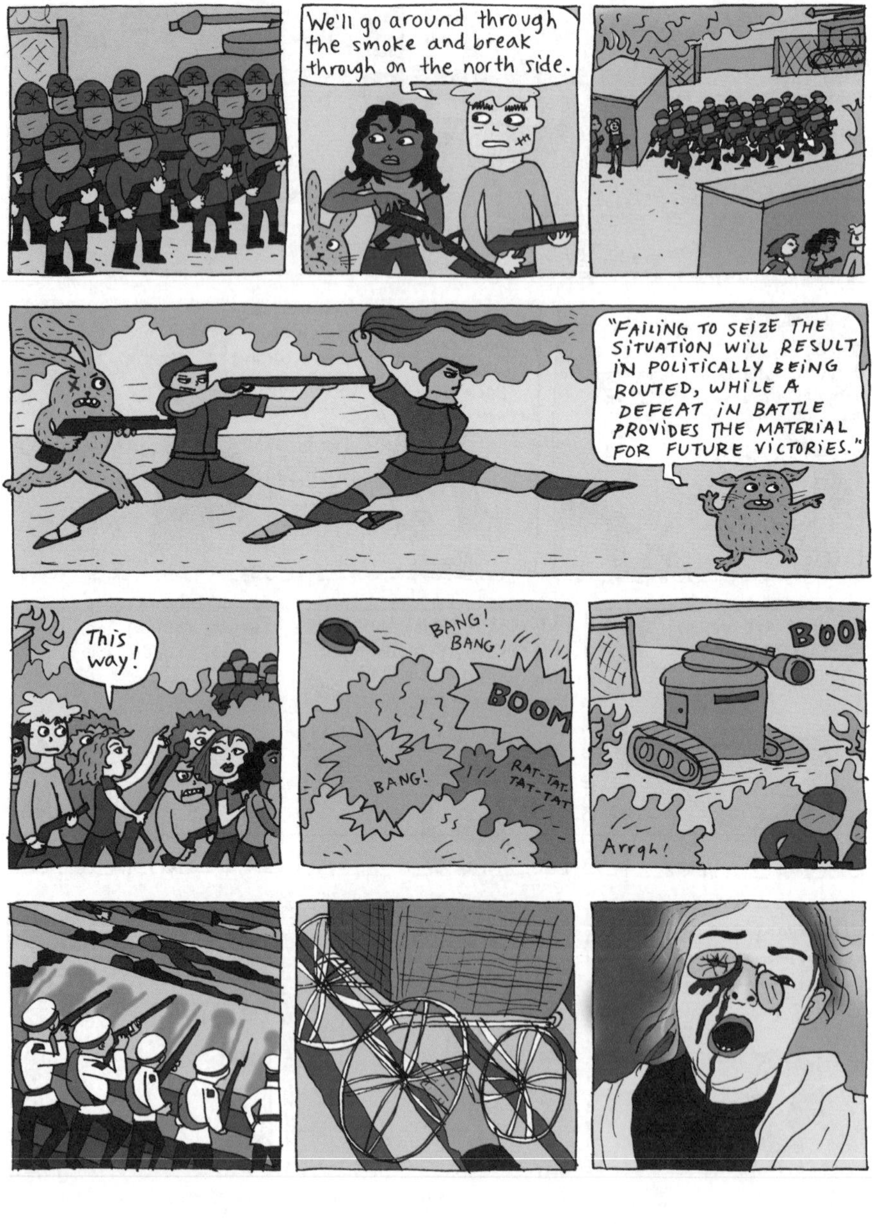
We'll go around through the smoke and break through on the north side.
"FAILING TO SEIZE THE SITUATION WILL RESULT IN POLITICALLY BEING ROUTED, WHILE A DEFEAT IN BATTLE PROVIDES THE MATERIAL FOR FUTURE VICTORIES."
This way!
BANG! BANG!
BOOM
BANG!
RAT-TAT-TAT-TAT
BOOM
Arrgh!

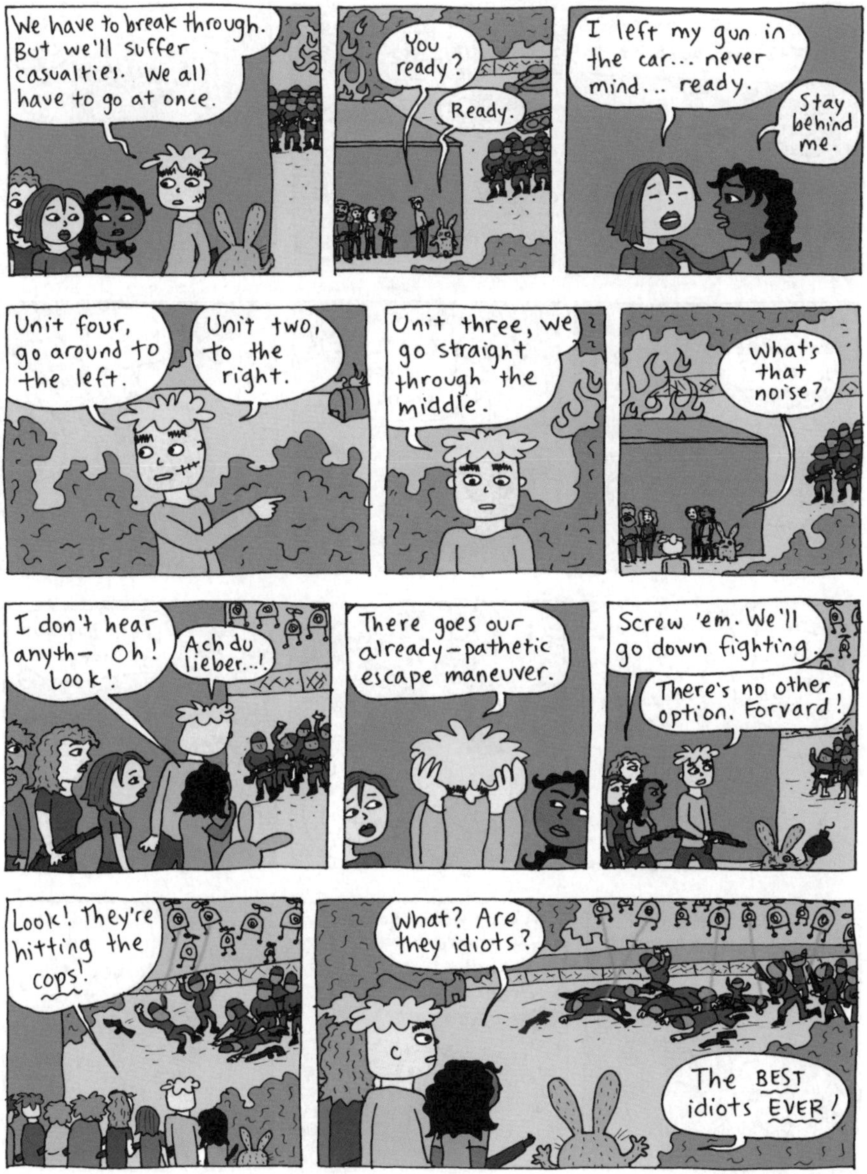
We have to break through. But we'll suffer casualties. We all have to go at once.
You ready?
Ready.
I left my gun in the car... never mind... ready.
Stay behind me.
Unit four, go around to the left.
Unit two, to the right.
Unit three, we go straight through the middle.
What's that noise?
I don't hear anyth— Oh! Look!
Ach du lieber...!
There goes our already-pathetic escape maneuver.
Screw 'em. We'll go down fighting.
There's no other option. Forvard!
Look! They're hitting the cops!
What? Are they idiots?
The BEST idiots EVER!

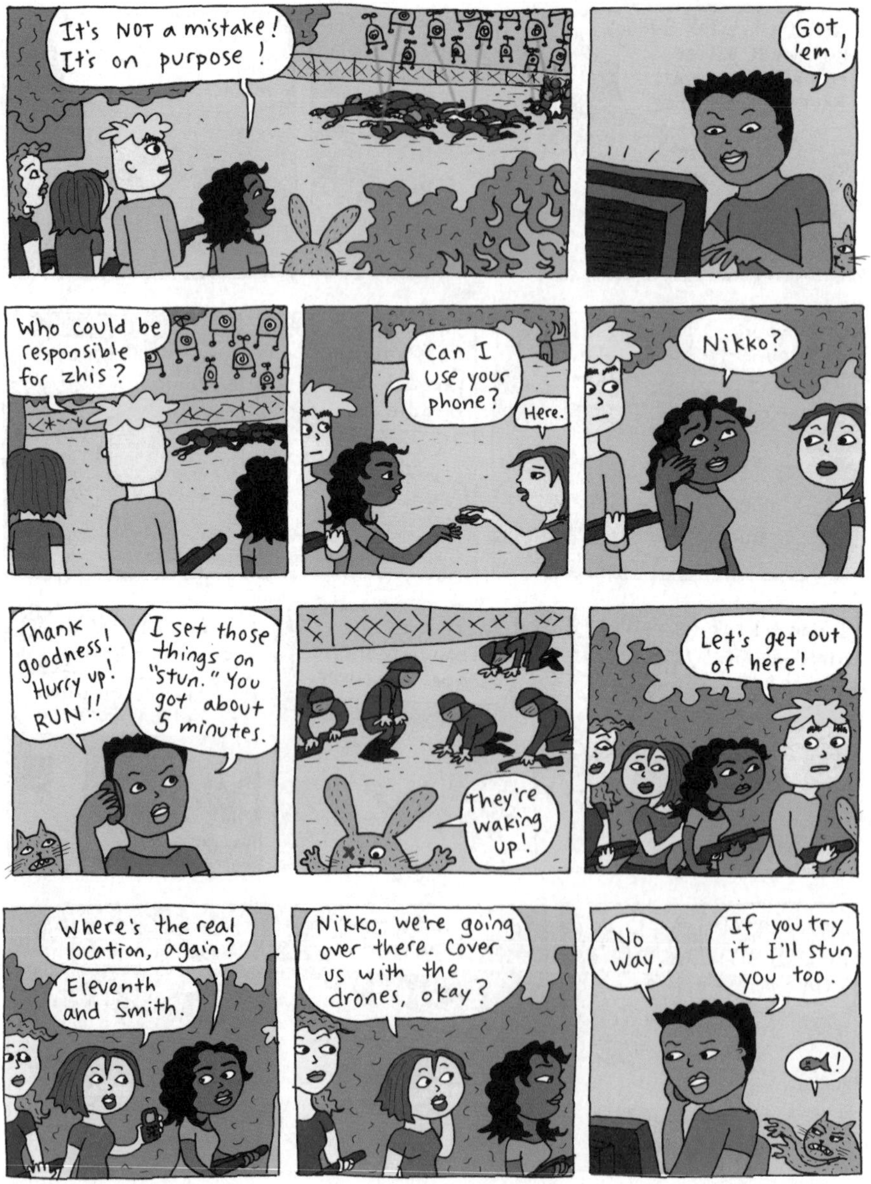

It's NOT a mistake! It's on purpose!
Got 'em!
Who could be responsible for zhis?
Can I use your phone?
Here.
Nikko?
Thank goodness! Hurry up! RUN!!
I set those things on "stun." You got about 5 minutes.
They're waking up!
Let's get out of here!
Where's the real location, again?
Eleventh and Smith.
Nikko, we're going over there. Cover us with the drones, okay?
No way.
If you try it, I'll stun you too.

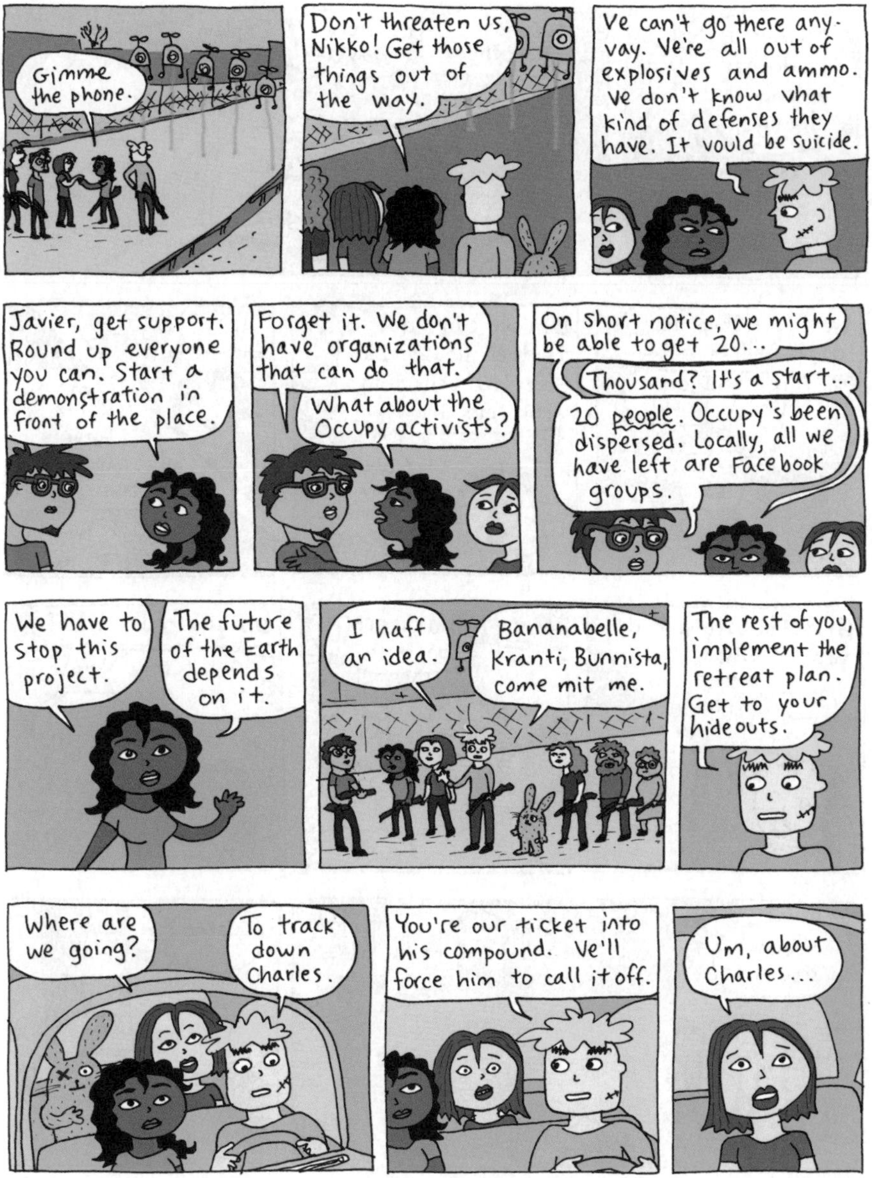
Gimme the phone.
Don't threaten us, Nikko! Get those things out of the way.
Ve can't go there any-vay. Ve're all out of explosives and ammo. Ve don't know vhat kind of defenses they have. It vould be suicide.
Javier, get support. Round up everyone you can. Start a demonstration in front of the place.
Forget it. We don't have organizations that can do that.
What about the Occupy activists?
On short notice, we might be able to get 20...
Thousand? It's a start...
20 people. Occupy's been dispersed. Locally, all we have left are Facebook groups.
We have to stop this project.
The future of the Earth depends on it.
I haff an idea.
Bananabelle, Kranti, Bunnista, come mit me.
The rest of you, implement the retreat plan. Get to your hideouts.
Where are we going?
To track down Charles.
You're our ticket into his compound. Ve'll force him to call it off.
Um, about Charles...

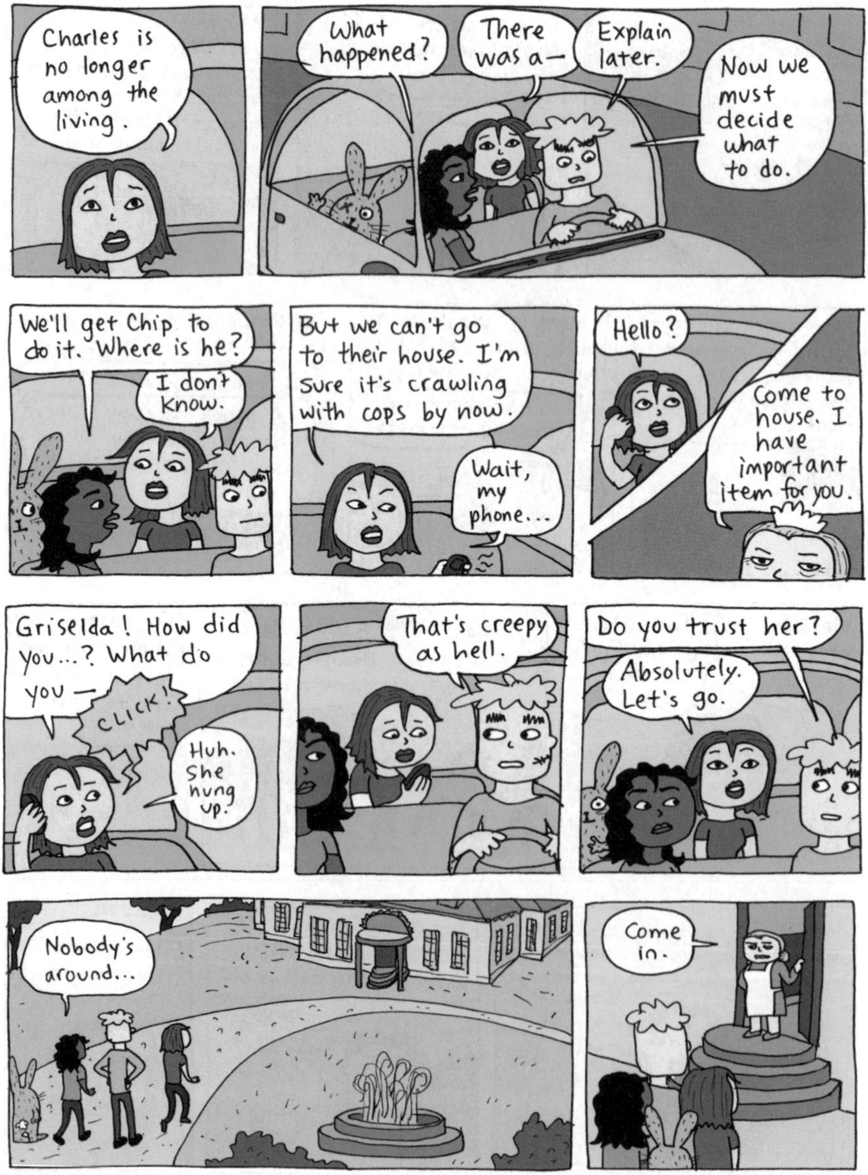

Charles is no longer among the living.
What happened?
There was a—
Explain later.
Now we must decide what to do.
We'll get Chip to do it. Where is he?
I don't know.
But we can't go to their house. I'm sure it's crawling with cops by now.
Wait, my phone...
Hello?
Come to house. I have important item for you.
Griselda! How did you...? What do you —
CLICK!
Huh. She hung up.
That's creepy as hell.
Do you trust her?
Absolutely. Let's go.
Nobody's around...
Come in.

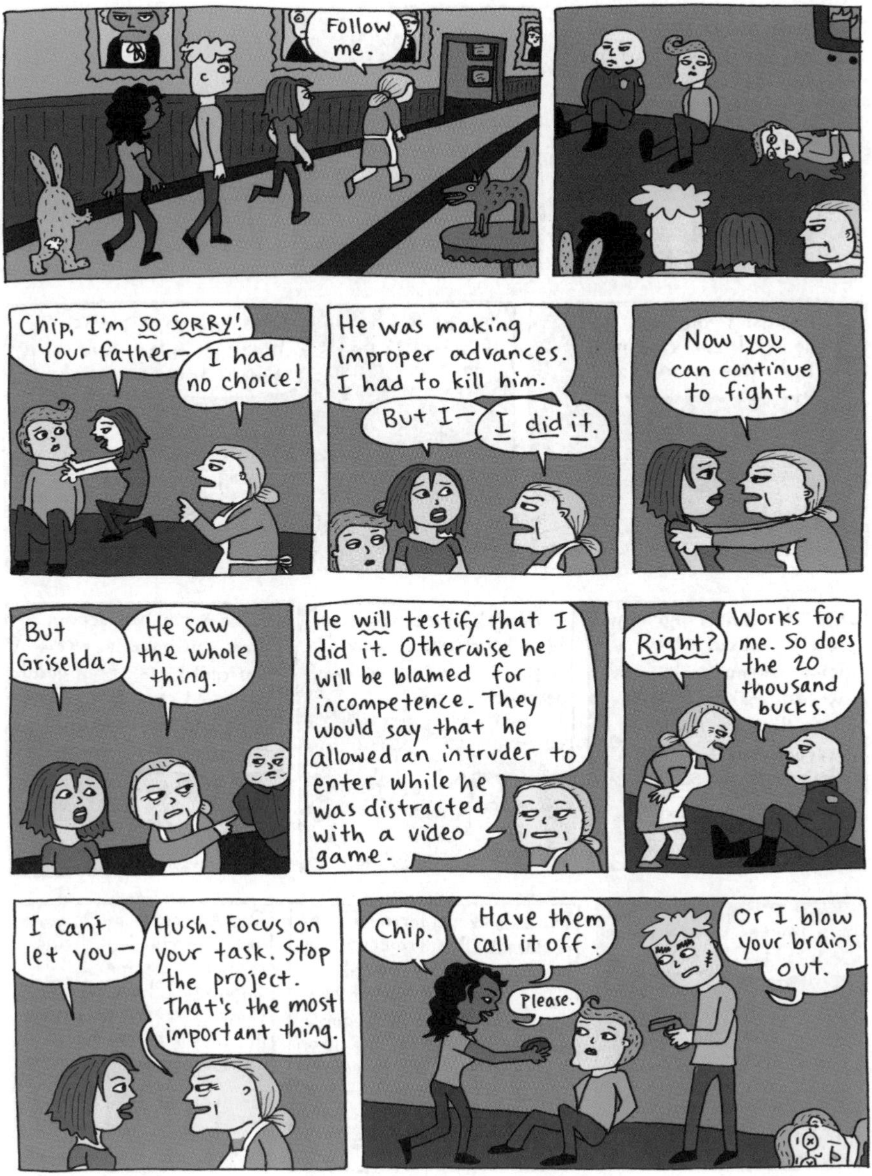
Follow me.
Chip, I'm SO SORRY! Your father—
I had no choice!
He was making improper advances. I had to kill him.
But I—
I did it.
Now you can continue to fight.
But Griselda~
He saw the whole thing.
He will testify that I did it. Otherwise he will be blamed for incompetence. They would say that he allowed an intruder to enter while he was distracted with a video game.
Right?
Works for me. So does the 20 thousand bucks.
I can't let you—
Hush. Focus on your task. Stop the project. That's the most important thing.
Chip.
Have them call it off.
Please.
Or I blow your brains out.

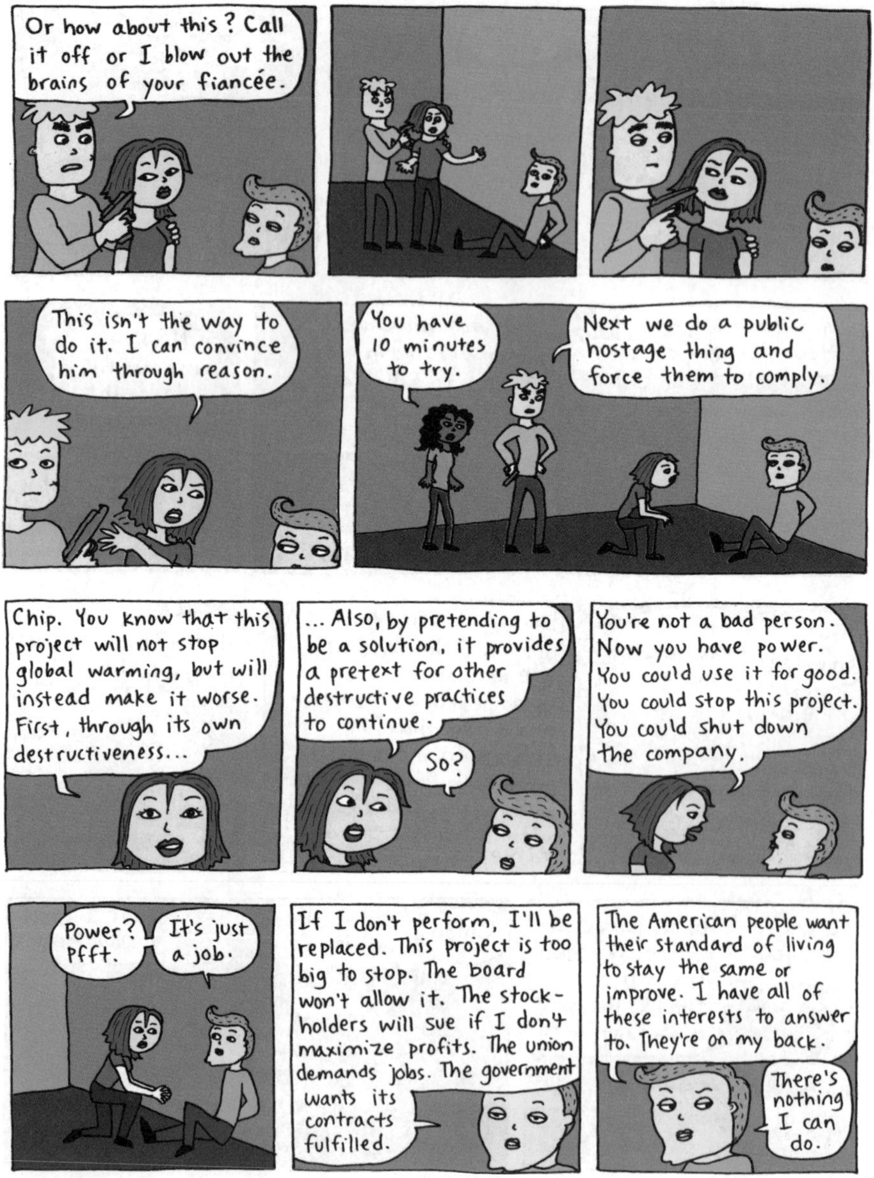
Or how about this? Call it off or I blow out the brains of your fiancée.
This isn't the way to do it. I can convince him through reason.
You have 10 minutes to try.
Next we do a public hostage thing and force them to comply.
Chip. You know that this project will not stop global warming, but will instead make it worse. First, through its own destructiveness...
... Also, by pretending to be a solution, it provides a pretext for other destructive practices to continue.
So?
You're not a bad person. Now you have power. You could use it for good. You could stop this project. You could shut down the company.
Power? Pfft.
It's just a job.
If I don't perform, I'll be replaced. This project is too big to stop. The board won't allow it. The stock-holders will sue if I don't maximize profits. The union demands jobs. The government wants its contracts fulfilled.
The American people want their standard of living to stay the same or improve. I have all of these interests to answer to. They're on my back.
There's nothing I can do.

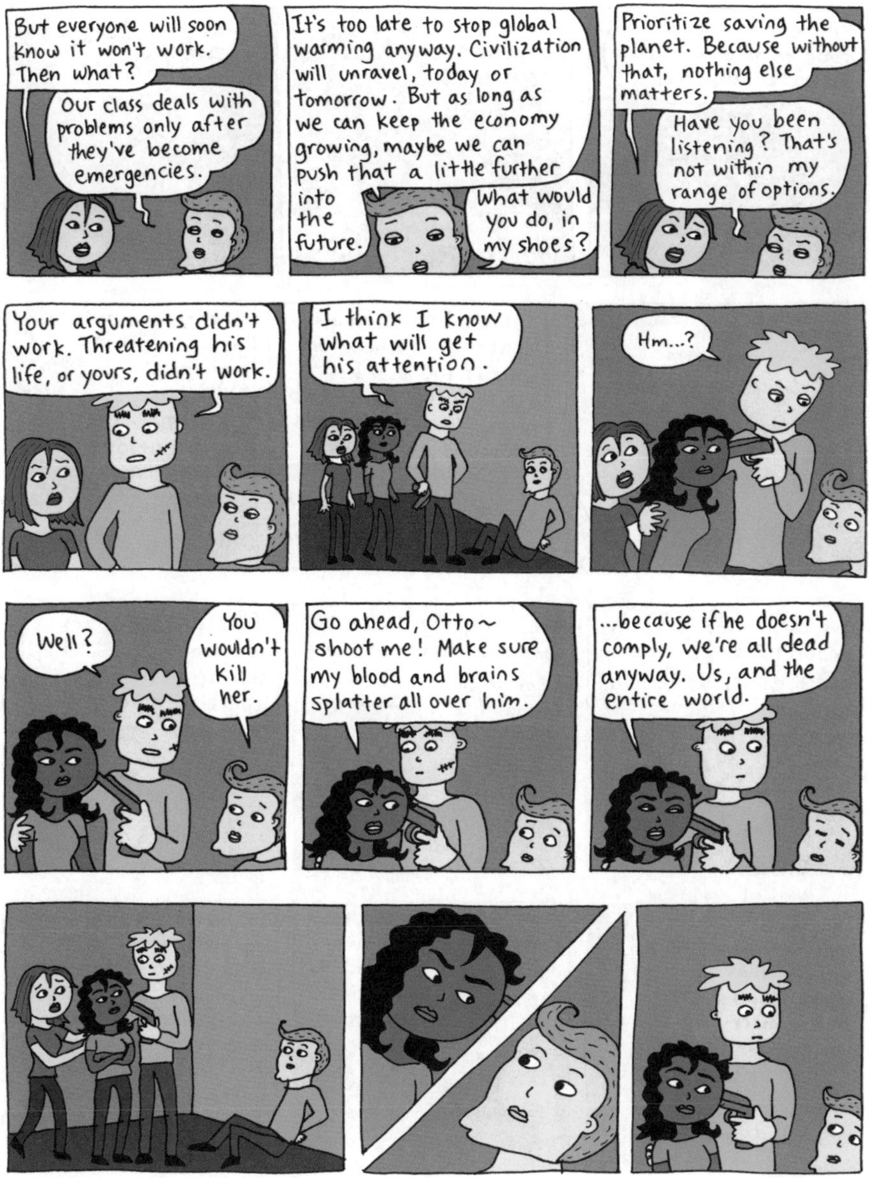
But everyone will soon know it won't work. Then what?
Our class deals with problems only after they've become emergencies.
It's too late to stop global warming anyway. Civilization will unravel, today or tomorrow. But as long as we can keep the economy growing, maybe we can push that a little further into the future.
What would you do, in my shoes?
Prioritize saving the planet. Because without that, nothing else matters.
Have you been listening? That's not within my range of options.
Your arguments didn't work. Threatening his life, or yours, didn't work.
I think I know what will get his attention.
Hm...?
Well?
You wouldn't kill her.
Go ahead, Otto~ shoot me! Make sure my blood and brains splatter all over him.
...because if he doesn't comply, we're all dead anyway. Us, and the entire world.

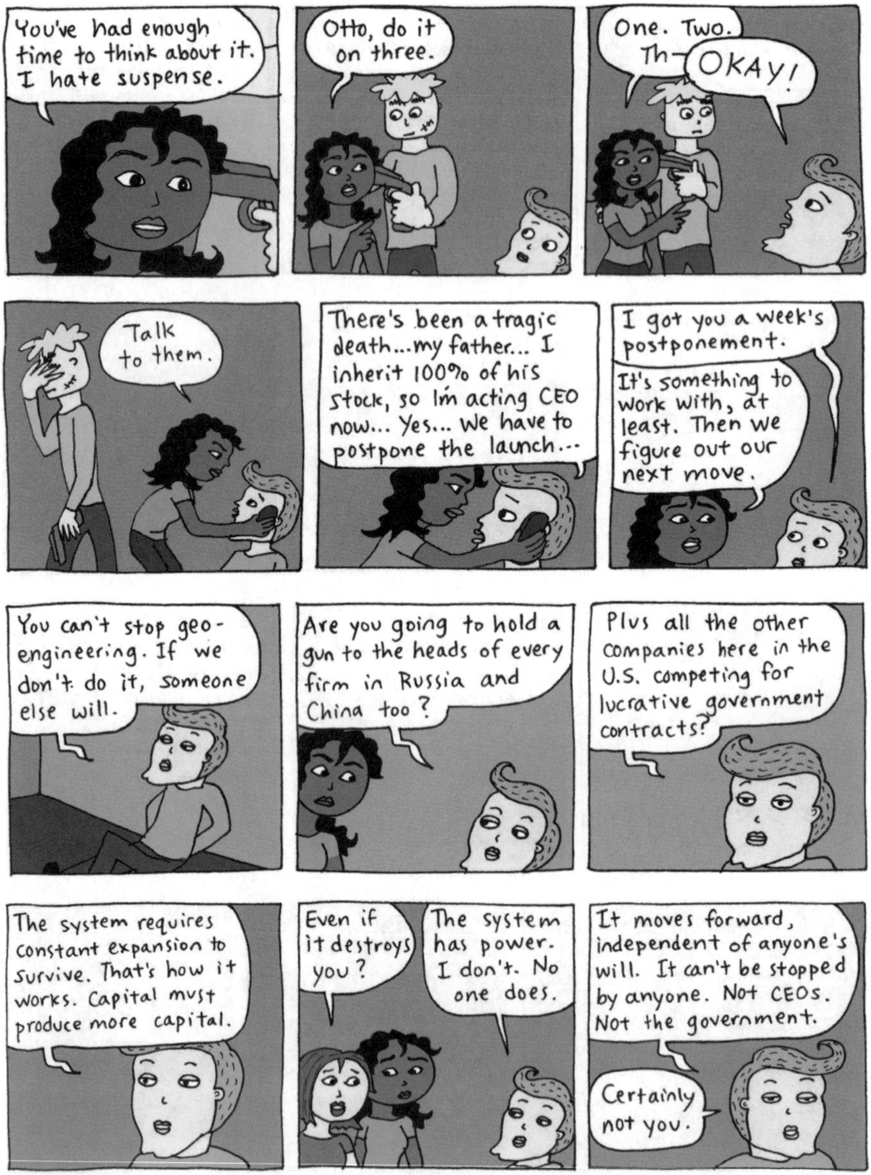
You've had enough time to think about it. I hate suspense.
Otto, do it on three.
One. Two. Th-
OKAY!
Talk to them.
There's been a tragic death... my father... I inherit 100% of his stock, so I'm acting CEO now... Yes... we have to postpone the launch...
I got you a week's postponement.
It's something to work with, at least. Then we figure out our next move.
You can't stop geo-engineering. If we don't do it, someone else will.
Are you going to hold a gun to the heads of every firm in Russia and China too?
Plus all the other companies here in the U.S. competing for lucrative government contracts?
The system requires constant expansion to survive. That's how it works. Capital must produce more capital.
Even if it destroys you?
The system has power. I don't. No one does.
It moves forward, independent of anyone's will. It can't be stopped by anyone. Not CEOs. Not the government.
Certainly not you.

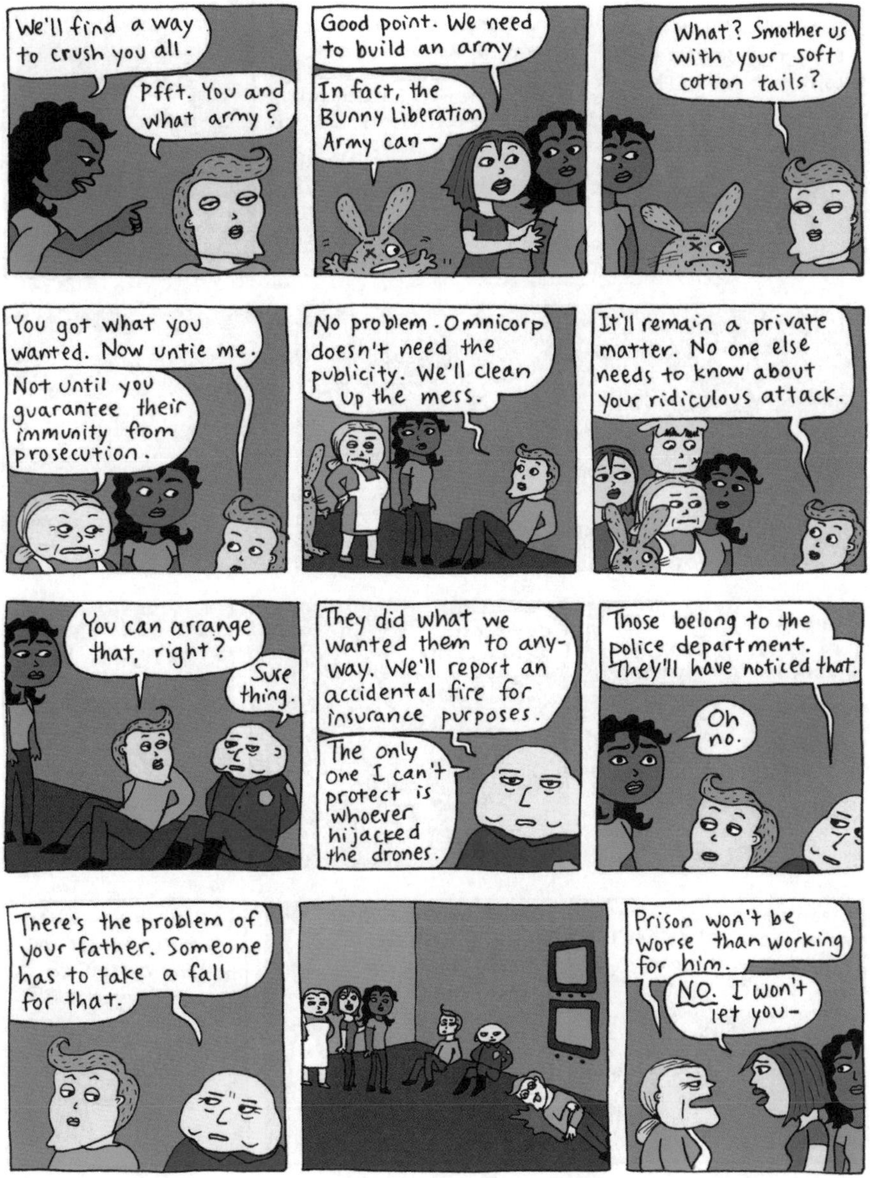
We'll find a way to crush you all.
Pfft. You and what army?
Good point. We need to build an army.
In fact, the Bunny Liberation Army can—
What? Smother us with your soft cotton tails?
You got what you wanted. Now untie me.
Not until you guarantee their immunity from prosecution.
No problem. Omnicorp doesn't need the publicity. We'll clean up the mess.
It'll remain a private matter. No one else needs to know about your ridiculous attack.
You can arrange that, right?
Sure thing.
They did what we wanted them to anyway. We'll report an accidental fire for insurance purposes.
The only one I can't protect is whoever hijacked the drones.
Those belong to the police department. They'll have noticed that.
Oh no.
There's the problem of your father. Someone has to take a fall for that.
Prison won't be worse than working for him.
NO. I won't let you—

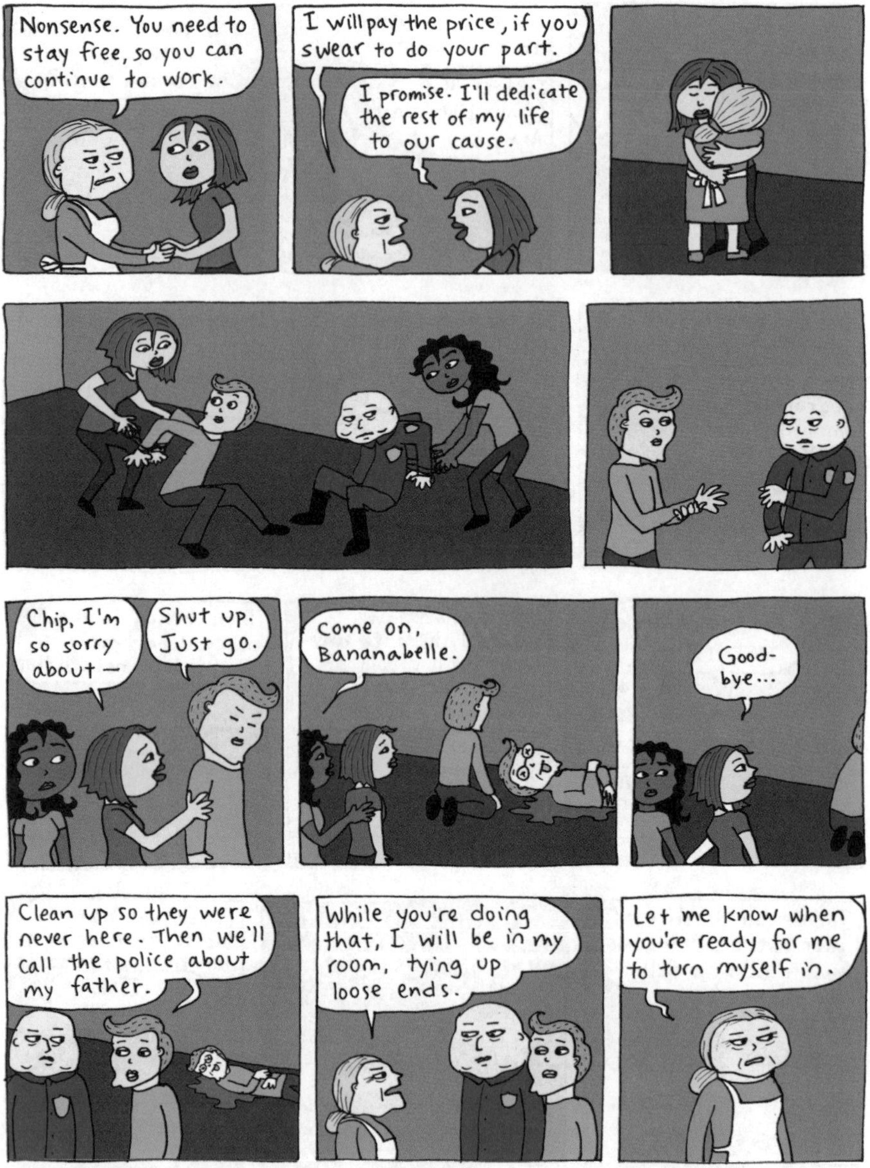
Nonsense. You need to stay free, so you can continue to work.
I will pay the price, if you swear to do your part.
I promise. I'll dedicate the rest of my life to our cause.
Chip, I'm so sorry about—
Shut up. Just go.
Come on, Bananabelle.
Good-bye...
Clean up so they were never here. Then we'll call the police about my father.
While you're doing that, I will be in my room, tying up loose ends.
Let me know when you're ready for me to turn myself in.

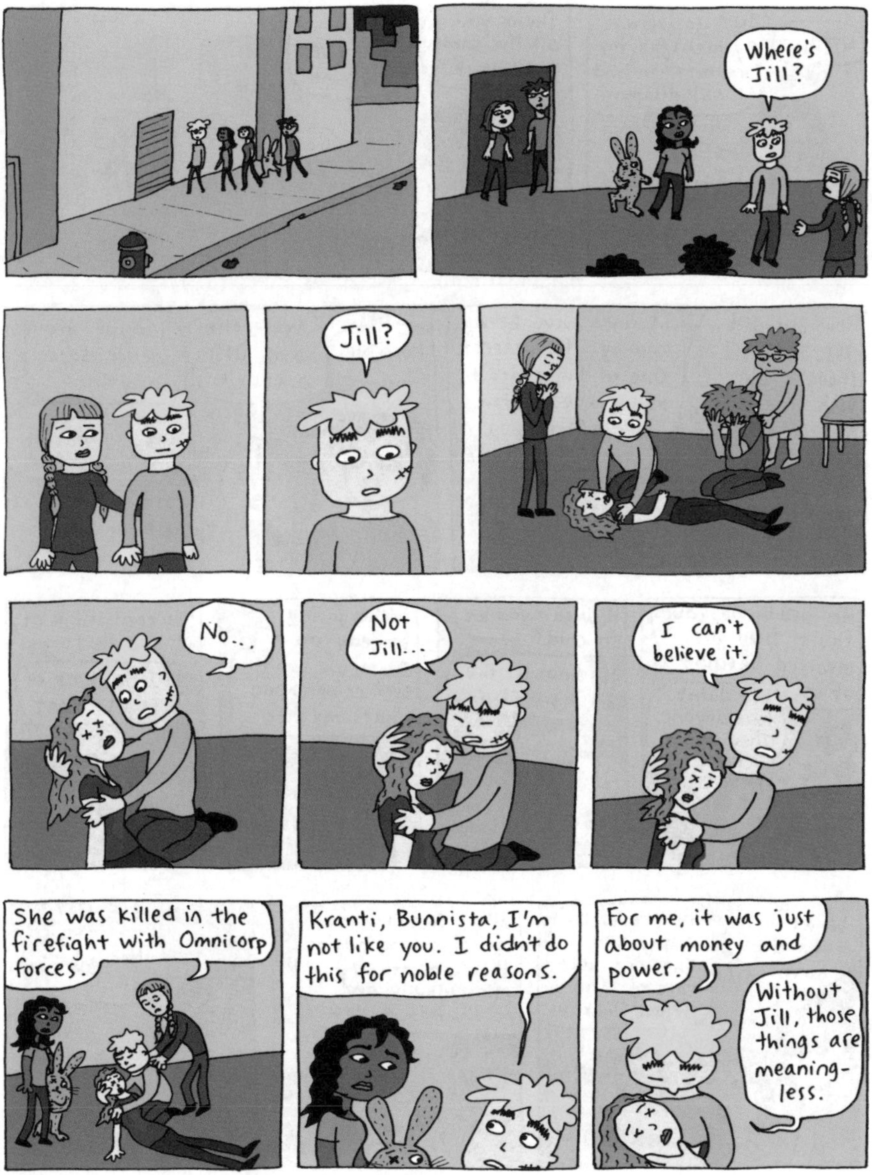
Where's Jill?
Jill?
No...
Not Jill...
I can't believe it.
She was killed in the firefight with Omnicorp forces.
Kranti, Bunnista, I'm not like you. I didn't do this for noble reasons.
For me, it was just about money and power.
Without Jill, those things are meaning-less.

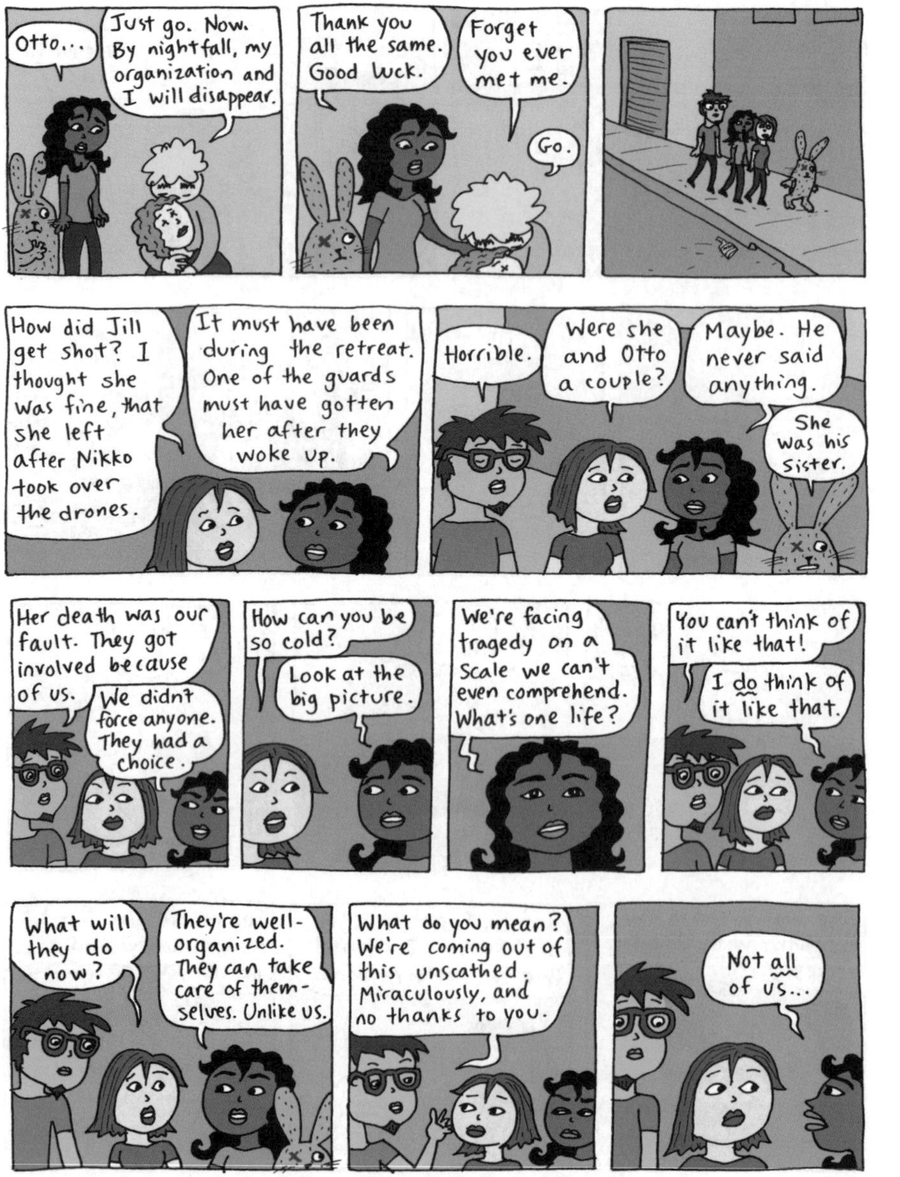
Otto...
Just go. Now. By nightfall, my organization and I will disappear.
Thank you all the same. Good luck.
Forget you ever met me.
Go.
How did Jill get shot? I thought she was fine, that she left after Nikko took over the drones.
It must have been during the retreat. One of the guards must have gotten her after they woke up.
Horrible.
Were she and Otto a couple?
Maybe. He never said anything.
She was his sister.
Her death was our fault. They got involved because of us.
We didn't force anyone. They had a choice.
How can you be so cold?
Look at the big picture.
We're facing tragedy on a scale we can't even comprehend. What's one life?
You can't think of it like that!
I do think of it like that.
What will they do now?
They're well-organized. They can take care of themselves. Unlike us.
What do you mean? We're coming out of this unscathed. Miraculously, and no thanks to you.
Not all of us...

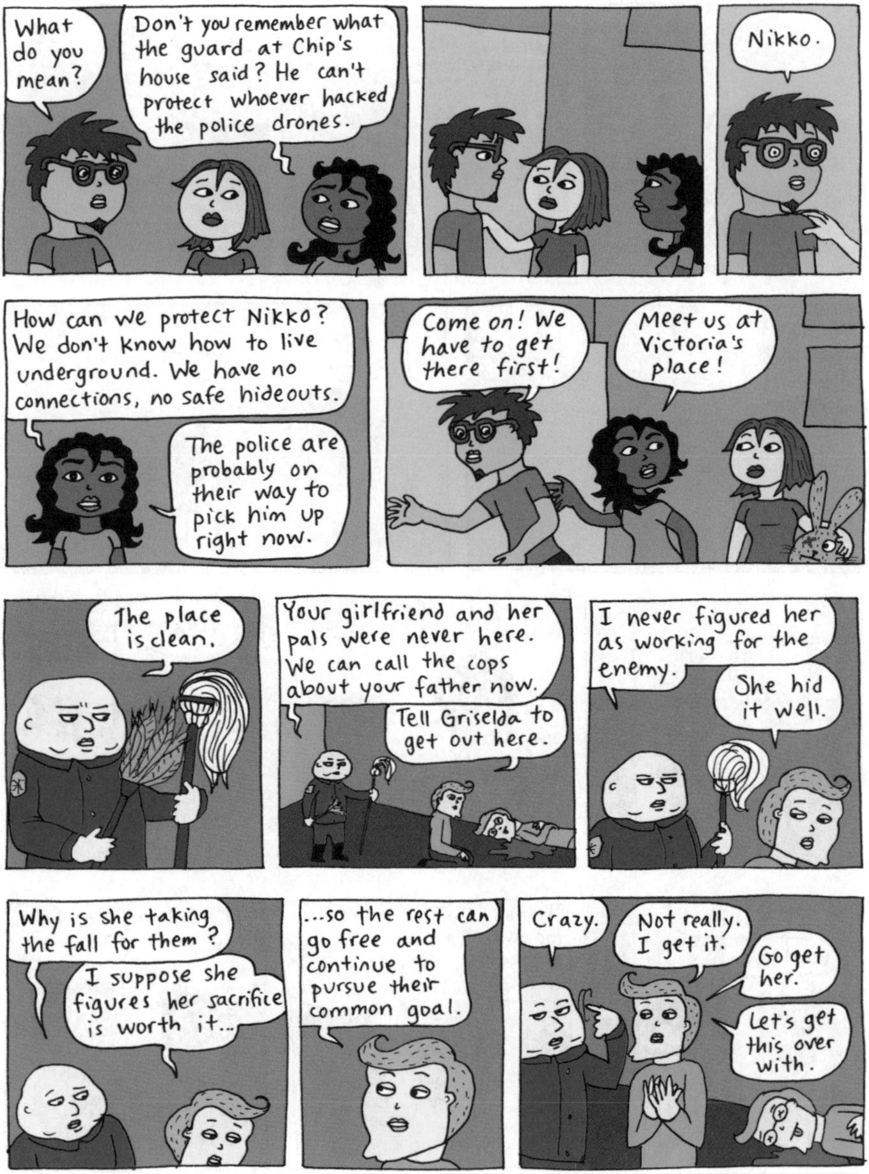

What do you mean?
Don't you remember what the guard at Chip's house said? He can't protect whoever hacked the police drones.
Nikko.
How can we protect Nikko? We don't know how to live underground. We have no connections, no safe hideouts.
The police are probably on their way to pick him up right now.
Come on! We have to get there first!
Meet us at Victoria's place!
The place is clean.
Your girlfriend and her pals were never here. We can call the cops about your father now.
Tell Griselda to get out here.
I never figured her as working for the enemy.
She hid it well.
Why is she taking the fall for them?
I suppose she figures her sacrifice is worth it...
...so the rest can go free and continue to pursue their common goal.
Crazy.
Not really. I get it.
Go get her.
Let's get this over with.

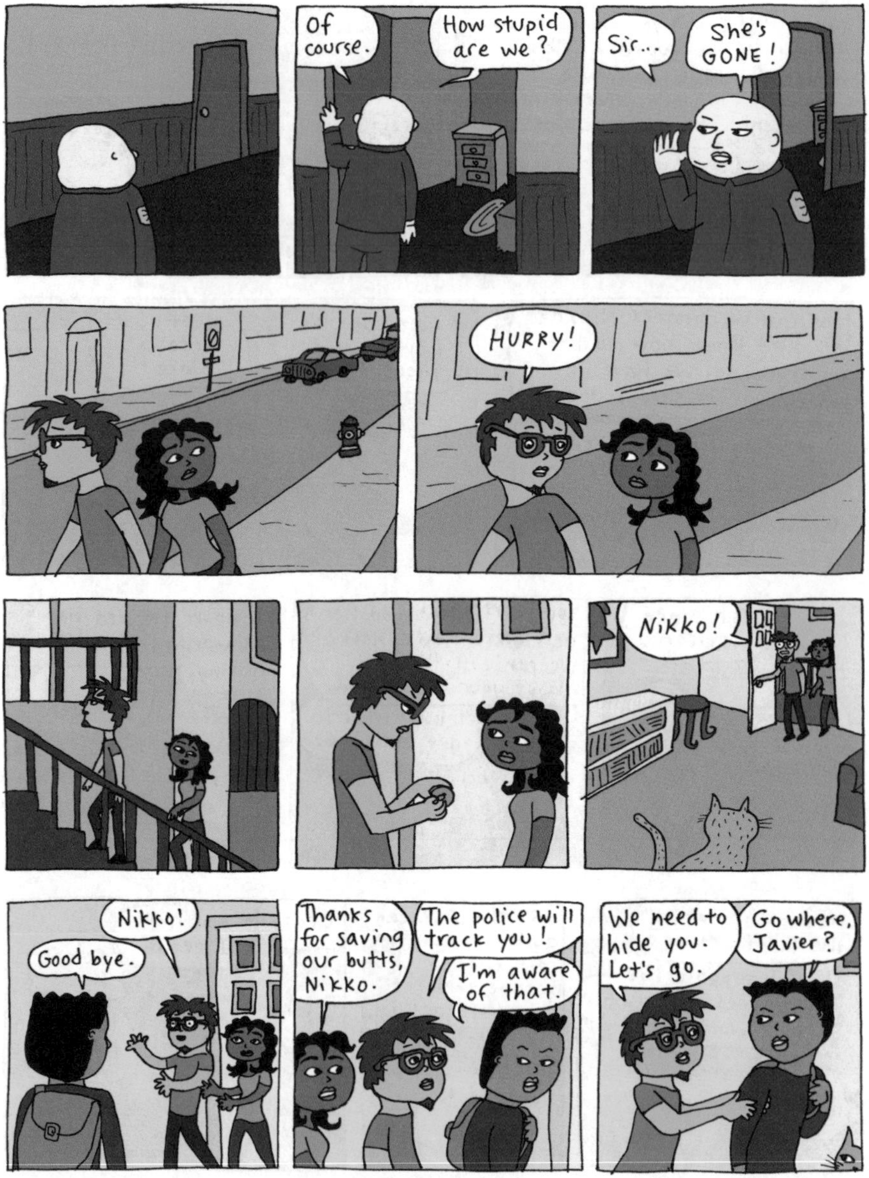
Of course.
How stupid are we?
Sir...
She's GONE!
HURRY!
Nikko!
Good bye.
Nikko!
Thanks for saving our butts, Nikko.
The police will track you!
I'm aware of that.
We need to hide you. Let's go.
Go where, Javier?

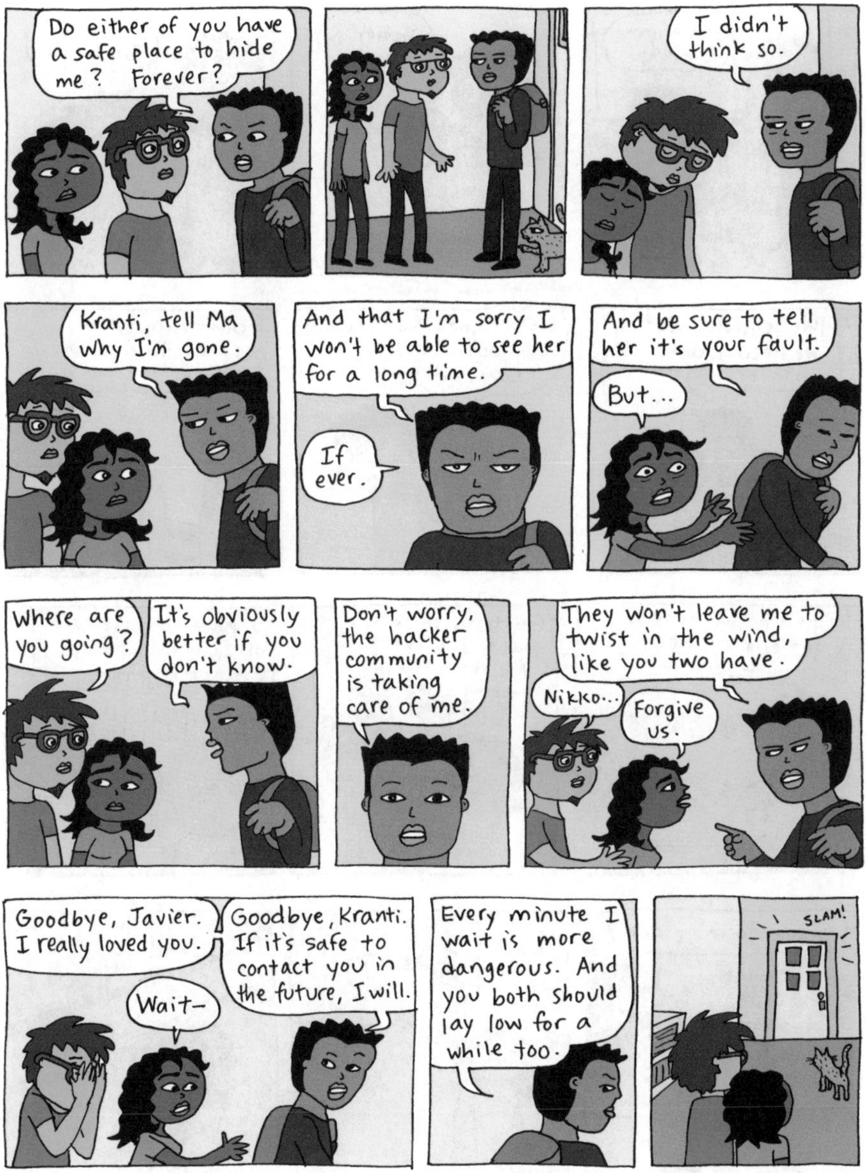
Do either of you have a safe place to hide me? Forever?
I didn't think so.
Kranti, tell Ma why I'm gone.
And that I'm sorry I won't be able to see her for a long time.
If ever.
And be sure to tell her it's your fault.
But...
Where are you going?
It's obviously better if you don't know.
Don't worry, the hacker community is taking care of me.
They won't leave me to twist in the wind, like you two have.
Nikko...
Forgive us.
Goodbye, Javier. I really loved you.
Goodbye, Kranti. If it's safe to contact you in the future, I will.
Wait-
Every minute I wait is more dangerous. And you both should lay low for a while too.
SLAM!

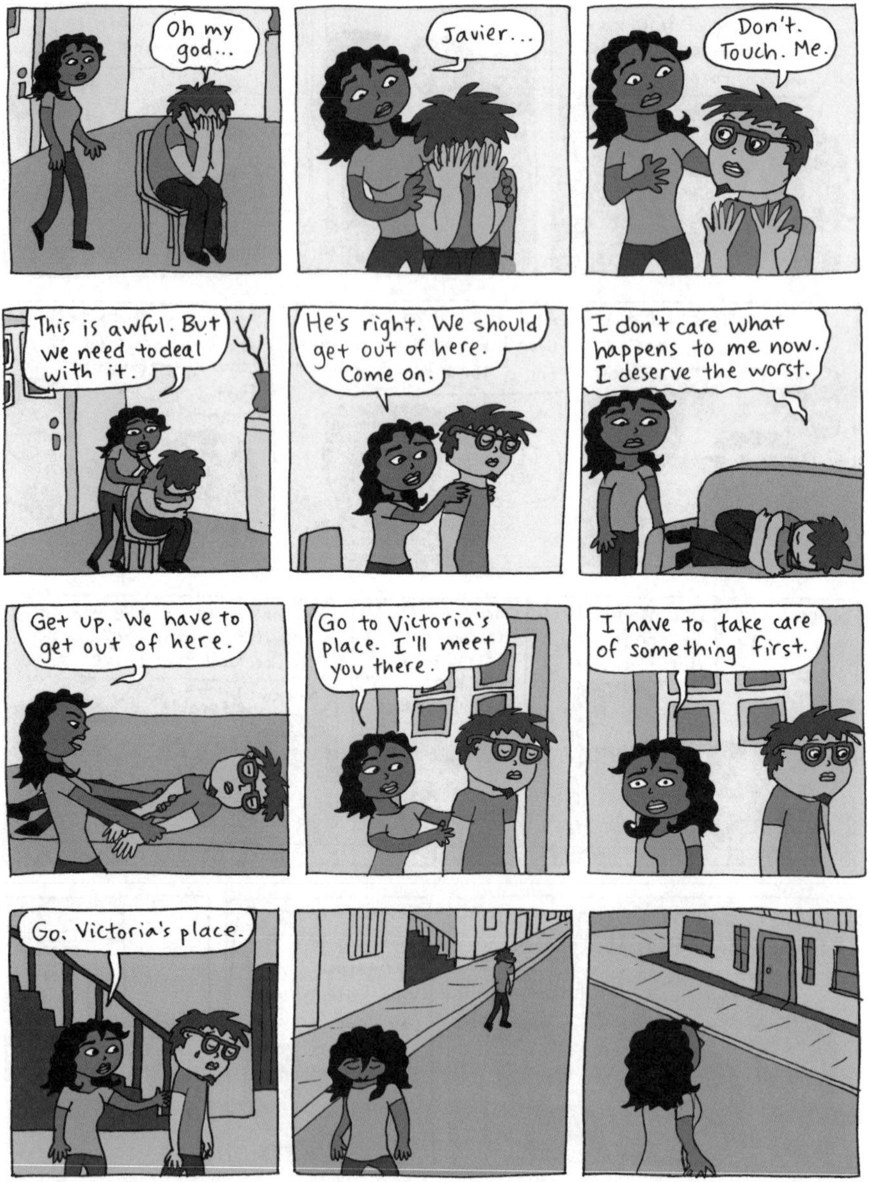
Oh my god...
Javier...
Don't. Touch. Me.
This is awful. But we need to deal with it.
He's right. We should get out of here. Come on.
I don't care what happens to me now. I deserve the worst.
Get up. We have to get out of here.
Go to Victoria's place. I'll meet you there.
I have to take care of something first.
Go. Victoria's place.

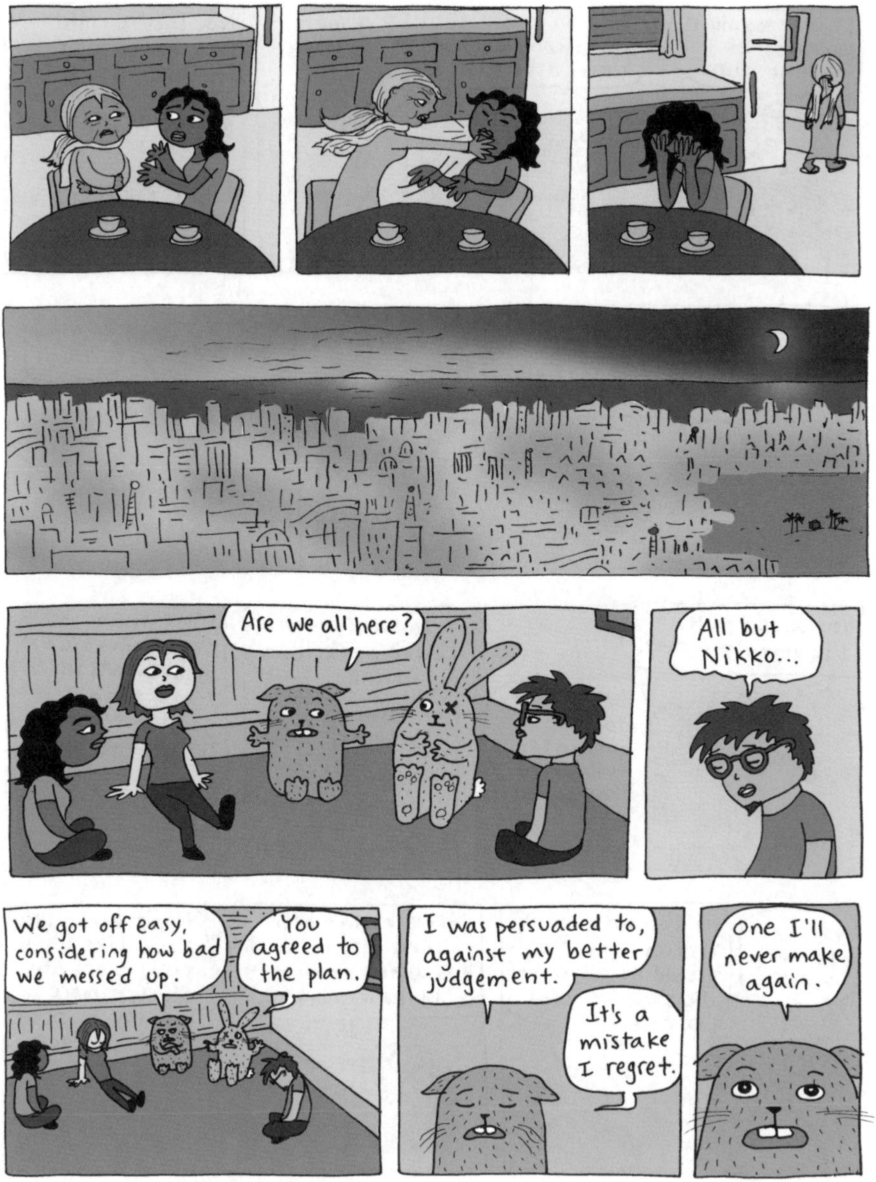
Are we all here?
All but Nikko...
We got off easy, considering how bad we messed up.
You agreed to the plan.
I was persuaded to, against my better judgement.
It's a mistake I regret.
One I'll never make again.

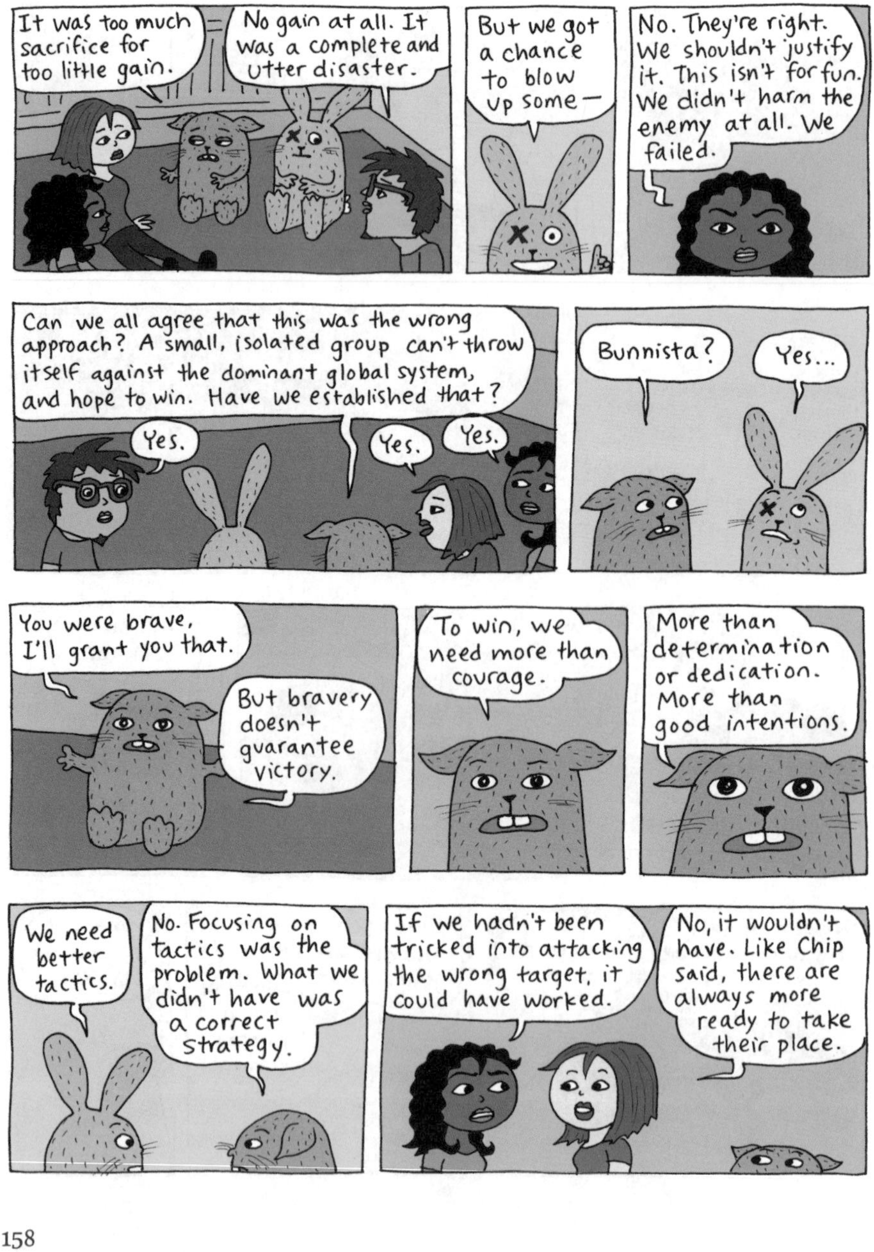
It was too much sacrifice for too little gain.
No gain at all. It was a complete and utter disaster.
But we got a chance to blow up some—
No. They're right. We shouldn't justify it. This isn't for fun. We didn't harm the enemy at all. We failed.
Can we all agree that this was the wrong approach? A small, isolated group can't throw itself against the dominant global system, and hope to win. Have we established that?
Yes.
Yes.
Yes.
Bunnista?
Yes...
You were brave, I'll grant you that.
But bravery doesn't guarantee victory.
To win, we need more than courage.
More than determination or dedication. More than good intentions.
We need better tactics.
No. Focusing on tactics was the problem. What we didn't have was a correct strategy.
If we hadn't been tricked into attacking the wrong target, it could have worked.
No, it wouldn't have. Like Chip said, there are always more ready to take their place.

We owe it to Griselda to get it right next time. And to Nikko. And Jill.
And the world.
You attacked one visible manifestation of a deeper, all-encompassing, structural problem.
To save the planet, the entire global economy has to be fundamentally transformed and restructured.
You can't do that by attacking its surface manifestations or effects. You have to destroy its core mechanism.
What is the system's core mechanism?
The system is capitalism. Its core contradiction is capital vs. labor.
Duh.
Working class revolution..? how?
To come up with the correct strategy, we need a theoretical foundation that coincides with concrete reality.
And we need to constantly test this theory in practice.
I'll do whatever it takes to win. Failure isn't an option.
I'm ready to start over!
We'll learn from those who came before us...
CAPITAL
COMMUNIST MANIFESTO
...and figure out how to deal with our current situation.
LENIN
The most important thing is to never give up.
We will persist!

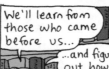